COD COLLAPSE

COD COLLAPSE

THE RISE AND FALL OF NEWFOUNDLAND'S
SALTWATER COWBOYS

JENN THORNHILL VERMA

NIMBUS
PUBLISHING LTD.
NIMBUS.CA

Nimbus Publishing Limited
3660 Strawberry Hill Street, Halifax, NS, B3K 5A9
(902) 455-4286 nimbus.ca

Printed and bound in Canada
NB1433
Editor: Simon Thibault
Editor for the press: Whitney Moran
Cover Design: Jenn Embree
Interior Design: Andrew Herygers
Interior illustrations: Natalie Thornhill Pirro
Front cover artwork by Jenn Thornhill Verma with guidance
from Gordon Harrison

*All photographs are provided courtesy of the author, and the author's family,
except where noted.*

Library and Archives Canada Cataloguing in Publication

Title: Cod collapse : the rise and fall of Newfoundland's saltwater cowboys / Jenn Thornhill Verma.
Names: Thornhill Verma, Jenn, author.
Description: Includes bibliographical references.
Identifiers: Canadiana (print) 20190162961 | Canadiana (ebook) 2019016297X | ISBN 9781771088077 (softcover) |
ISBN 9781771088084 (HTML)
Subjects: LCSH: Thornhill Verma, Jenn. | LCSH: Thornhill Verma, Jenn—Family. | LCSH: Newfoundland and Labrador—Biography. | LCSH: Fishers—Newfoundland and Labrador—Biography. | LCSH: Cod fisheries—Newfoundland and Labrador—History. | LCSH: Newfoundland and Labrador—Economic conditions. | LCGFT: Biographies.
Classification: LCC FC2177.1.A1 T46 2019 | DDC 971.8/040922—dc23

Nimbus Publishing acknowledges the financial support for its publishing activities from the Government of Canada, the Canada Council for the Arts, and from the Province of Nova Scotia. We are pleased to work in partnership with the Province of Nova Scotia to develop and promote our creative industries for the benefit of all Nova Scotians.

There
once was a
Thornhill
from Fortune
Bay...
He fished...
and he fished
all day...
His name   was Reg
and Emily   was his
wife... together, they lived a   modest life.
Reg and the missus had four sons... The b'ys
didn't go at the cod — not one. The oldest was
Clyde, then came John, next was Reg,   and the
youngest was Don.   Don met Pauline and two turned to five
Nat first, Angie second, and Jenn was last to arrive.
Jenn married Raman and they had a daughter.
Lil Navya was born not knowing her great grandfather. This book is
dedicated to all of those above... Our history (and more)   on paper for
you with all
my love
♥

Table of Contents

Prologue

Cod recovery still far off: DFO
—*The Telegram,* St. John's, Newfoundland and Labrador, January 30, 2019

That was the headline in the daily newspaper. I kept a copy, holding on to it like a lotto ticket one number short of the big win.

The news was expected given the previous year's Fisheries and Oceans Canada (DFO) report, which found a 30 per cent decline in the cod spawning stock—and its prediction of worse years to come. Only a few years earlier, research had shown the stock was recovering. Somehow, this formidable species seemed on its way back from the brink. But the hope of a true comeback proved too good to be true.

While cod both was and is not on its way to reclaiming its historical levels of abundance, I still hang on to hope that a recovery, in some form, is possible.

The summer before that headline I was standing next to my father outside what had once been the Thornhill family home, out in Little Bay East, an outport fishing community surrounded by other outport fishing communities. The house now belonged to another family, with no connection to me, my father, this bay, or this community. I note the irony in my feeling of belonging here, on this soil, in front of this house: I hadn't been here in over a decade.

The house overlooks Fortune Bay on the Burin Peninsula on the southeastern shores of Newfoundland—Newfoundland being the island portion of Canada's most easterly province, Newfoundland and Labrador. Little Bay East isn't big enough to get its name on the sign approaching the turnoff from the Trans-Canada Highway. It's overshadowed by places like Bay L'Argent and Jacques Fontaine, places that get their names in white letters on the green roadside signs.

"It's Bay Large-ent and Jack's Fountain," Dad reminds me on the drive.

"Right, right," I reply, having mistakenly pronounced the names in French. Perhaps it's a sign I've been living on the mainland too long.

Standing behind the chain-link fencing, I'm feeling even more like an outsider. I can't go inside the house—a home that welcomed the Thornhills for the better part of a century—because the couple who recently bought it aren't here. They paid fourteen thousand dollars, a staggeringly low price for a property anywhere in Canada in 2018, especially a waterfront one. And that's still eleven thousand dollars cheaper than the original asking price set by my uncles Clyde and Reginald (Reg) and father, Donald (Don), after its last owner, Uncle John, died. If that sounds like a lot of unnecessary names to you, trust me, it isn't. At least not to this house. At least not to me. And not right now, as I stand in front of this fence.

The house feels like living history to me, my history. My family's history. John owned the house, but it belonged to my paternal grandparents before that. It's where Reginald (Pop) and Emily (Nan) Thornhill raised their four boys and it's where I visited with my father each summer throughout my childhood, maintaining a connection to my outport fishing roots. This visit marks the first time I won't be able to set foot inside. John is gone and our stake in this house is no longer ours to claim.

For over two centuries, the Thornhills and the Clarkes (Nan's side of the family) lived on this peninsula, our ancestors having crossed the Atlantic Ocean from England to settle in this place. A place that promised plentiful cod fishing. In the late fifteenth century, explorer John Cabot had famously referenced these waters as teeming with cod, so much so that he hypothesized one could walk across their backs in this part of the Atlantic. My ancestors could never have imagined a day when the cod population would collapse, shuttering the cod fishery and outport communities all along these coasts. Could they have imagined we'd be standing on the outside looking in, too?

But that's what has happened. I was twelve when the Canadian government announced an end to cod—and what I thought was the fishery, too. That likely sounds like an odd thing for a twelve year old to think about, but I did. I thought fishing was done and the people were, too. In the years leading up to the "cod moratorium," I was a preteen, finding myself in the world. In those formative years, it felt as though my family and province were losing their identities. As cod plummeted from plentiful to piddling, the human population dwindled too, with people abandoning the outports in droves.

Moratorium stories dominated the supper-hour news in those days. Fishers and plant workers acted like a school of fish out of water: forced out of their element, their livelihoods, and with all they had ever known yanked out from underneath them. The bleakness and despair of those news stories was repeatedly broadcast into living rooms and kitchens throughout the province and across the country. Some got a front-row seat as wharves and docks were left to rot, clapboard siding on saltbox houses exposed joints, and schooners and dories sank into their surrounding harbours.

The moratorium was meant to last two years—presumably long enough for the cod population to bounce back after rampant overfishing. It wasn't. In 2019, it is still in effect. At least you can count on some things to never change in this place.

For the Thornhills, the losses started before the 1992 cod moratorium. Pop was the last fisher in our family and his fishing career—from a dory fisherman on the Grand Banks, once the richest cod-fishing grounds in the world, to schooner-fishing inshore—had long-ago ended. Pop died in 1987, five years before the moratorium. Looking back, it was a personal family loss foreshadowing a population's loss. Our links to the cod fishery were forever severed in those moments.

Throughout my childhood summers and into my teenage years, I returned to the Thornhill family home, or what I then called Nan and Pop's house—later Uncle John's house—with my father. I grew up on Newfoundland's west coast, mostly in Corner Brook, a pulp and paper town. The trips with Dad to Little Bay East helped me connect to my family's fishing outport roots. Life seemed simpler there—yet not necessarily easier. Like, if something broke, you didn't do what city folks did and call in a repairman. You fixed it yourself. You figured it out. As a child, I took pleasure in combing the beach for shells and rocks or climbing the nearby mountainside, where I could look out past the peninsula of Little Bay East to where Fortune Bay disappeared into the horizon. Somewhere out there in the deep blue beyond, Pop and others like him fished.

But at the age of twenty-five, when I returned for Nan's funeral, my connection to this place had dulled. It was at the burial when I realized I had more family members six feet under than I did living in Little Bay East. Only Uncle John remained. My family's sense of place and permanency in the community was disappearing. And the distance between my unfolding life on the mainland and the traditions from which I came were growing farther and farther apart.

It wasn't until eleven years later, when Uncle John died in Little Bay East, that I started to feel the full significance and space of that distance. Then, the following year, my husband, Raman, and I saw a pixellated flicker of white pirouetting on a sonogram: a steady, unmistakable heartbeat. That's when I realized it was time to finally attend to what I'd been ignoring for more than a decade: I needed to go home. That's where the answers to who I am and where I'm from could be found. And I'd need those answers to address my child's future questions, too.

As I stand here now, outside the former Thornhill family home, I'm gutted thinking the house is no longer ours. All that remains under our namesake is in the graveyard. In this moment, at thirty-eight, I'm a new mother to my seven-month-old daughter, Navya Amelia Verma. I'm nearly the same age my father was when his father died. Right now, my father is undergoing palliative cancer care. If he's lucky, he'll reach the same age Pop was at the time of his death. Dad is seventy and his doctors tell us he has a few years to live; Pop died at seventy-four.

Time feels precious and precarious. I feel the weight of brand new life and imminent death, frightened equally by both. *What will I tell Navi about where we're from? How much time do I have with Dad?* These are the kinds of questions I mull over. If I don't carve out the time and space now to unearth my roots, then I may never have the chance to do so.

Now, a quarter of a century after the cod moratorium and more than half a century since Pop was a fisherman—the last in our lineage—I'm sharing my family's story before it's too late. I'm also sharing the stories of descendants of Newfoundland and Labrador fishers like me, whose families left the fishery or the fishing outports. Together, we tell the story of what happened to Newfoundlanders and Labradorians when the cod fishery collapsed: one of the greatest collective traumas in the history of our province and one for which no one has ever truly been held to account—except, perhaps, the cod.

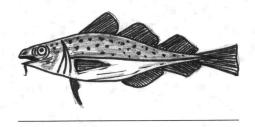

PART I. ROOTS

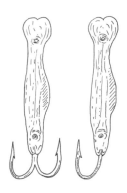

CHAPTER 1:
Salt Water in Our Veins

"Don't fall me down, Pop, don't fall me down," I fearfully repeated. I remember holding my grandfather's hand when I was a child as we walked along the wharf across the road from his home. Pop's tight grip revealed he, too, was apprehensive, but his hands were incapable of letting go. Those same hands flipped the pages of my storybook, his index finger slowly tracing the words. I thought that was for my benefit. Only later did I learn it was for his. When we came across a word we didn't know he'd say, "Let's call it wheelbarrow": code for *we'll borrow this word until we figure it out.* If there were too many wheelbarrows, Pop would close the book and tell his own stories, often returning to tales of the sea.

Pop, as we called him, was my paternal grandfather, Reginald Thornhill, a fisher from the Burin Peninsula on the southeastern shores of Newfoundland. Newfoundland is the most easterly point in North America and the island portion of the Canadian province, Newfoundland and Labrador. Commonly called "The Rock" for its windswept rockfaces, jagged and exposed to the North Atlantic Ocean, you could almost say its people are like rocks, too—sharp, solid, and reliable. As was my grandfather. His daily dose of sun and sea salt with a dash of cold winds had the effect of giving Pop's skin a creased and leathery appearance. He was a smallish man, but agile and able. His hands, calloused from a lifetime hauling fishing gear, were his livelihood. The gear he handled

(Left) Grandfather "Pop" (Reginald) Thornhill holding salmon in his dory, Fortune Bay, c. 1864. (Right) Pop holding dried and salted cod, Little Bay East, Newfoundland, c. 1979.

over the years changed from natural fibres to synthetic ones, contributing to the bristly, scratchy canvas that became Pop's hands.

My delicate child's hand in his was the closest I'd ever come to the fishing labour and legacy that put me here. I can picture Pop, his wool fisherman's cap or *beanie* covering his short, silvery hair. He wore rubber boots over corduroys with a collared plaid shirt and sweater along with a bomber-style jacket on cooler days. His attire was as understated as the man himself, but I'd come to learn his life was anything but.

At the peak of his career, my grandfather spent more time at sea than on land. Fishing took Pop, and those before him, to the seawaters off our coasts—be it nearby Fortune Bay, off the southeast coast to the Grand Banks, or farther afield to the seaways off northern Newfoundland, Labrador, or the neighbouring province of Nova Scotia. Pop couldn't swim, but he survived at least five shipwrecks on the same waters that downed the *Titanic* and birthed a tsunami.

When Pop arrived in the world in 1913, the supposedly unsinkable *Titanic* already lay 12,500 feet under water, more than 500 kilometres southeast of Newfoundland. The year he started fishing, 1929, a wrecking ball of a tsunami rose up out of an earthquake rumbling under the ocean, about 260 kilometres south of the Burin Peninsula, on the southern ridge of the Grand Banks fishing grounds. The Banks were once the world's richest cod-fishing grounds, spanning an area three times the size of Newfoundland. When the Banks shook, it created a landslide, triggering a series of waves that became a tsunami. The trough of the tsunami reached the peninsula's shores first, sucking back the sea in a single gulp, exposing the ocean floor underneath its deep blue rug, and toppling schooners docked at harbour as that rug was pulled out from under them. The crest of the tsunami followed with three successive waves hurtling toward landfall—at least two-dozen communities dotting the coast—at initial estimated speeds of 140 kilometres per hour. Losing velocity as it neared shore but gaining height, the 40-kilometre-per-hour waves still packed sufficient punch to level fishing stages and wharves, uprooting houses from their concrete foundations and careening unsecured structures out to sea. Water levels rose anywhere from 7 to 25 metres above normal, drowning the sparsely populated outports. Twenty-seven people died and nearly one hundred buildings (including homes) were destroyed. It would take days to assess the losses and damages. With the Great Depression poised to create its own economically destructive wave, more casualties were yet to come.

That's the backdrop marking the year my grandfather, then sixteen years old, started fishing. Surely he was aware of these events in all their gruesome detail and, surely, that awareness, combined with his own close calls, removed any sense of security he may have had about a life at sea. What does it mean to a community or to one's character to live and work so far outside of a basic sense of security? Or for things so abnormal to be normalized?

And yet, Pop would continue a life at sea as a *saltwater cowboy*—this is not a term he would have used, but it fits, given he routinely escaped the dangers of shadowed icebergs, rogue waves, and other ocean calamities

Fishers on the wharf. Grandfather "Pop" (Reginald) Thornhill is likely centre; others may include Eli Clarke, Reuben Clarke, and Sidney Green. Likely taken in North Sydney, Nova Scotia. (Source and date unknown)

threatening to capsize much more than the day's catch. Other fishers also don't use the term and although the similarities abound—wrangling fish not cattle, riding waves not bucking horses, and wearing sou'westers not cowboy hats—fishers lack the cavalier attitude. That's because fishers know they are no match for Mother Nature.

Pop, three of his brothers, his father, grandfather, and great-grandfather fished. So too did the father and grandfather of my paternal grandmother, Emily Thornhill (*née* Clarke), or Nan. It was Pop's second great-grandfather on his paternal side and great-grandfather on his maternal side who first left England for Newfoundland. I don't know what professions or lives they left behind, but I do know what brought the Thornhills, Clarkes, and many other settlers to Newfoundland: cod. In truth, they came because they were put here—the British colonized Newfoundland and Labrador to ensure financial futures, turning the fishery into a resident rather than migratory industry. A self-governing British colony since 1855, Newfoundland would later attain Dominion status (1907–1949) comprising the island of Newfoundland and the continental mainland of Labrador.

More than five centuries ago and at the request of Henry VII of England, Italian explorer Giovanni Caboto (better known by his English name John Cabot) undertook an expedition from Bristol to the west in search of a northern spice route. While the journey took Cabot to what he would call *new found land*, the land was neither *new* nor *found*. The Portuguese and Basque are thought to have fished the Grand Banks before that time. The land was also briefly staked by Vikings five hundred years earlier and had been inhabited by Indigenous peoples, the Beothuk, even before that. But what Cabot saw in the waters off Newfoundland dazzled. The backs of cod, shining like crinkled foil just below the surface, offered the promise of a plentiful food source fit for a hungry kingdom. It wasn't the riches of the Orient, but it was precious just the same.

"They affirm that the sea is covered with fish which are caught not merely with nets but with baskets, a stone being attached to make the basket sink in the water," wrote Raimondo di Soncino, the ambassador of the Duke of Milan in London to the duke in 1497, following Cabot's expedition. "And said Englishmen, [Cabot's] companions, say that they will fetch so many fish that this kingdom will have no more need of Iceland, from which country there comes a very great store of fish which are called stock-fish."

The Basques and other fishers had safeguarded these fishing grounds, foregoing claiming the land for anyone. But for an explorer like Cabot, this discovery would only be considered a find worth claiming by telling the world and claiming the land as England's. With di Soncino's letter in the hands of the British presses, the secrecy ascribed to the Grand Banks was out. At the time, cod was a profitable commodity worldwide. Catholicism, which forbade parishioners from eating meat on Fridays, over the forty days of Lent, as well as during other religious events and holy days, contributed to the rising demand for cod and other groundfish such as halibut, haddock, and pollock.

Cod attracted seasonal European fishing fleets from England, Ireland, France, Spain, and Portugal to the Grand Banks for a century or more, before permanent European settlers began to arrive as early as the seventeenth century. My family arrived in the eighteenth century, as did the majority of Newfoundland's settlers, when my third- and fourth-great-grandparents settled in Newfoundland from England. The Thornhills and Clarkes hailed from southern England—Dorsetshire, or Dorset as it's called now, Wiltshire, and Somerset—all in the region of Wessex as it was once known, or the West Country as it's known today. They would have called themselves "planters"—a term for those who volunteered to remain for a longer period in Newfoundland and Labrador rather than return to England at the end of the fishing season. People overwintered for any number of reasons, some as caretakers for fish merchants or ship owners, others to hunt or trap animals, and still others to build boats. My second-great-grandfathers on both sides (William Thornhill and Samuel Clarke) still bore the title of "planters" (based on census records), which also indicates they owned their own fishing boats. Perhaps some planters still considered a return to England, but leaving the rock and the roots they had forged with their wives and children would have made leaving a titanic task—good in theory, but not in practice.

Some of the Thornhills first settled on the 20-square-kilometre Brunette Island at the mouth of Fortune Bay, a large bay on the southeast coast of Newfoundland. The bay, which appears on maps in the early sixteenth century, likely received its name from the Portuguese word *fortuna*, meaning "place of good fortune." The French likely named the island *brunette* meaning "brown," a reference to the island's vast peatlands. By the mid-nineteenth century, there were as many as 300 settlers on Brunette Island, attracted to its proximity to rich fishing grounds. Across Newfoundland, tens of thousands of settlers (as many as 80,000 by 1840, doubling the population from 40,568 in 1815 and quadrupling from 21,975 in 1805), dotted the coastlines, preparing dried salt fish for mostly European and Caribbean markets. By then St. John's, the island's commercial centre, was the hustle, while the bustle, the island's cultural beating heart and burgeoning soul, was found in the outports. Salt codfish exports from Newfoundland saw a threefold increase during the beginning and middle of the nineteenth century, despite the cold-water conditions hampering cod's productivity mid-century. Pushing the fishery to northern Newfoundland and Labrador opened up new fishing grounds, but per-fisher catch rates had started to fall. There's some evidence to suggest overfishing began at that time. The promise of maintaining incomes—and at a time when the price of cod was dropping—likely overshadowed the pitfalls of plundering what still seemed to be a plentiful resource (more fishing could maintain incomes, but for how long?). And so, Newfoundland's population grew and so, too, did the fishing. In the 1870s, it is estimated that the Newfoundland commercial fishing fleet alone had grown to eighteen thousand small boats and twelve hundred larger vessels. Those are remarkable numbers, given the Canadian-wide commercial fishing fleet today (based on 2016 numbers) is about eighteen thousand vessels—more than 85 per cent of which fish the Atlantic. By the 1890s, there were double the number of fishers than in the 1850s; over half the population fished; and 85 cents of every dollar of the colony's export earnings could be attributed to the cod and seal fishery (with salt cod providing the majority of revenues).

The annual spring seal fishery (or seal hunt, as it was called) was well underway by that time, conveniently operating in the months prior to the cod fishery. Seal meat, pelts, and oil (extracted from blubber) helped fishers make up for declining incomes from cod. The seal hunt continued into the mid-1900s, but has faced difficulties ever since, particularly as hunting methods became the subject of international controversy from animal rights and conservation groups.

Meanwhile, even with a declining market for salt cod by the end of the nineteenth century, the general sentiment was that the fish were thriving. English biologist Thomas Huxley remarked in 1883 at a fisheries conference, "With existing methods of fishing, it is inconceivable that the great sea fisheries such as those for cod, herring and mackerel, could ever be exhausted."

On Brunette Island, the peat and turf that dominates the land is an accumulation of partially decaying vegetation in swaths of mustard, rust, and sage. Low-lying plants, mosses, and berries blanket the rugged terrain, choke-holding ponds, yet are stonewalled by the island's cliffs. In Mercer's Cove, a fishing community on Brunette Island whose residents were resettled elsewhere in the late 1950s and has remained vacant ever since, the decay of life is even more apparent. Concrete headstones in the cemetery and slab foundations from an old church, homes, and sheds: all evidence of people and places lost in transit, returning to dust. Even the wildlife brought here—the bison and moose introduced as part of a provincial wildlife reserve in the 1960s—have died off (some from natural causes, some surely poached), although Arctic hare and caribou continue to inhabit this land.

By the late nineteenth century, families were already moving off Brunette Island to mainland Newfoundland, settling nearby to continue cod fishing. The Thornhills would settle in places like Little Bay East, Bay L'Argent, and Grand Bank on the Burin Peninsula, and Harbour Breton and Stone's Cove on the western shores of Fortune Bay. My immediate family eventually landed in Little Bay East, a sheltered peninsula at the bottom of Fortune Bay. My great-great-grandparents (on my paternal grandmother's side), William Miles (or Myles; names often had alternative spellings because they were recorded phonetically by the British during the census periods and many Newfoundlanders lacked the literacy skills to correct them) and Phoebe Thornhill, were the first of the Miles clan to settle in Little Bay East. On September 27, 1872, they moved from Terrenceville (the head of the community of Fortune Bay

Cod Drying on the Flakes, Quidi Vidi, Newfoundland, c. 1886. (Library and Archives Canada PA-139025)

at the southernmost tip of the Burin Peninsula, or Fortune Head, as it was originally called). William and Phoebe were first cousins, which was common at the time, and make me a Thornhill on both of my paternal grandparents' sides of the family.

In Little Bay East and all along Newfoundland's coastlines, codfish was split, salted, and dried on flakes—raised wooden platforms on the beaches. The process entailed cleaning the cod (removing its head, spine, and guts), salting it for several days, washing off the excess salt, and then laying it to dry in the sun on wooden flakes. The wooden flakes were flat platforms, positioned three to four feet off the ground, constructed of bows and twigs and strong enough to walk on.

The word "flake" is of Nordic origin, deriving from Old Norse, a language spoken by Vikings or Norsemen, who would have used the word *fleke*, meaning "a rectangular frame." The word was used by English settlers in Newfoundland in the seventeenth century and was recorded in Richard Whitbourne's 1620 book, *A discourse and discovery of New-found-land*. By the time my ancestors were living in Little Bay East, flakes were common, one of the visible influences of the salt-cod fishery. Indeed, this influence would penetrate every aspect of Newfoundland's existence— its settlement patterns, architecture, art, cuisine, and traditions.

That influence would continue for generations in spite of the salt-cod industry's struggles, never regaining its market share. In fact, the global market price for salt-fish dropped at the end of the century, saw a brief comeback, then tanked again after the First World War (between 1929 and 1936, fish exports declined from $11.5 million to $7 million). According to Heritage Newfoundland and Labrador, the original decline was "due partly to the ecological strain on cod stocks, but the [Great] Depression was largely responsible for later reductions as capital became scarce and demand dropped." Another factor may have been the influence of large trawlers, as "many independent fish harvesters blamed these larger vessels for the 1920s price drop in salt fish that ricocheted into other fisheries," reports the non-profit Canadian Council for Professional Fish Harvesters. Census data between 1921 and 1945 also show the number of Newfoundland fishers fell by half over that period. By the 1930s, one-quarter of the population was dependent on government relief. Many fishers were indebted to merchants, who traded in gear, food like salt beef, pork, sugar, butter, and barrels of flour, as well as other supplies on a credit-based system, taking catch, usually salt fish, as payment. If there was no merchant at the outport, a travelling merchant would visit by

Boy with cod fish on gaff, Flowers Island, Bonavista Bay, 1939. (The Rooms Provincial Archives)

schooner, transporting fish and keeping a below-deck store fully stocked with trading supplies.

Since colonization, Newfoundlanders and Labradorians have relied on imported foods, particularly over winter. Even during summer, as Newfoundland and Labrador's climate and soil conditions are generally non-conducive to growing fresh local produce, imported foods are necessary. Today, Newfoundlanders and Labradorians still rely heavily on imported goods with produce from the province comprising just one-tenth of what's consumed.

With so many fishers collecting relief payments in the early to mid-twentieth century, bankruptcy became a serious concern for the colony, prompting Britain to assume responsibility for Newfoundland's finances and replace its elected government with a six-person commission (three Brits and three Newfoundlanders) along with the governor in 1934. A defibrillation attempt maybe the best way to describe what the commission was attempting to do: offering a jolt to the fishery by subsidizing new fishing vessel construction and encouraging modernization in fishery production and marketing. This was a defining era for Newfoundland, also marked by the Great Depression and the Second World War.

Despite government relief programs, many Newfoundlanders lived in abject poverty, whether they worked in the fishery, forestry, mining, or other growing industries like pulp and paper. Poor and inadequate nutrition as well as limited access to health care contributed to growing disease, with conditions like beriberi (caused by vitamin B-1 deficiency, often leading to heart failure) and tuberculosis spreading rampantly.

Meanwhile, salt-codfish trade exports fell by half, and fifteen thousand fishing jobs were lost in the decade following 1947, a period economic historian David Alexander calls the "demoralization" of the fishery. It was within that context that just over half of Newfoundlanders voted, in 1949, in favour of joining the Canadian Confederation. The other half wanted to revive their own responsible government. The fishery was by no means dead, but it was in the midst of a massive overhaul: what control the colony had of its fishery would soon be taken over by Canada. The changes in the fishery would result, in the years that followed, in the relocation of tens of thousands of people. Many were relocated through government assistance across Newfoundland and Labrador, from areas that were no longer economically prosperous to areas considered more economically viable. To top it all off, the speed and accuracy of new fishing technologies were blowing Newfoundland's proximity to the fishing grounds, once its greatest competitive advantage, out of the water.

Forty-plus years later, the cod fishery collapsed. The government of Canada issued an end to cod fishing on July 2, 1992. The glorious cod that John Cabot boasted about five centuries earlier were nearly gone. The collapse of the cod stocks and the shutdown of its fishery shook the identity of this fishing nation to its core, unearthing a monster of a tidal wave whose destructive waters still ripple through communities today. The cod moratorium, as it came to be known, marked a closure of groundfishing, predominantly cod, in the waters off the coast of Newfoundland and most of the Gulf of St. Lawrence. It remains the largest industrial layoff in Canadian history, putting some thirty to forty thousand fishers and plant workers across Newfoundland and Labrador out of work.

The moratorium, which was meant to last two years, continues to this day. The economic devastation was immediate, deep, and lasting. And there was a social cost to the moratorium, too. Thanks to overfishing and a collective sense of denial on the part of nearly everyone involved, the fishing days of my grandfather's youth were over almost as quickly as they had started. The collapse didn't happen overnight, history tells us, but for those who lost their jobs, homes, and communities, it surely felt like it did.

The Thornhill family home sits on a floodplain between two bodies of water in Little Bay East. While that may sound precarious, it's immeasurably safer than other settler homes, treacherously perched on seaside cliffs. Here, a short beach runs along Fortune Bay to the northeast and a longer stretch of beach runs along the *barasway*, as Newfoundlanders call a barachois or coastal lagoon, to the southwest. Rolling hillsides and the main entry to the community are to the southeast (facing the side

Thornhill family home (second from left) facing Fortune Bay, Little Bay East, Newfoundland and Labrador, over the years: 1967 (top and middle, Lloyd Green) and 2017 (bottom, Clayton Burton).

porch and main entrance to the house), while the rest of Little Bay East, a small peninsula of a town, is accessible to the northeast.

The house was constructed in the 1930s, but due to renovations over the years, some of the home's original features—which, admittedly, I don't remember, but have admired in old photographs—are gone. At one time, the house had six front-facing windows and was clad in wood siding, its garden surrounded by a short picket fence. Now, there are four smaller front-facing windows, white vinyl siding, and a partial chain-link fence. The painted green door and steps to the front porch offer some seaside sensibility.

I'm sizing things up from behind the chain-link fence when the home's new occupants return. In Newfoundland and Labrador, generally speaking, if you meet a stranger at the corner store or while asking for directions, they are just as likely to tell you their life story as they are to invite you over for coffee or tea—and there's an even greater likelihood they'll do both, all while referring to you as *sweetheart, my love,* or *me ducky.* Often, coffee or tea then naturally segues into a dinner ("lunch" for mainlanders) or supper (dinner) invitation, depending on the time of day. Politely declining is generally futile where food is concerned, and in this place, food is always concerned.

That is, except in this case. Mr. and Mrs. Owner, as I'll refer to them, have returned and their hellos and eye contact are politely brief, so I find myself in the awkward position of forcing a short conversation. Mr. Owner indulges me—his stance, a twisted side-lunge, as if ready to dart toward the house, tells me he's reluctant to talk—while Mrs. Owner ducks inside carrying grocery bags. Perhaps it's because we're family of the previous owner. In any case, I learn the Owners are in the middle of renovations, having already knocked down walls on the main floor and partially gutted the kitchen.

"We like things open," Mr. Owner says, "but it's kind of rough." Part of me wants to press to see what they've done with the place, but the other part knows to leave well enough alone. If Newfoundlanders want to invite you inside, they'll invite you inside. Besides, I want to retain the small luxury of showing my face around here, even if it's on the wrong side of the chain-link. Meanwhile, Dad joins in the conversation and remarks on the work he's put into the house, most recently the roof.

"That roof will outlast the whole place," Dad offers, laughing.

"Oh, is that so?" the man replies, feigning mild interest.

"Yes, I'm the one who did it!" Dad continues, not catching the rhetorical nature of the question, instead taking it as an invitation to drone on. Dad is known to drone on, but usually only does so in the company of immediate family. It could be about anything, but usually centres on some common topics like chess (the winning move), astronomy (the latest discovery), my mother (her latest evangelism), money (there's never enough), how bad the food was at such-and-such a place (it's always bad), and how many things he has remaining on his to-do list (too much to ever accomplish in three lifetimes). The latest topic Dad goes on about, and who could blame him, is his cancer. A prostate cancer that was removed more than fifteen years ago, when Dad was fifty-two, recently metastasized to his bones. Since early last spring Dad's been taking a new medication. The meds showed early progress but six months later, the cancer is spreading again. He's now undergoing a round of intravenous chemotherapy as part of his palliative care, which means the cancer is incurable and the treatment is to help comfort, possibly prolong life, but not cure.

"I thought I was off scot-free again," Dad had said in an earlier conversation between just the two of us. He was recalling how quickly the doctors acted to remove his prostate more than fifteen years ago, and how the meds had an immediate effect. "But now I'll wait and see what my next doctor appointment tells me. We don't know if I'll have a year or five years, but I feel like a stranger in my own body."

Dad's a man who appreciates science. A former x-ray technician, he knows most men die *with* prostate cancer, not *from* it. But he's expecting a bad report on account of how he's been feeling. Some days are better than others. On good days, he eats what he wants, takes day and even overnight trips into the woods, and fiddles with his latest hobby: repairing accordions, mostly of the button variety. On his worst days, food lacks taste and his body has only enough energy to endure the persistent pains and aching. Now, I find myself watching my father shrink under the weight of his own cancer-addled body.

I pinch my eyes and steady my emotions, my grip on the chain-link tightening, not that anyone has noticed. My brief mental absence has meant I've missed the window to clue Dad into Mr. Owner's polite cue. But I'll hold my breath a moment longer to indulge my father's ramblings and laughter because it's bringing back memories of our father-daughter time, before the cancer, here in Little Bay East.

Dad and I made the six-and-a-half-hour drive from Summerside (and later Corner Brook) on the *T-C-H*, as we called the Trans-Canada Highway, countless times. Along the way, we'd list and laugh at the names of Newfoundland communities. Joe Batt's Arm, Placentia, Dildo, and Conception Bay were in high rotation on our list, even before I understood their connotations. How I'd memorized the trees, lush and full forests on the west coast shrinking to tilted, sparse creatures on the southeast coast. Once we reached the barren, moon-like terrain of this wind-whipped peninsula, I knew we were closing in on the turnoff. I marvelled at the uprooted trees and *erractics*, the enormous rocks set out on the barrens, seemingly placed there by giants. It's a fair description, as these boulders are leave-behinds from retreating glaciers at the end of the last ice age. Past the turnoff, we'd drive around the base of sheltered mountains, thick with bush once again and rising up between the long, luminous seaways. Every so often, a rockface bore a declaration of love: *Don* ❤ *Pauline* (my mother's name) was one such proclamation, though my parents denied it was them.

Those drives often started chaotically. Dad would haphazardly pack his bag just minutes before we hit the road. This was something of a character trait, likely evidence of the lasting influence of outport life. For example, he was the kind of man who had to be told by his wife, *Don, you're in desperate need of a haircut.* He allowed his shock of straight, jet black hair to grow long around his ears and into side-swept bangs across his forehead, the hair resting on the shelf created by the frame of his glasses. Mom, my sisters, and I endlessly bought Dad new clothes for his birthdays and Christmases too, not that he ever wore them. He favoured the dishevelled look on account of always getting up to something in the garage or the yard, often for someone else.

Most trips to Little Bay East entailed Nan putting Dad to work, especially after Pop died in 1987. As I was left to explore Little Bay East on my own, Dad replaced siding, painted windows and doors, even levelled the second storey of the next-door house (formerly owned by my now-deceased great uncle and aunt) into a second shed. John, who assumed ownership of the Thornhill home, was handy but couldn't get up to big jobs like that. He walked with a limp and a cane on account of having a prosthesis on his right leg and a sore left leg—the result of his being an innocent bystander in a drunk-driving accident in his twenties. That accident is what brought John back home to Little Bay East (on disability insurance) and kept him there all those years later. (*It would have to be by accident,* my teenage-self would later think. What made me marvel about the outport as a child became dreadfully mundane as a teenager.)

By now, Dad is wrapping up his lengthy summary of repairs to the homestead. We move onto exchanging contact information, thanking Mr. Owner for his time while he thanks Dad for his labour. A good outcome, but my mind keeps trailing elsewhere: *Will Dad and I ever return home together again or could this be it?* All those trips with Dad, all those years, I failed to appreciate how that time offered me a chance to get to know my roots. But how was I to know whether my roots needed getting to know or were at risk of not fully knowing at all?

My first clue should have been what had happened here on this porch, the same one Mr. Owner just stepped over. In 1987, just shy of his seventy-fifth birthday, Pop walked out the door like it was any other Sunday. In a betrayal of his heart, a plaque dislodged from his artery, fatally blocking a blood vessel. Hearing the commotion, Uncle John limped to the front stoop, thinking Pop had lost his footing. But he had lost his life instead.

Somehow, this was a fitting death for my grandfather: a quiet man, unsinkable as he was, having survived at least five shipwrecks, succumbing to a sudden and quiet death. In that moment, five years before the cod fishery collapsed, my family's connection to the fishery was gone. Though the loss was deeply personal, it foreshadowed an entire population's loss for generations still to come.

The phone call from Uncle Clyde in Little Bay East to my father across the island in Summerside marked one of the rare occasions I saw Dad cry. Unaware I was there, Dad had his back turned from where I was standing in the doorway to the master bedroom. I saw him holding onto the phone receiver with two hands, like it was a life raft. He sat on the bed, his head low and shoulders hunched. There was silence before the deep sobbing, somehow controlled, maybe so us girls wouldn't overhear. Just shy of his thirty-ninth birthday, my father was fatherless.

Until then, I always thought my parents' bedroom was magical with its sparkling stucco ceiling and mesmerizing pale blue wall, where horizontal lines of stucco interchanged with stripes of swirl-patterned wallpaper. This was my father's handiwork. But as Dad sank into the royal-blue bedding, I worried the room might swallow him whole like an angry sea. Seven at the time, it was likely my first encounter with the dull pain of stress reaching across my shoulders. I attempted to blink away the tears, but I couldn't stop the flow once I learned what had happened.

Now, more than thirty years later, I'm standing steps away from Pop's porch, my grip once again tightening on the chain-link. As I feel

Grandfather "Pop" (Reginald) Thornhill (left) and one of his shipmates, Sandy Evans. (Source and date unknown)

the pressure radiate across my shoulders and a sting behind my eyes, I too feel as though I'm shrinking, somehow becoming seven again. On this spot, my grandfather took his final breath. And now, I can't help but wonder when Dad will take his.

Pop came and went on this porch since 1940 or 1941. Pop's older brother, Ches, built the house while living in Grand Bank, about 120 kilometres southwest from here. Their father, my great-grandfather, George Thomas, living in Little Bay East at that time, put a lot of work into it. Everything was new except for some salvage lumber that had come from Pop's eldest brother Will's old house, found just across and up the road (Will's house was entirely gone by the time Dad and his brothers came on the scene). Everything has a purpose or can be repurposed in the outports; there was no sense letting good lumber go to waste. Pop bought the house in 1940 or '41, and he stayed for nearly half a century. Some days, he surely must have wondered, *Will I ever return home or could this be it?*

One of those days was in late September of 1940. Pop was a dory fisher in the Banks fishery by then. In those days, offshore schooners fished the Grand Banks. The schooners launched smaller boats, called dories, to haul longlines using hundreds of baited hooks on a single line set on the ocean floor. The Grand Banks and the Flemish Cap sprawl over an area of 280,000 square kilometres—almost triple the size of the island of Newfoundland (108,860 square kilometres). As part of the Canadian continental shelf, it's one of the widest continental shelves of its kind in the world. More than 700 kilometres off the south and east coasts, it's an area where marine life has flourished, especially groundfish like Atlantic cod, haddock, pollock, capelin, Atlantic halibut, redfish (ocean perch), Greenland halibut (turbot), yellowtail flounder, witch flounder, and American plaice, as well as shellfish like crab, shrimp, and scallops. The fish are attracted to the cold of the Labrador Current meeting the warmth of the Gulf Stream over a terrain of elevated ocean floor plateaus, creating shallow, warm, sunlit depths where sea life flourishes. The humans came, from all over the world, for the fishing.

Pop likely started as a deckhand or *catchee* (sometimes called *cadgy*, *kedgie*, or *kedgy*) onboard a Banks schooner. In a September 2017 article for *The Southern Gazette*, the local newspaper published in Marystown, reporter Allan Stoodley tells the story of a Newfoundland sea captain who started as a catchee, a jack-of-all-trades job that entailed everything from "launching and retrieving the dories, doing odd jobs for the skipper, assisting the cook, manning the fog horn to help guide the dories back to the mother ship and sometimes even taking the wheel." In Raoul Andersen's 1998 book, *Voyage to the Grand Banks: The Saga of Captain Arch Thornhill*, Andersen describes a kedgie as a "deckhand, cook's assistant and sometimes replacement for adult dory fishermen." That's how my father and uncles recall Pop's accounts of his earliest fishing days. My grandfather took whatever work he could get. He'd even cook.

"The grub on board was pretty rough stuff. Salt beef, mostly," Uncle Clyde tells me. "They probably ate a lot of salt fish too." Being the eldest, Clyde has the sharpest memories of Pop's fishing days. A meal of *fish and brewis* (pronounced *brews*), salt cod boiled with hard bread, and *scrunchions*, salted fried pork fat, would have been a particular favourite among crews. It was also a meal that sailors likely invented and is still popular across Newfoundland and Labrador today. With no cold storage on board, everything the captain and crew brought or prepared for food had to be non-perishable. That's why all the cod caught in the nineteenth-century cod fishery was salted—it was the only way to preserve the catch while fishing at sea for lengthy periods. So, when Pop stepped in as cook, his main course was necessarily simple. Still, since mealtime was cherished (it was the only part of the day interrupting the work, other than sleep), Pop prepared another suppertime favourite: baked beans.

A story Pop often told Uncle Clyde went like this:

Fellow crewman: *Something wrong with these beans.*
Pop (thinking his career might be cut short): *Oh?*
Crewman (laughing): *Wasn't enough of them.*

Many fishers and even captains started out as deckhands. Captain Archibald (Arch) Thornhill, whom Pop would later work for, began his career as one. (With the same last name on the same peninsula, Captain Arch and Pop were likely distant relatives. Both had Thornhill roots on Brunette Island and a great-grandfather named William James Thornhill. But the William James on Pop's side married Hannah Hepditch, while Arch's married Mary Ann Green.) As for his experience as a deckhand, Captain Arch recounted to Raoul Andersen, when interviewed for his book, "I wouldn't make as much money as a man in a dory, but it would be a great help to my family." Deckhands would earn a small sum for the season as well as any fish they managed to catch off the side of the vessel when time permitted. If a deckhand was lucky, he'd fill in for a dory fisher who had fallen ill. He'd earn a share of the day's catch, putting some extra cash in his pocket at the end of the season.

As for Pop's work advancing from a deckhand to a doryman, Uncle Clyde told me during one of our interviews, "They wouldn't want a partner who couldn't do anything, so he must have done all right. Once you found a good match, you could be dory mates for years."

Pop picked up work dory fishing all over the Burin Peninsula. Grand Bank was for many years the centre of the Grand Banks schooner fishery, but Pop also worked for skippers in nearby Bay L'Argent, down the Burin Peninsula in Burin or Footes Cove, on the western coast of Fortune Bay in Tibbos Hill and Harbour Breton, and elsewhere across the island, off Labrador, and Nova Scotia. The kind of dory Pop would have operated on the Banks fishery was a double dory, narrow but easily rowed by two men and with adequate bottom length (stem to stern, approximately fifteen feet) to accommodate a sail rig. A dory like this, outfitted with a long overhang in the bow and stern, could be navigated in rough gales and seas.

A good day on the Banks may have gone something like this: Before dawn, the crew baited their trawl lines, often using capelin—a small, plentiful and oily fish—as bait. This happened aboard a schooner, or what they called the *mothership*, which had the dories stacked on the deck. One trawl line measured about 60 feet long (or what they would have measured as 10 fathoms), with smaller lines extending from the main long line. The smaller lines bore the baited hooks. One trawl line could have hundreds of hooks. The men would bait about ten lines each and set them aside in a tub. Each dory could accommodate two to four tubs of gear per dory mate. Once anchored in a good fishing location, the mothership would drop off the men as early as four or five in the morning, two to a dory, to begin setting and hauling their trawl lines. The dories were launched and would return to the mothership from their fishing grounds several times each day to unload their catch. It was typically the dory mates' responsibility to row back to the schooner. Commonly, they would do so with codfish packed to the gunwales (sometimes called gunnels)—a visual of how plentiful cod was in those days. When the day was done, some time in late afternoon, they would hoist the dories aboard the mothership before turning their attention to cleaning and preparing the cod for salting. After splitting and washing the catch, the crew would cure the cod with salt, then stow it in the schooner's hold. There would be a brief reprieve to eat and sleep, and the next day, they would start all over again. As soon as the schooner's hold was full, the captain would sail back to harbour to unload.

At port, the salted cod was scrubbed, then taken by horse and cart to the beach to dry by the "beach women," women in the community who spread and tended the fish as it dried. It took as long as four to six weeks to dry the fish properly on the flakes. Every day, the women would spread and turn the fish, piling and covering them overnight.

For the fishers, turnaround at port was often quick. Each trip could take weeks. The entire season took up half the year, from as early as March, but more typically late April or May, through to the end of October. The schedule varied by community, but fishers on the southern shores were afforded a longer season given their proximity to the Banks. Most of the crew would stay aboard the schooner, away from their families, until the season drew to a close.

Pop was nearing the end of his season in fall of 1940, and likely eager to return home to Little Bay East. That's because that year, he had the closest call of his career while dory fishing on the Grand Banks. Pop spoke to Clyde, throughout his life, about what happened. Here's what Clyde recalls from those conversations: Pop and a dory mate were out on the Banks. Pop turned to see the mothership, as fishers would periodically do to gauge the distance between their dory and the schooner. Pop spotted the schooner but saw there were no masts on her. It was an odd sight, given that the mothership had no power (no engine) and relied on her sails. As Pop looked more closely, he saw she was in some kind of trouble, unable to right her sails. Pop and his dory mate hauled up their trawls and rowed back to the schooner, which Clyde recalls Pop said was called the *Florence*. They and the other dorymen boarded the schooner, working quickly to salvage what they could. The situation turned from bad to worse, forcing the captain and crew to bail. They abandoned their catch, too, just as another schooner arrived to their rescue, hoisting all ten dories from the *Florence* onto its decks. The captain and crew were saved, but because the catch went down with the mothership, they all went home penniless.

It's a shipwreck that sounds eerily similar to one Captain Arch Thornhill would share in detail before his death in 1976. Captain Arch, as he was known, spoke with Raoul Andersen, an anthropologist, historian, and professor at Memorial University of Newfoundland in St. John's. The account in Andersen's 1998 book neither names my grandfather, Reginald Thornhill, nor any of the dorymen directly, but one cannot ignore the commonalities in what Clyde recalls from Pop's account and Captain Arch's version of events aboard the *Florence*.

In his account, Captain Arch acknowledges two important background details. First, he had kept no detailed captain's log or diary during his time working in the Banks fishery. This was the norm at the time. Second, Captain Arch, not wanting to be faulted for inaccuracy, and Andersen, not seeing the *who's who* as fundamental, did not name those involved. Andersen writes: "it might be interesting to learn *who* did or said this or that…[but] it was unnecessary to our purpose." Furthermore, Andersen quotes Captain Arch as follows: "I can name the names as if it were yesterday, but I'm not going to. I'm not mentioning any names."

Periodically, Captain Arch does name names, but it's of his family members or colleagues with whom he worked closely throughout his career. In his account of the *Florence*, Captain Arch also indicates the crew mostly came from Fortune Bay. He also talks about his affinity for Little Bay East. That's where his mother was from and it's where he made his first trip on a sailing boat, and later aboard a Banks schooner. It's also where he made his decision, at twenty-six, to captain a vessel. This combination of information leads me to believe Pop was aboard the *Florence* with Captain Arch.

The only other person to write about the *Florence* is Grand Bank writer Robert C. Parsons. Parsons specializes in stories of shipwrecks off Newfoundland and Labrador. He's written more books on the subject than anyone and keeps a public record of over 1,100 Newfoundland schooner men who have lost their lives at sea. Parsons wrote about the *Florence* shipwreck in his 1992 book, *Lost at Sea, Volume II* (later reprinted in 2001 as *Lost at Sea: A Compilation*). As part of his research, Parsons chatted with William Tom Thornhill (I cannot determine a family relation) in Grand Bank. Thornhill recalled nineteen crew, Parsons tells me, but my grandfather, Reginald Thornhill, wasn't one of them.

"Mr. Thornhill may have forgotten Reginald," Parsons wrote to me by email. "Regrettably William Thornhill passed away several years ago."

When I later met Parsons in Grand Bank, we chatted about the likelihood my grandfather was aboard the *Florence* on that fateful day.

"If your family remembers the story of the *Florence*, then it's probable your grandfather was there," offered Parsons.

The *Florence* was an American-made Bank fishing schooner considered a "dummy" schooner at the time she set sail on her last voyage, on September 10, 1940. She earned the unfortunate title as she was among the last Newfoundland sailing schooners awaiting an engine promised by her owners. She was the first American-built vessel Captain Arch ever sailed, having survived an August hurricane with her earlier that season, on another fishing trip. He was confident in her abilities, but she was set lower than other vessels, which carried the risk of taking on water on the deck, particularly when weighted down—for example, with a load of fish. She also sailed slow and steady, trailing the engine-fitted schooners that steamed by on their way to and from the fishing grounds.

In the account told by Captain Arch to Andersen, before the *Florence* set out to the Banks in September, the men stopped for bait: frozen squid from a bait depot shop in Fortune Bay. They set sail for the same location as in August, anchoring there and aiming to gather 4,000 kilograms of fish (or what they would have measured as 40 *quintals*). In a couple of weeks, they had reached their aim, but with a few days of bait remaining they opted to head to St. Pierre Bank. When they arrived, the weather didn't allow for fishing. As the following day was shaping up nicely, Captain Arch called his crew out in the wee hours of the morning to ready their gear. That day, the skipper opted to "fish under sail" (versus at anchor, as was usually the case), launching the dories every 30 to 40 metres, each two-man dory crew setting sail southeast. Captain Arch explains fishing under sail:

> You would tow them along in this direction, each dory would go
> down, and they'd drop their buoy overboard and tow out their
> buoy lines. When you got a little distance from one dory, you'd

drop the next one and go on until all your dories were out. And
when the last dory was dropped, you would sail down the length,
the reach of that gear, to pick them up again.

The day continued this way until it was time to pick up the dories from their last run. As Captain Arch maneuvered the vessel to initiate this process, the *Florence* caught a headwind, flattening its sails. The jib stay, which affixes the forward-most sail, had broken from the masthead, the highest point of the schooner's mast. The mast was well over the gangway (the narrow pathway connecting one end of the ship to the other) at this point, water gushing up over the stern, where the masts had broken off entirely. Water started coming in the cabin. All ten dories were out, and began making their way back, having noticed the mothership's wrecked sails. Surprisingly, all of the dorymen came aboard within the next hour. Aware that the *Florence* would sink, they gathered their belongings and whatever fishing gear was salvageable before setting back out into the dories.

Meanwhile, Captain Orlando Lace and his crew of the *Mahaska*, from Lunenburg, Nova Scotia, were also fishing in the area. They could see there was a "slab on the water" where the *Florence* had been. With the Second World War having recently begun, they worried that a submarine might have sunk the *Florence*. The captain, a native of Rencontre East in Fortune Bay and a First World War veteran, braved the scene, despite the apprehension of his crew. By the time he reached the *Florence*, she was sinking and most of the men had their belongings and gear aboard their dories. Before Captain Arch abandoned his ship, he poured gasoline across her decks and set fire to her as a visual warning to other skippers in the area. The *Mahaska* hoisted the ten dories and stacked them next to her own ten on deck. The *Florence* sank in a few hours, with her "head up high, stern first," as Captain Arch would proudly report.

Had everything gone according to plan, the captain and crew of the *Florence* would have arrived home early that morning with another 10 quintals of codfish (making their total catch 50 quintals or 5,000 kilograms). Instead, their voyage home took another eight days. The *Mahaska* was making a fresh-fish run, so had ice on board to preserve the catch, but her crew would have needed to return to unload their catch at home port. A strong gale-wind changed their plans, but eventually they made it to Sydney, Nova Scotia, where Captain Arch and his crew spent four days in a hotel before being transferred to Halifax, where a boat, likely another fishing boat, transported them home to Newfoundland.

If Pop was aboard the *Florence*, then he returned, as I do now, to this porch in Little Bay East. Mr. Owner has closed the door behind him. Dad is already at the end of the driveway. Uncle Clyde, Dad's eldest brother, and his wife, Aunt Hattie, have a cabin next door. Hattie's on the cabin's porch, waving us inside. My mother, husband, and seven-month-old daughter are already inside. We all made the drive from Grand Bank together. I take a deep breath of fresh, salty air—the smell of fish noticeably absent—take one last look at Pop's porch, and then head up the stairs to Clyde and Hattie's with Dad.

CHAPTER 2:
The Thornhill Boys

I can see the wharf from Clyde and Hattie's cabin. Beach, water, wharf, dories, fishing stages—all the similar structures are there, if not the sounds and smells I recall from when fishing was in its prime. Now, it's the lost spirits and stories I'm after.

Stories like how, when Pop would return from his work at sea to the local port, his boys would greet him. From oldest to youngest, Clyde, Reg, John, and Don Thornhill would light up like brushfire, wild and sweeping over the wooden planks of the wharf, hollering and whistling their approval.

Today, the wharf is quiet. We're all crammed inside the cabin: Clyde and Mom are on the chesterfield, Raman is holding Navya on the armchair, and Hattie, Dad, and I are at the kitchen table. Multiple conversations are underway, which is a common occurrence and always cues me to tune out. Everything looks familiar in the cabin, and it all looks fake in some way: the vinyl tablecloth, instant coffee, and evaporated milk on the kitchen table, the model tall ship, the toy rifle, and mounted moose head on the wood-panelled wall. But two things grab my attention and feel real in this ghost of a place: Aunt Hattie's homemade partridgeberry jam on the counter, and Pop's glass fishing floats hanging from the ceiling. On their own, patridgeberries have a slightly acidic taste, but these scarlet berries have been cut with sugar, making the jam a perfect combination of tart and sweet. The glass floats were once used by fishers like Pop to hang their nets and lines in place on the fishing grounds. No longer in use by most fishers, they often hang from ceilings in houses and cottages like this one as decor. On the refrigerator door, I spot the recreational cod fishery (what locals call the *food fishery*) schedule, scrawled on a piece of scribbler paper. My attention returns to Dad as he unpacks a six-pack of dark red ale and the bucket of fried chicken he insisted on picking up. Bringing these kinds of goods from the nearest town is usually met with delight by locals, but Uncle Clyde is already having a beer as he and Hattie just wrapped dinner. The rest of us—my mother, husband, and I—are still full from breakfast and my seven-month-old daughter isn't ready for fried chicken, having only recently started eating solid foods. That leaves Dad as the only one interested in chowing down, which I take as a positive sign of how he's feeling today. Clyde and Hattie are not exactly locals— they live in St. John's, but own this cabin in Little Bay East, next door to the old Thornhill family home. When they are here, they do as locals do— which can often mean doing without unless you're prepared to make the fifty-minute drive into Marystown (or elsewhere) for something you can't make or don't have at your fingertips. Dad's gesture isn't lost on them because bringing in treats like this is also part of what people here do.

Growing up, the drives Dad and I took to Little Bay East were punctuated with unhealthy-but-delicious deep-fried food choices like fries, stuffing and gravy, fish and chips, and old-fashioned plain donuts, usually from the seemingly ubiquitous Irving Big Stops. You could give someone fairly decent directions by telling them how many Irving gas stations they needed to pass to get wherever they were going. Fried-chicken joints or fish and chip shops could likely work as reliable road-markers too.

Back at Clyde and Hattie's kitchen table, we're discussing the possibility of flooding. "Never has any water came in on the floor of that house," says Clyde, pointing to Nan and Pop's old place, "but it has come up to the stairs of the porch." That was the closest the house ever came to the threat of flood waters. Nan went running up the stairs to her bedroom, afraid the water would start pouring in over the porch, says Clyde. But Pop shrugged it off, wondering what all the fuss was about. Water rising was never a good sign, but it came without the fear of drowning—or freezing to death, in this case. Still, no one wanted water in their house, so when Clyde and Hattie built their cabin, they propped it up three feet off the ground, safely above the threat of rising tides or flooding, with a spot to store their boat. "I put my boat around the [back of the] house and tie her on," Clyde says. "The plug is out of her anyway, so if water comes in, the boat fills up and empties out again."

Clyde and Hattie built this cabin back in the eighties and have been making the three-hour drive from St. John's a half-dozen times a year ever since. Clyde speaks softly and slowly, uncharacteristic of a Newfoundlander, but he makes up for it by having minimal silences between his words, which are spun together with hissing *S* sounds, a periodic *you know,* and smiles and chuckles out of the side of his mouth. Clyde dresses casually, yet is always pressed and groomed, with his moustache and hair neatly trimmed. He speaks with the authority granted to eldest siblings but doesn't flaunt it. Hattie is a cute, mousey creature with square-rimmed glasses and short, white hair. She's always at risk of being drowned out in a room of talkers, which is a common risk at kitchen tables in Newfoundland and Labrador. Still, she's effective at making her guests feel at home, scurrying unnoticed between the talking heads, whispering with her breathy voice in your ear, *Would you like some tea or coffee, my love?* I nod a quiet *yes* to the tea and take it, as my Aunt Hattie breaths a *luh,* meaning *look, there it is* (the tea), and I offer back a quiet *thanks.*

I trace my fingers over the crocheted doily in the middle of the table. The lacy pattern is a familiar texture. Some of my earliest memories here in Little Bay East are of examining and admiring the latest handcrafted or repurposed thing. The over one-metre-tall wooden model lighthouse across the road on the beach, where Clyde's boat is tied on during the season, is Clyde's own handiwork. Most of the knitted and stitched things around here are Hattie's doing. What stories the quilts might tell if you traced each square, each triangle of once-rejected fabric, back to its original source.

I remember the old Singer sewing machine Nan used to make quilts. It has a story too—Pop smuggled it back to Little Bay East during his time working on the coastal schooners, avoiding the necessary tariffs. The sewing machine was top-of-the-line and a total game-changer for Nan, who was accustomed to mending clothes and linens by hand. Everything—even the oldest, out-of-date-looking things—had a purpose. If it wasn't immediately obvious what that purpose was, then you simply hadn't had it long enough to figure it out.

Hang on, I have just the thing, is a common phrase of the outport-living do-it-yourself types. If this or that needed repair, then someone would duck out to their shed and be back with the fix. I remember Uncle John returning from the shed to hand me a plastic salt beef pail. Lightweight with a handle, it was perfect for my childhood beachcombing. I used it right over there, near where Clyde's boat and model lighthouse are now.

Uncle John always seemed to be fresh out of the shower: his black hair combed back with hair cream, a shine to his face and sparkle in his eyes behind wire-rimmed glasses. He wore slacks with a small black comb at the ready in his back pocket to sweep his mop back in order. He always seemed to be wearing a clean white undershirt, like he hadn't yet had the chance to press or pull on a proper one. He also had a perpetual grin on his face, which gave a fullness to his cheeks and made you think whenever he was about to speak, it was to let you in on some juicy piece of gossip. It was a harmless "crying wolf" case most of the time with John, but I enjoyed the lead up just the same. John's limp, a reminder of the drunk-driving accident, didn't dampen his spirits either, at least as far as I could tell. It certainly didn't prevent him from getting around. In fact, often he'd have a collection of seashells already started in the pail. I imagine beachcombing was a pursuit of patience for John, practically having to strike a yoga pose, forward-dips and balancing on his one good leg, to retrieve a shell.

I'd collect anything I thought to be of value, which for me, as a child, meant something with a seemingly rare quality. Did it sparkle or shine? Did it have an odd shape? Was it smooth? Rocks and pebbles, beach glass and bits of pottery, coral, driftwood, and even bone fragments all suited me fine. I'd climb over seaweed, driftwood, and anchoring ropes affixed to dories in the shallows of the bay, looking out for sticklebacks, two-inch and three-spined carnivorous fish, as they darted this way and that. I'd walk around lobster pots, wood piles, and buoys and overturn stones and

Uncle John Thornhill, about five years old, and father (Donald) Thornhill, not yet one year old, playing with chicks in the fields in Little Bay East, c. 1949.

(Left) Grandmother "Nan" (Emily) Thornhill standing in the garden, summer 1966.
(Right) Grandfather "Pop" Thornhill in the living room of the Thornhill home at Christmas, c.1980.

whatever debris stood between me and a good find. I took special care over the holes in the sand, worried they might be razor clams.

Who's the girl down in front of the Thornhills' place? A passerby would ask.

Oh, sure that's Don's youngest. Here for a nice visit is all, they'd respond. With the local dialect, it sounded more like:

Oo's dat girl down h'in front h'of de Tarnell's place?

H'oh, sure dat's Don's h'youngest. 'ere for h'a nice visit h'is h'all.

It's easier to write than to say—adding *Hs* (what sounds like *haitch*) in front of vowels and removing them where they naturally belong. All over this province, there are vestiges of the French and English languages, but the accents and dialects—of which there are hundreds—are uniquely their own, playfully called *Newfy* or *Newfinese*. There are academics who propose Newfoundland English is its own unique language—and author Russell A. Bragg wrote an entire book about it called *Traditional Newfoundland English: The First English Language of North America*. For me, being in Little Bay East has always offered an immersion into local dialects and the nature of language.

In 1984—the year I held Pop's hand on the wharf and learned about his own linguistic quirks, like his *wheelbarrows*—my oldest sister, Natalie, had received an autograph book as a gift. The book was called *Special Lines from Special People*, and the cover featured the cartoon character of Love-a-Lot Care Bear fishing in a heart-shaped pond. Inside, coloured pages awaited notes and words of the book owner's choice. "I asked Pop Thornhill to write something," says Natalie, recalling her excitement at filling the pages. "He wrote it all in there, very slowly, taking careful time to write it; like he really put a lot of effort and care into writing in it." But even with Pop's careful and slow writing, what he produced was almost illegible. "I remember saying to Mom or Dad 'What is that?'" Natalie says, seeing Pop had signed off as *hohhy*. "They told me it read 'Poppy,' and Poppy didn't go to school because he was a fisherman." The words Pop wrote in her autograph book were simple yet memorable, "dear natalie, just a few words to say I love dear natalie. love hohhy thornhill." Later on as a teenager, Natalie would tear Pop's autographed page from her book, fold it into her wallet, and keep it close by as a cherished memento.

Meanwhile, Uncle John, who was once a teacher, would tell us that words like *apple* and *h'apple* or *evening* and *h'evening* were like synonyms. We knew in fact they were not, but we weren't about to correct him. You didn't go into people's homes and tell them how things are, even when those things were decidedly not how they imagined them to be. Besides, what these language lessons lacked in accuracy, they made up for in culture and history.

Take nearby Tarnell Cove, for example, a small cove near Little Bay East. "Whoever did the original mapping wrote what he heard, and

The Thornhill boys (left–right): Donald ("Donnie"), one, Reginald (Reg), three, John, five, and Clyde, seven, Little Bay East, c. 1949,

whoever told him the name of that cove said Tarnell's," observed Cora Scott, who, born, raised, and still living in Little Bay East, adds the 's, as locals do. "And who knows, maybe way, way back the surname *was* Tarnell until someone changed it to Thornhill." This topic came up recently, as a few of us debated in a town Facebook group whether the cove ought to be renamed Thornhill's Cove.

"Not on my dead body," was Cora's reaction to the renaming suggestion (mine and my second cousin Frank's) and the Little Bay East town council had long-before agreed with her. Having this context helped me to understand some of the oddities in the census information too. When the British government gathered vital statistics from Newfoundland, there were entries for family names like Miles (also spelled Myles) and my grandmother's maiden name, Clark, was also spelled Clarke. But Dad says Nan shortened it from Clarke when my great-grandmother Emily (Miles) Clarke passed away, not wanting to pay for the extra E on the headstone. Indeed, he was right, as all the other Clarkes in the Little Bay East graveyard appear to have their full name spelled out, whereas my great grandparents' shared headstone has the abbreviated version. I can't verify the penny-pinching part, but it certainly fits the penny-pinching time and place.

By far the most important language lesson I learned was from Pop. For everything he could do—having survived shipwrecks and close calls, even though he couldn't swim—Pop couldn't read or write. He reported as much in the 1945 Newfoundland census. At the time, he was thirty-two, Nan was twenty-eight, and their first two boys, my uncles Clyde and John, were three and one. According to the census, my uncles *could* read and write. It was an interesting report given the contradictory record of 1935, which cited Pop could write but not read. Then there was the anomaly of two toddlers being profoundly literate. Were they child prodigies? No offence to my uncles, but likely not. In fact, the census appears to have multiple incorrect entries, but I like to think it reflects Nan and Pop's determination to ensure their boys—all four of them, including my uncle Reginald and my father, Donald, by 1948—would gain the classroom education Pop never had.

Either you get your education, or you go away and get a job was the stance Nan took. I can see her laying down that law—one of her many roles in the family. Bob-cut hair, furrowed brow, and puckered frown, Nan could look severe for such a petite woman. Despite her size, her personality towered above everyone around her. The way she took up space gave her a greater presence, too, as she would often flail her arms to give emphasis to what her scratchy and sometimes indiscernible voice would be saying. Nan had a sternness about her that often came off as just plain mean (she wielded her words like weapons—sharp, accurate kill-shots), but she was more well-meaning than anything. Above all, she was practical. Families were paid a stipend when their children attended school, so there was undoubtedly a financial incentive to Nan's *go to school or get a job* ultimatum, but mostly she and Pop wanted a better life for their boys. A better life: that was, and still is, the outport dream.

My uncles and father—The Thornhill boys—arrived on the scene like clockwork. Nan and Pop married on October 12, 1941, and then, from 1942 to 1948, they welcomed a new son into the world every two years. A healthy growing family, in and of itself, was a sign of riches in a place where there were few riches to go around.

But an embarrassment of riches also meant more opportunities for the grim realities that many faced: death in the family on and off the water was common, as young lives were lost at work, to illness, and on battlefields. Pop's older sister, Winnifred (Winnie), died in childbirth at nineteen (though public records indicate she was only fifteen at the time of her death in 1921), giving birth to a stillborn. In 1938 Pop's younger brother, Francis (Frank), and Nan's younger sister, Caroline (Car), who were married and lived next door to Nan and Pop (two brothers married to two sisters), lost an infant son in a tragic accident. Little Reginald died from accidental strangulation in his crib sheets at only four weeks. Frank and Car had more children but experienced miscarriages along the way. Meanwhile, Pop's older brother Ned lost his first wife, Blanche, at thirty-two in 1939 after the couple had already lost two sons—Chesley, nine months, in 1936, and another son in 1931. The details of their lives and deaths are scarce, but one surviving son was taken in by Ned's second wife, Sadie, and the new couple would have more children besides.

On Nan's side, sometime before 1935, her older sister Ida drowned, supposedly while rinsing her baby's dirty diapers in a nearby watering hole. Ida's death was all the more awful given that it orphaned her three children: from oldest to youngest, John Thomas, Stan, and Stella. Ida's husband and the children's father, James Henry Brown, was in no position to care for his children, given his seafaring work. My great-grandparents, Ida's parents, John Samuel and Emily Clark (with no e), adopted John Thomas and Stella, while Stan was adopted to another family. It would have been too much for one family to take in all three children. The separation—a common experience, given the realities of life and death

Three of the Thornhill boys (John, about twelve years old; Reg, about ten; and Don, about eight) with Nan (Emily) Thornhill, thirty-nine, while Carol Randell (Stella Randell's daughter) looks on, Little Bay East, c. 1956.

at sea—meant John Thomas and Stella lost touch with Stan and all of them lost touch with their father, who later drowned, supposedly on a rum run aboard a ship between Barbados and Newfoundland. "They were coming back in a storm and two men got washed over and my father was one of them," Stella, now eighty-six years old, told me.

Stella's adopted grandfather, my paternal great-grandfather, John Samuel Clark, drowned too—about four years later. John Clark was an early fisher and later boat-builder and carpenter. On December 23, 1946, Great-Grandfather Clark and Great Uncle Elias (Eli, also a fisher who likely did carpentry work too) took their dory a short distance south, around Little Bay East and across the bay to Bay L'Argent.

"They were doing work," says Stella, fourteen years old at the time, "carpentry work in a kitchen—they had a job over there, so I guess he wanted to finish it maybe before Christmas. And of course, they went out in the storm and their boats swamped, I guess." Others in my family tell me they heard John and Eli were transporting a wood stove. They also shared the supposed conversation in Little Bay East that day, which, in its simplicity, captures the stark reality of how two lives could have been spared had they known or heeded the weather warnings.

You're not going out today? asked one man to a skipper on the wharf.
No, not today, the skipper replied. *The weather is not fit. Too stormy.*
Sure, John and Elias Clark are gone up to Bay L'Argent in the dory, said the man.
But did they make it? asked the skipper.

Maybe it was the weather or maybe the motor gave out or maybe the dory took on water in a rogue wave, already weighed down by the stove. Whatever the case, the men never made it back for Christmas. "I remember very well, walking up the road on a frosty day with snow flying and hearing the news," Stella says. "It was a couple of days I think before they had found my grandfather, washed up on the shore. I think both of them did, washed up on the shore close to the cemetery."

Eli was the first one found on shore, supposedly, and without a stitch of clothing, seated upright at the high-water mark by a pile of his clothes, near a place colloquially called Ragged Rock. Those clues could indicate Eli made it to shore but froze to death once he got there, his attempts to get out of his wet clothing futile. John washed up later in a similar spot. By the time my great-grandmother Emily was given the men's clothing, she noticed their wallets were missing. *They'd take the coppers off a dead man's eyes if you'd let 'em.* Those are the words Dad remembers my great-grandmother saying about that occasion in the years that followed. She would retrieve the wallets, but the anecdote shows the desperation of those times. It wasn't that people were malicious; they were *dirt poor,* Dad says.

This is the world in which the Thornhill boys, Clyde, John, Reg, and Don, arrived and spent their earliest years. "We didn't ask a lot of questions then," says Clyde. "I don't know why, but we had our lives and our parents and grandparents, so we thought we were in pretty good shape." By all accounts, life was good. Besides his family, Pop had steady work and a roof of his own over his head. "If he had a good season, he'd make a hundred dollars a year," says Clyde. Pop did a bit better than that, based on his entry in the 1935 Newfoundland Census. Over the 1934–1935 season, at twenty-two and still living at home with his parents and younger brother Francis (Frank), Pop reported earning $150 NF. (Newfoundland had its own currency from 1865 to 1949; the Newfoundland dollar was on par with the Canadian dollar.) His father, George Thomas Thornhill, who was sixty and also a fisher, cleared $300 NF and owned the family home, valued at $600 NF. His older brothers, Ches (thirty, living in Grand Bank with his wife, Beatrice) and Edward (or Ned, twenty-seven, living in Little Bay East with his wife, Blanche, and son, Chesley) Thornhill, also did well: both owned their homes (Ches's valued at $450 NF; Ned's valued at $700 NF) and they made decent yearly wages (Ches made $300, while Ned cleared $450 NF). The 1945 census valued Nan and Pop's home at $1,000 NF and Pop earned a respectable $500 NF that year, though he had been unemployed for twenty-six weeks. Pop's jump in earnings between those census years coincides with what the average Newfoundland fisher experienced: "many fishers quadrupled their earnings, and between 1935 and 1945, their average annual income jumped from $135 to $641" (NF dollars), writes Jenny Higgins in an article for Heritage Newfoundland and Labrador. This wage increase coincides with the spike in the value of cod during the Second World War. With less fishing during wartime, cod sold for three times its pre-war rates.

But that wage increase didn't continue. My father remembers Nan saying during the 1960s (Dad would have been twelve in 1960), the family needed at least $35 Canadian dollars (CAD) a month to survive—that's less than the $41.67 NF/month (or roughly $9.62 NF/week) Pop made in 1945. And while that wage represented an increase over the wartime years, it was still well below the rest of Canada. In 1939, $28.50 CAD/week was the minimum budget for a family of five in Canada; and that average had risen to $40.11 CAD/week by 1947.

Given the seasonal nature of my ancestors' work, fishers took whatever odd jobs they could to supplement their earnings during the off-season, income they didn't necessarily declare. They would have also qualified for government relief and, later, when Newfoundland joined Canada, employment insurance, given their seasonal earnings couldn't tide them over for the year.

Fishing put money in Pop's pocket, but it meant being away from home, doing hard physical labour, and facing miserable or even dangerous conditions at sea. It was common for fishers to take ill during or after a fishing trip. One time, Pop returned home suffering from double pneumonia and rheumatic fever.

I thought you were dead, the doctor in Grand Bank told Pop after a brief hospital stay and recovery, Clyde told me. This had to have been sometime in the late 1940s or early 1950s, because Pop had access to chest x-rays. A normal x-ray would have shown the lungs as hollow, shadowless, and black with a clear definition of the ribs. In Pop's case, white, crystal-like flecks appeared in the hollows—a clear indication of damage. From what, Clyde doesn't know. Pop likely encountered similar bouts of sickness in his earlier years, but without access to medical diagnostics, advice, and treatment, Pop would have had to let these conditions run their course. The same was true of infections like tuberculosis, which plagued Newfoundland at a rate far higher than Canada, Great Britain, and the United States, mostly due to the poorer living conditions.

Pop had already retired from the Banks fishery by this time, and surely was aware that the writing was on the wall for the cod fishery. The *Florence*, which went down in flames off the St. Pierre Bank, was among the last deep-sea fishing vessels of her kind. Throughout the 1940s and 1950s, any schooners that weren't wrecks had been converted to gasoline and diesel power, but they were still no competition for the steel draggers and trawlers that had arrived on the scene. And it wasn't just the type of fishing vessel but the nature of the industry that was changing: the traditional inshore, salt-fish fishery was moving toward a contemporary offshore, dragger, fresh and frozen fish fishery.

As their name implies, draggers were equipped to drag nets along the ocean floor, scooping up everything in their path. They carried ice and made shorter trips to and from port to bring their fresh fish to market. Meanwhile, the introduction of centralized fish plants in Newfoundland and Labrador supported a frozen fish market—frozen catches were shipped abroad to markets direct. The new industrial fishery demanded more reliable vessels, equipment, and processing and marketing techniques, all of which capital-poor Newfoundlanders simply couldn't afford.

"The fishery as Pop knew it went out when the draggers came in," Dad says. "Pop took any job he could get." Over this period, some men joined draggers as crew or worked in the local fish plants. It was a pivotal time in the fishery, with technology heralding a new era, stripping locals of their competitive location-based advantage. The new fishing fleets, with their more powerful winches, echo sounders for detecting the location of fish, and automated factory freezers, were at the forefront of a more efficient fishery. It didn't matter that Newfoundlanders and Labradorians lived at the gateway of the fishing grounds because the newer fleets could get to the grounds and secure their catch faster. That meant cod and other fish species were being caught at rates never before seen.

Those without new gear or technologies were forced to find work elsewhere. Some continued working on the ocean in coastal freighting or the merchant navy. Others turned to land-based operations, such as the building of the railway, mining (predominantly iron ore but also copper and fluorspar), forestry, or pulp and paper industries. Overall, hardworking labourers remained hardworking labourers. These changes to the job market happened quickly. Reading, writing, and arithmetic were prime tickets out of these labour roles and outport communities. This was especially true for the younger generation, and the older folks knew it. For people like Pop, the best and only option was to stick with what they knew.

Pop, his older brother, Ned, and their younger brother, Frank, acquired their own schooner for inshore fishing sometime during the 1940s. Since the time of the Great Depression, merchant schooners had been sold off to Newfoundland owners and, with the demise of the traditional schooner fishery, had become more affordable. Buying the schooner was Ned's idea. He and Pop did the lion's share of the labour, especially on account of Frank's failing health. Frank had a crippling disease that was never diagnosed. His youngest son, Frank (Junior at the time), says his father's condition may have been caused by tweaking his back, either falling through a fish flake or as the result of a polio infection. The condition worsened over the years and Junior remembers fishing with his father only once in a dory. Frank's back became bowed like the handle of a teacup, and his speech was affected too. It got to the point where his own family could hardly understand him. The condition caused Frank to spend his final years, in the 1980s, in a long-term care facility in St. John's. But back in the '40s, Frank helped his brothers as best he could. My father remembers how Uncle Frank dragged his feet, frequently fell, and needed assistance because he couldn't get back up on his own.

At that time there were many small vessels operating out of Little Bay East and the neighbouring communities, primarily owned and operated by locals. On an average day there might be four or five schooners in the harbour, my father and uncles recall. There's a photo of Uncle Reg, then about two or three (1948–49), dressed in overalls and a long-sleeved shirt, hands up in the air and clearly yelling out loud, proud as a peacock. It was likely Nan behind the camera and Dad would have been close by, given he was still an infant. Reg is on the landwash, the place marking high and low tide, in Little Bay East, where I would later beachcomb, though I'd never see Pop's schooner in the background. The schooner had sails in the front and back and was fitted with two engines. One was an Atlantic Marine Engine or what was more commonly called a *make and break*, recognized for its *putt-putt* sound when the engine fires, then coasts, then fires again to maintain speed. These engines took gasoline, but many fishers opted for cheaper fuel like kerosene or diesel. The make-and-break ignition stands out in Dad's memory, reminding him of a man in town, Jimmy Miles, who lost his arm to such an engine. "He had a stump for an arm, but managed to be the best kind of carpenter just the same," Dad says. Though the engines were simple ignitions, caution needed to be paid to their operation, as parts of the engine were exposed and visible when running.

In the spring through to early fall, Pop and his brothers spent their time cod fishing near shore, often using handlining techniques. Handlining involves deploying a line with hooks, lures, or bait (squid or capelin for attracting cod) over the side of a boat like a dory. The line is pulled in by hand once the fish bites. Jigging is a version of handlining not requiring bait (though many do use bait just the same), but using a hooked lure or series of hooked lures (that look like small fish or bait), pulled up and down, to attract cod or squid.

Fishers had started using other techniques too, towing large nets called *cod seines* that encircled entire schools of codfish, dropping box-shaped nets called *cod traps* that could be left unattended and returned to later to collect the catch; *gillnets*, weighted to the sea floor, with surface floats, in effect creating a net wall requiring daily checking to ensure the catch, their gills becoming entangled in the netting, was retrieved at its most fresh; and *longlines*, which use a series of baited hooks. Handlining and trapping are considered more sustainable methods, given they selectively target their species, whereas seines and nets can catch anything in their path. Meanwhile, dragger gear offshore can be especially damaging, disrupting entire wildlife and habitat on the seafloor. The rise in these new methods were all attempts at keeping catch rates as high as possible. Some methods, like seines, traps, nets, and longlines, were in use as early as the mid-1800s in the global fishery.

"Some argued the gear left too few fish behind for handliners, who could neither compete with nor afford the intrusive equipment; others worried the new technologies were depleting inshore cod stocks," this, according to Heritage Newfoundland and Labrador. "Government inaction compounded the handliners' discontent and a frustrated few began to sabotage seines and other gear. Eventually, however, other fishers either had to adopt the gear out of necessity or, if they could not afford them, work for those who had adopted them, recognizing that few jobs existed on the island outside the fishery."

This same story would play out as longliners replaced dories, schooners, and punts. But for a time, at least, my grandfather and great-uncles enjoyed schooner fishing.

When Pop and his brothers returned home from fishing, they would cure the catch with salt, laying it to dry in the sun on wooden flakes. The flakes were lined up on the beach by the barasway behind Pop's and Frank's houses. People strung their fish on clotheslines to dry too. Drying might take weeks or over a month, especially if the weather called for rain, requiring the codfish to be covered or brought inside.

By late November and early December, the herring fishery was in full swing, with Pop and his brothers using gillnets. Getting herring to market required less work than cod. After they were caught, herring were easily frozen with natural frost, then sold by the early new year. Herring was in demand across the island and elsewhere—both as food (fresh, frozen, smoked, cured, canned, or as roe) and bait.

The influence of the fishery was all around in those days. In Little Bay East, there was a lobster factory, a herring factory, and salted cod being dried on flakes, clotheslines, and beaches. At the bottom of Fortune Bay, inland from the ocean, the Thornhill boys enjoyed their sheltered cove on the western side of the Burin Peninsula. It was considered a safe harbour and, at its peak, was home to a population of between 250 and 300, all of whom were making a good living:

> Everybody had nice houses, quite a bit of land, and they kept cattle, sheep and goats. In those years quite a few men own and commanded their own vessels. Most were small and carried crews of from eight to ten men. Many came to this place to wash the fish they caught on the Grand Banks and off the southern Labrador Coast. The women and children 'made' the fish on the fish flakes all along the water front. They used the dollars they earned from this work to beautify their homes.

This description from 1913 comes from Raoul Andersen's book *Voyage to the Grand Banks: The Saga of Captain Arch Thornhill*. That was also the year Pop was born. My father and uncles remember their outport home similarly, some forty years later, save for the women and children preparing the cod flakes. Right up through high school, the boys would periodically catch their own fish to make a bit of pocket money, getting seven to ten cents CAD a pound. They mostly sold the fish fresh; if the fish required cleaning and salting, they would ask Pop to help out, but it wasn't as common a practice by then.

The Thornhill family had a vegetable garden, tended to by the women. With limited space and poor soil, Pop's mother and aunts worked hard to keep potatoes, turnip, carrots, onions, cabbage, beets, parsnips, pumpkins, and rhubarb. The women also foraged for blueberries, patridgeberries, and bakeapples (also known as cloudberries in other northern climates; bright orange berries which grow well in marshlands), while the men hunted for moose and game birds, and snared rabbits. Families kept livestock too. My father recalls they had three or four sheep for making home-knit wool garments, and a few hens for eggs. Some families kept goats and cows for milk and making butter and cheese, but there was limited grazing land in Little Bay East. "[The sheep] roamed everywhere," Dad recalls, "eating freely the wild grass, down on the other side of the harbour. Funny thing is, they seemed to migrate to different spots depending on the wind direction and other climate conditions. It was not nice dodging sheep shit on the road though, especially while running back and forth to school!"

The school in Little Bay East was affiliated with the United Church and of the one-room variety. Not having adequate numbers of students to accommodate separate classes, the schoolchildren up to grade five shared their own classroom, while those from grade six onwards shared their own. The teacher for each class assigned curriculum according to each student's level of education. The highest level of schooling one could acquire in Little Bay East was grade eleven—the highest standard anywhere in the province—but the grade levels available each year depended on whether there were students to fill them.

Dad was the only student to pass the grade nine exams one year. In grade ten, there were only two students—him and Eric Green. When spring broke, Eric left for lobster fishing, leaving Dad as the only candidate for grade eleven: "Myself, I went to Bay L'Argent in a dory, to stay there for a week doing my grade ten public exams," Dad says. "Knowing better now, I could have walked each day the 2.5 miles by road. The fresh air could have done my brain thinking much better. Instead it was a thing to do to cram as much as you could before writing [the exams]. I could guess within a few marks what my results would be."

As Dad would have guessed, he passed that year. Not liking the prospects of being the lone grade-eleven student, he moved to Grand Bank with his uncle Ches and aunt Beat for his final year of high school. By that time, Ches had long retired from the Banks fishery and was working at the local fish plant. The school in Grand Bank was the John Burke Regional High School, and is still in operation today. That year, 1964–65, Dad was one of about fifty students in grade eleven and there were close to two hundred in the school overall, affording him a far richer learning experience than Little Bay East ever could.

There were other opportunities, too. Dad was into making model wooden dories as a pastime. He planned to sell a particularly beautiful one in Grand Bank. *Before we sell it, let's put it in the fair,* said Uncle Ches, encouraging Dad to showcase his craftsmanship at a local exhibition. Sure enough, Dad won a twenty-five-dollar prize for his handiwork and went on to sell the dory, too. It was good pocket money for my father, who by now was realizing his family might be considered poor as he compared his life to those of his classmates in Grand Bank. Pop was already paying room and board to Ches and Beat for Dad's lodgings, so if Dad didn't make his own cash, he would almost certainly go without.

Father Donald (Don) Thornhill during his teaching year in Winterland, Newfoundland c. 1965–66.

Eager to start earning his own money, Dad did probationary teacher training the summer after grade eleven, and was assigned a teaching job in Winterland, between Marystown and Grand Bank. Clyde and John would follow similar paths, completing their grade eleven in Little Bay East, and then taking teaching jobs. Clyde taught in Boat Harbour while John taught in Harbour Mille and Little Bay East. Meanwhile, Reg followed his own path—or, more specifically, the more common path: dropping out of high school.

Instead of continuing grade nine, Reg started working on a coasting or freighting boat, sailing between outports on the island and throughout the region to support local merchant trading. He went on to fishery college and took a small-engine repair course in St. John's after that, but having grown restless with the outport lifestyle, he eventually said, *To hell with this.* He and a crowd of boys from the area packed up for Renfrew, Ontario, where they found work repairing old railroad tracks. Getting to know the surrounding area, he eventually found mining work further north in Timmins, where he still lives today.

I came to know Uncle Reg least, because of the distance between us— he in northern Ontario, we in western Newfoundland. There was one family vacation when we drove from Corner Brook to Timmins, but it was the only time. My father was afraid of flying, so our vacations were mostly relegated to the island. What I did gather about Reg was that he continued on as a *To hell with this* kind of man. Case in point was his ongoing bargaining with his family doctor upon finding out he had high blood pressure. If revealed, the health information could threaten his work in the mines. *I don't have high blood pressure doc, right?* Reg would say to his family doctor. He'd rather die providing for his family than live on welfare. Year after year, the doctor obliged, granting him the clean bill of health he needed.

I could tell Reg kept working with Newfoundlanders in Ontario because he had the thickest accent of all of the Thornhill boys, save for his dropping in a mainlander *eh* for the Newfoundlander *hey.* He was also the first person I ever heard swear unapologetically. It wasn't an occasional curse word, either. Reg dropped F-bombs in all of their glorious forms—as a verb (*so-and-so fucked that person over*), a noun (*that guy is a fucker if ever I saw one*), and as an adjective (*ain't that fucking beautiful*). It wasn't that Reg was a cantankerous man; he simply said things as he saw them. In some ways I learned a superior grammar lesson from Uncle Reg, the scholastic underachiever, than I ever did from Uncle John, the only university-educated one.

The three Rs—reading, writing, and arithmetic—were essential learning for the Thornhill boys. All of them learned the *wheelbarrow* lesson from Pop.

Dad, do you know this word? John, do you know this word? Reg would commonly ask.

Ah, call it wheelbarrow, Pop would respond. The boys knew there was only so much Pop could do, and *wheelbarrow* became more or less a joke between them. But while they joked, Pop was learning from the boys' questions—and their answers, too. As the boys' literacy skills improved, so too did Pop's. When I came into the picture, I also learned Pop's wheelbarrow lesson, which is as helpful to me now as it was to me back then as a new reader. The lesson was this: be resourceful. Don't let that one word or fact or tidbit of information or one *thing* prevent you from seeing the big picture. Don't perceive that small road bump as a barrier. Keep going. And that's just what Pop did. Over the years, he taught himself to write—I think so he could communicate with his sons, who, one by one, were leaving the outport.

Each of the Thornhill boys left with the intention of settling elsewhere, away from the rural fishery lifestyle they'd only ever known. After high school John pursued the army, but they told him he was *not suitable*. He heard the same when he tried out for nursing, so he pursued a Bachelor of Arts instead, becoming the first in the family to get a university degree. After his teaching gig, John moved to St. John's to take up work as a door-to-door salesman selling Electrolux vacuums. City life had its excitement, but for boys from around the bay, the city's hustle and bustle could be nerve-wracking at times. "When I was thirteen, looking over the water, I could only imagine what St. John's looked like," Dad once told me, considering his first days living in the city. "I was afraid to cross the road at the top of St. Clare Avenue. I'd wait until someone else crossed first a couple of times until I got used to the traffic signals."

Meanwhile, John was taking to city life quite naturally—moving up in his career, in fact. He had just started working for the Canadian department store Zellers when the accident happened. John was standing at the open trunk of his Ford Pinto station wagon parked on Scott Street when a drunk driver came barrelling around the corner toward him. The driver sandwiched John between the front bumper of his car and the back bumper of John's. The impact pinned both of John's legs before catapulting him through his station wagon with such force that his upper teeth left an imprint on the plastic dashboard and cracked his jaw, leaving it dangling out of place. At the hospital, the doctors could not save his right leg, and so amputated it below the knee. He continued to have trouble with his left leg given the considerable impact it, too, had endured. John would have two scars tracing from the corners of his mouth to below his chin, forever revealing the severity of that broken jaw. The impression of John's teeth in the dashboard was a constant reminder of the accident too. Since Dad bought the station wagon as our family car, I had plenty of opportunity to run my fingers over the indentation, allowing my imagination to fill in the rest of the horrid details.

He had his education, he could have gone on teaching, Reg would say, always tough as nails. But John lacked confidence and maybe always had, say Clyde and Dad. During the lengthy healing process, John collected an insurance payout and secured disability insurance, opting to move back to Little Bay East to live with Nan and Pop. The move home was a decision no one was particularly thrilled about. For Nan and Pop, the boys moving out was a sign of success and this decision, despite the circumstances, flew in the face of that philosophy. John, too, was unhappy. *If I had the choice to live as I do now, all banged up, or live on one cent a day, I'd choose the one cent a day*, John once told Dad. He wanted his health and mobility back. I don't think he intended to stay living in Little Bay East or with his parents all those years, but that's how it turned out.

Meanwhile, Clyde and Dad left teaching to take advantage of a trade bursary program in the province training technologists in laboratory science and diagnostic imaging. They loved math and science and likely could have pursued medicine, but were limited by the expense. The boys, now young men, could be as resourceful as they liked, but they could not ignore their humble beginnings. The reality of being born into a family of outport fishers—and turning their backs on it—was never distant.

"I did *not* want to go on the water," my father once told me. I had been interviewing him, trying to pinpoint the time when our family's link to the fishery was severed. "My father was shipwrecked too many times for me to like that," said Dad. "Also, the captain is the last one to leave the ship. While I would have done good with navigation, I was just not fond of being out to sea. I remember fishing boats that took on frozen ice and became top-heavy and went beneath the sea, all hands lost! There were too many reminders of these things happening."

One of those memories was back in the late 1950s, when the boys were still in grade school. It may have been around 1958, when Dad was ten and Clyde was sixteen or so. They recall the wool coat Pop showed up wearing when he returned home. That coat was memorable because it was a *new-to-them* jacket. Pop had received it from the Red Cross after having been rescued with only the clothes on his back.

That season Pop had agreed to fish for swordfish aboard a longliner as part of a small crew of four or five. The rest of the crew came from English Harbour on the northeastern Bonavista Peninsula, so they likely picked Pop up and headed to the Grand Banks from there. Longlining was a relatively new practice for the Canadian swordfish fishery at that time, having been formally introduced in 1962, though many had already initiated the practice. According to the federal Fisheries and Marine Services (now the Department of Fisheries and Oceans), swordfishing came about after reports of accidental swordfish catches by foreign longliners fishing for tuna and mackerel. Previously, swordfishing was exclusively carried out using harpoons, but now *longlines*—a main line with baited hooks set on branching lines—could be set near the water's surface to lure the swordfish. Longline fishing boats were relatively small compared to other vessels involved in the Banks fishery.

Whatever happened, the vessel Pop and the other men were on caught fire, forcing them to disembark quickly to a lifeboat without any of their personal belongings. Three vessels, likely Spanish and Portuguese, formed a triangle around the lifeboat, using ropes to secure physical communication with the lifeboat and bring the swordfish crew to safety aboard one of the other vessels. The men were dropped at a nearby port where they received the Red Cross clothing donations. Pop arrived home wearing a wool coat with a checkered white pattern. It was not exactly something Pop would normally wear, but it did fulfill the most crucial job—keeping him warm.

On another occasion, Pop recounted how he and a dory mate were knocked overboard hauling in their gear. They weren't sure what upset their balance, but they talked about everything from a whale to a shark to a rogue wave. They held on to the trawl line to pull themselves back aboard the dory. There were countless second-hand accounts Pop told too. In one, a man fell overboard and his quick-acting dory mate grabbed him by the hair on his head. In another, a man fell through the ice. With quick thinking, he slapped his wet wool mittens on the ice. The mittens froze in place, creating a place the man could grip onto and hoist himself out of the frigid waters.

The boys heard these first- and second-hand accounts and they witnessed the effects of marine storms and hurricanes from the lookout spots above Little Bay East, where they would climb to the tops of the hills near their home to storm-watch—to see the waves roll way out, then way back in. "There was seemingly no pattern to it and to watch it that way, from a theatrical perspective, was something wonderful," Dad recalls. Perched behind the rocks on the mountain, the boys would wait for the wind to rip until it blew off somebody's roof. Even on a beautiful day, an ocean swell might come in and docks, boats, and people would get swept out, some for good. Not that the boys would wish that upon anyone of course, but that was the power of nature they encountered.

What the boys didn't witness themselves, they could hear about. They eavesdropped in real time on sea captains' ship-to-shore radio conversations using their own shortwave radio. They heard many a stressful conversation—enough to animate the stories they heard of the devastating shipwrecks of their time. Wrecks like the *Blue Wave* trawler in 1959.

In early February of that year, a winter storm wreaked havoc across Canada's eastern seaboard. The wind gusted to well over 100 kilometres per hour and the temperatures dipped to thirty below. The *Blue Wave* was on a course from the Grand Banks after securing its staggering fifty-thousand-plus kilograms of fish. Despite the ship's veteran captain and crew, the conditions created icy buildup that the crew couldn't contend with quickly enough. Icy cold ocean spray froze to the vessel's structure. This was a common occurrence in inclement weather, the waves reaching heights of twenty-five feet, but potentially catastrophic if the vessel becomes top-heavy. In such a case, a ship is susceptible to rolling over and capsizing.

The *Blue Wave* sent a mayday signal and while many ships sought to respond, the dense fog made the vessel impossible to locate. Into the second day of the search, two of the *Blue Wave*'s unmanned dories and her unmanned lifeboat were spotted off of Cape St. Mary's on Newfoundland's Avalon Peninsula. The sighting gave a clear indication that all had been lost. That year, 1959—when Dad was eleven, Reg thirteen, John fifteen, and Clyde seventeen—was a particularly fateful one for Banks fishers. *The Western Star* newspaper in Corner Brook reported in its February 12, 1959, issue the sinking of an astonishing 142 ships in the North Atlantic over the previous two weeks alone.

Even knowing these gruesome details, the boys took plenty of risks of their own. In a game of *copy*, a version of follow-the-leader, they would trace each other's footsteps, one-by-one, jumping from one floating ice pan to another in the bay. In the spring, pack ice broke up in Fortune Bay, providing plenty of opportunity for this dangerous game. With each pan sinking under the weight of each boy, it could quickly become a fearless rivalry of who would dare stay out in the harbour the longest or travel the farthest.

They played other games, all in pursuit of passing time in the outports. Games like *puss-and-duck*, also called *piddly sticks*, played with sticks and

Wintertime looking down Harbour Road in Little Bay East, Newfoundland, February 1956. (Source unknown)

stones; *Red Rover* on the wharf brought the added risk of someone falling in. Sometimes it was as simple as using a branch to stir up some dust on the road or throwing rocks in the cove; other times, they fashioned bows and arrows or slingshots by tying a rock onto a stick, like a fishing rod. Somehow, everyone came away from these games unscathed. It was all part of making one's own entertainment and it wasn't just the boys who took part. The men in the community enjoyed an occasional dangerous game of their own, and they loved practical jokes, too.

Dad remembers one such gag. One of the men in town would catch, skin, and hang rabbits on a line in his yard. On several occasions, he realized someone had stolen the rabbits. Having a fair idea of the thief's identity and being of the opinion that the thief was too lazy to do his own hunting and didn't deserve someone else's goods, the man sought revenge.

By the way, did you enjoy your meal of rabbits? the man asked the supposed thief.

What rabbits?

Meow, said the man, catching some laughs from those around him who were in on the joke. He had skinned a few feral cats, hanged those out too, and the same thief made off with the meat. Unless the man was wrong about the thief's identity, then the thief may never know the difference. Word must have reached the thief, though, as the thievery ended immediately.

Climbing hills, jumping ice pans, dodging sheep shit, taking Pop's dory out to neighbouring communities, or catching and curing a few fish—it all meant that Nan was forever mending the boys' clothes. This was yet another task she did by hand (until the arrival of her sewing machine) as if the farming, cooking, and cleaning were not already enough on top of raising four boys mostly alone. Adjustments had to be made as the same pair of trousers worked their way from Clyde to John, Reg, and Don.

"With the wear and tear we gave our clothes, it's a wonder I had any pants to my name," says Dad, the youngest and most at risk of going pantless. It was such a common occurrence the boys remember a limerick they would recite about losing one's pants:

There once was an old man from Belleorum,
who bought a pair of pants and wore 'em.
He went to St. Jacques and got a new axe
and went in the woods and tore 'em.

By the early 1950s, when many schooners had been forced out of the fishery by the factory freezer trawlers (in effect, floating fish factories) and a number had become coasting vessels carrying freight to and from various ports, Pop joined a coastal schooner service sailing between ports in Nova Scotia and Newfoundland while still periodically fishing for the next decade. Pop likely would not have recognized the Banks fishery by then. Diesel-engine trawlers from all over the world—Canada, the United States, Russia (then the Soviet Union), France, Iceland, Norway, Portugal, Spain, Germany (West)—were competing for cod, processing and freezing their catch onboard, then delivering it directly to their markets.

"By 1953, more than 500 trawlers were fishing the northwest Atlantic," writes Graeme Wynn in the foreword to Dean Bavington's book *Managed Annihilation: An Unnatural History of the Newfoundland Cod Collapse.* "[A] decade later, the number approached 1,000, and many of them were among the largest fishing vessels in the world." Catch rates soared at that time and many fish stocks, including cod, may have been at their healthiest, as fishing had slowed during the Second World War, potentially allowing the stocks a chance to rebound and flourish. But the growth in the cod stocks would turn out to be no match for the growth in technology, which allowed greater precision and efficiency in catching cod and other fish.

It was also at that time that Newfoundland was officially handing over control of its fishery to Canada. The *Terms of Union*, the agreement outlined on March 31, 1949, and governing Newfoundland's relationship to the rest of Canada, granted the federal government control over the "[p]rotection and encouragement of fisheries" (draft term 5, no. 8); however, the terms provided for a five-year transitional period. And so, in 1954, the federal Department of Fisheries took over from the Newfoundland Fisheries Board (Term 22).

Folks like Pop, who had moved onto other careers, likely looked on and wondered how all of this was possible. While today we would consider traditional fishing methods more sustainable, at the time, were considered outmoded, even antiquated.

Pop continued to enjoy a career at sea, as the lifestyle on the coastal boats was much the same as on the schooners, though the food was better given they had ice on board, allowing for perishables. The coastal boats or *steamers*, as they were once called, were owned and operated by the Canadian National Railway (CNR), carrying mail, freight, and passengers. In fact, these boats would have been the only mode of travel available at the time for those from remote communities. Pop spent much of the next ten years aboard such a boat in and out of Lunenburg, Nova Scotia. He grew accustomed to the luxuries freighting afforded, using the ice for his food preserves, and smuggling items back to Little Bay East, like Nan's sewing machine and a new stove.

The shipping service operated over the same seasons as the fishery— about six months of the year spring to fall. Pop spent most of his time aboard the SS *Clyde Valley*, an old steel boat used as an ammunition ship at one time, but owned and operated by shipping companies like the Riverport Steamship Company in 1946, and Lake Shipping Company in 1955.

It was aboard the *Clyde Valley*, sometime in the 1950s, that Pop would have yet another close call. Again, details are scarce. Just off of the coast of Labrador, probably near Nain, the vessel ran aground on the rocks in 145-kilometre-per-hour winds. Stuck in the shoals, the vessel required assistance and had to be patched by divers, no doubt delaying Pop's trip. This time, the close call did not threaten his life, but reminded him that accidents can happen.

People were of the god-fearing variety in those days and with good reason. Prayer kept fishermen and coasting crew safe and families fed, but it was often recited as ritual more so than religion. There was a Congregational Church erected in Little Bay East in 1909 that lasted until the late 1950s or early '60s. Jimmy Miles, the carpenter who lost his arm in the make-and-break engine, was the main builder of the new United Church of Canada (a joining together of the Congregational, Presbyterian, and Methodist churches). The new church was far more open than the previous. It had a base of rock with a metal frame that supported its high ceilings and a steeple roof. Another church would later replace this one and still stands today.

There wasn't always a Sunday church service, given that one minister serviced the churches of Pool's Cove, Anderson's Cove, and Little Bay East. Still, there was the Sunday etiquette. Work ceased as of Saturday evening and Sunday was the time to dress your best and take a stroll. When a service or ceremony was needed at the same time in multiple communities, ministers were replaced by laymen trained to act on their behalf. (Pop's father, George Thomas Thornhill, served in this role; someone in town had even given him a piece of clapboard engraved *Reverend George Thomas Thornhill*.) Before funeral homes came into existence, such arrangements were the responsibility of the church, too. Caskets were built from the same long boards people used to craft their dories. Whether you died dory fishing or died on dry land, it was the same lumber you would go down in.

Just as one minister served multiple communities, so too did one doctor. There was a doctor in Bay L'Argent who would take house calls, but typically required patients to travel to his clinic. Nan Thornhill called the doctor to drop in when Great-grandmother Emily became ill at eighty-three. A few days earlier, her sight had been so sharp she could spot a dime on the floor. Suddenly she had come down with flu-like symptoms. One evening she asked Nan for a spot of brandy, gulped it down, and died. Great-grandmother Emily had lived with Nan, Pop, and their boys since Dad was five or six years old.

It would have been close living quarters then and still was with five bodies in the Thornhill house: a three-bedroom house with a closet that later became the washroom on the second storey; and a kitchen with a pantry, small sitting room, and a sizeable living room on the main level.

Wood was the primary fuel for heating the house and for cooking. In the kitchen, there was a wood cookstove that warmed the kitchen and pantry but did little for the rest of the house in the dead of winter.

Somehow Nan knew exactly when to put the bread in the oven and when to take it out. Years of practice making a dozen loaves a week to feed her hungry boys helped. Bread was the staple food. When there were no more meat, potatoes, and gravy, bread was always on hand. Of course, the family ate fish too, but meat was the premier choice. Meat was a marker for how well economically the family was doing. Even bologna— as questionable a meat source it may appear to outsiders—was (and to some degree still is) considered a delicacy, certainly enjoyed on the island of Newfoundland more so than anywhere else in Canada.

By the time they were ready for bed, the boys would head upstairs, change into their pajamas, and climb into bed as quickly as possible. The cold penetrated the second floor something fierce in winter. To stay warm, each boy had his own rock—long and smooth, something the shape of bologna—which he would heat on the stove, wrap in a blanket, and place at the foot of his side of the bed. Clyde and John occupied one room and a bed, while Reg and Dad shared the other. Another reason to get into bed quickly was that the last one in had to turn out the kerosene lamp. The boys had a small battery-operated flashlight too, but Nan didn't feel safe with batteries inside the house, and so made the boys keep the flashlight in the shed. When they awoke the next day, they couldn't see out the window given the frost and, if they were lucky, the *piss pot* in the hallway and the *slop bucket* in the closet had frozen over, eliminating the smell.

Nan ruled the roost, always. It was only right. Long trips at sea took their toll on the women and children left behind in outport communities. The endless tragedies certainly had their effect, but even the time men spent away doing seasonal work had its challenges. The absence of husbands, fathers, and sons placed great pressures on women. Tensions and conflicts could be high during the short period men were home, with mothers, children, and others competing for their attention. Nan had a simple and effective solution to all of this, the Thornhill boys recall. *Your father needs to go to bed*, she would tell the boys. That was one way of handling any lovemaking problems. As the boys grew older they, too, would encounter their own, similar problems.

"Becoming of age was a real problem [in Little Bay East]—few choices of girls to no girls to be had as friends," Dad told me. "Also, it could generate too much small talk." Not only that, but most people were related in some way. While that was at one time acceptable (take my Nan's sister Edith marrying her cousin Simeon just a generation before as an example), it was no longer acceptable to knowingly get involved with a relative, even a distant one. I write "knowingly" because many in the area and even the island have a distant familial connection.

Even more challenging in a small community was handling the incessant gossip. It was so bad that Dad asked a girl he once dated if she wouldn't mind walking on opposite sides of the road during their time together, all in an attempt to throw the town off the scent and curb the community small talk. She obliged, but the relationship didn't last.

Perhaps most challenging of all was Nan's attitude and constant meddling. Dad recalls one instance when he had a serious girlfriend, Audrey. Dad was heading away for school and had earned enough money to pay for dentures to replace his upper teeth. Embarrassed to see the girl during the transitional time when he had all of his top teeth removed, he initiated a breakup, giving Audrey vague reasons. If it was meant to be, they would find a way to rekindle the relationship, Dad thought. Turns out the girl remained in touch. She mailed letters to Dad via his parents' address. Only when it was too late did Dad learn Nan had kept the letters from him. She had decided the young woman wasn't worthy of Dad's attention. Later, when Dad met my mother and married her, Nan complained he should have stayed with Audrey.

"I had my mind set on her," Dad says about the first time he saw my mother, Pauline Marshall, at a student union meeting before asking her to a school dance. To see photos of them now is like looking at John Travolta and Olivia Newton John from *Grease*, except Dad didn't have a car so took photos leaning up against a half-dozen others. There's a collection of photos of Mom and Dad playing checkers. Ruffled clothes and wide grins show neither are preoccupied with the game.

"I more or less said eff this, I've got to live my own life," says Dad. Nan's growing disdain for my mother mostly came down to religion. Mom was raised Catholic and Nan could never deal with that reality. To Nan, the differences between her United Christian faith and Mom's Catholic Christian faith were insurmountable, which is why she refused to attend Mom and Dad's wedding. The wedding took place in a Catholic church and was officiated by a priest joined by a United minister—it was an important gesture, but not enough to please Nan. Pop supported the wedding, but couldn't go against Nan. Married folks stuck by one another, even when it wasn't deserved.

Meanwhile, Nan took more to Reg's wife, Lorna, and Clyde's wife, Hattie, who were not only of the same faith as Nan but were from the same region. Mom, on the other hand, hailed all the way from Corner Brook, the pulp and paper city over six hundred kilometres away on the west coast of the island. Mom also worked as an x-ray technologist just like Dad, while Lorna and Hattie were stay-at-home wives, just like Nan. As it happened, John would never marry. It's difficult to imagine how he could have while living under Nan and Pop's roof. That fact alone surely plagued John's already poor self-confidence. Pop was not the kind to interfere, but he quietly disagreed with Nan all the while, making visits in Little Bay East bearable for Mom and eventually the rest of us too.

While the boys were settling into their new lives, Pop's health was worsening. To continue working on the coastal boats, he had to pass regular physical exams. He found out he had high blood pressure, so the SS *Clyde Valley* refused to clear him for work and sent him home. Pop kept working well into his mid-sixties, mostly doing his own thing, dory fishing around Little Bay East. He had a lobster license around that time with about thirty-five lobster pots that he would set around the bay, catching about five lobsters a day in season. His lobster license, a small piece of tin that fishers would attach to their dories, is still in the Thornhill shed and dated 1974. He had a license for salmon fishing and carried on catching herring, too.

By 1974, twenty years had passed since Canada assumed responsibility from Newfoundland for the fisheries. That year also marked the low point, pre-moratorium, of the inshore cod fisheries. Northern cod followed a migrating season that entailed heading offshore to the banks in fall for spawning, then returning inshore for summer feeding on capelin. With cod fishing on the offshore banks having reached an all-time high over the last decade, the result was a decline of cod in the inshore fisheries in the 1970s.

Although it was no longer his primary career and hadn't been for decades, Pop continued to fish cod and salmon in those days. In a 1979 letter to my father, Pop wrote about his intentions to "gig [*sic*] a few codfish" that year, preferring it to the "salmon racket."

Did Pop know the extent of the problem with the cod stocks? I can't be sure, but the troubles were there.

"The stock had sustained an annual fishery in the neighbourhood of 250,000 metric tons for about 200 years (until the 1970s)," writes Art May, former Deputy Minister of DFO in a 2009 article, "THE COLLAPSE OF THE NORTHERN COD," for *Newfoundland Quarterly*. "With the buildup of offshore fishing, the total catch in the late 1960s peaked around 800,000 tons. The seeds of the northern Cod's destruction were therefore planted during the 1960s."

Others have made similar hypotheses. Perhaps most scathing are the estimates by fisheries biologists Jeffrey Hutchings and Ransom Myers, who reported the northern cod caught between 1960 and 1975 roughly equalled the catch between 1500 and 1750. Many took the poor inshore catch rates at that time to mean overfishing in the inshore cod fishery. In reality, overfishing was happening everywhere, but the high catch rates offshore during cod's spawning seasons was surely the greater issue.

My uncle Clyde told me about a time he borrowed one of Pop's dories to get to and from Anderson's Cove one stormy evening. Clyde pulled the dory onto shore in Little Bay East, but it must have drifted around the cove in the weather. The dory suffered a beating with the waves pounding it against the rocks, causing it to break into pieces. It's astonishing how something that lasts so long in a rugged environment can one day just be gone. The same could be said for fish. And people for that matter. People like Pop.

Pop's high blood pressure caught up with him, and he succumbed to a heart attack in 1987. His death was just shy of the cod moratorium in 1992. By 1995, all major cod and flounder fisheries on the Grand Banks were closed and the catch levels of many other fish species such as Greenland halibut and redfish were sharply restricted.

The moratorium was the nail in the Newfoundland cod fishery coffin, but Pop didn't live to see it come to fruition. Nan continued running the Thornhill home until she died, in 2005. I was twenty-five by then, trying to find myself as a woman in the world and hesitant about embracing my Newfoundland and Labrador roots. Then, by the time Uncle John died in 2016—likely of a heart attack, but possibly a stroke—the island had changed. I had too.

More than 2,600 kilometres away, I experienced a miscarriage on the same evening John died. My uncle's death meant the Thornhill home would be put on the market. Clyde still had his cabin next door to John's in Little Bay East, but the physical connection to Pop felt nearly gone for good and, with it, my family's link to the fishery. Dad did not yet know his cancer had returned, and I was growing pessimistic that a baby was ever in the cards for my husband and me. My world was out of sorts, and all I knew was that I needed to go home.

CHAPTER 3:
Growing up *Newfie*

Nearly forty years after Pop died, I'm holding one of the many letters he wrote to my father. It's written in blue ink with cursive writing on scribbler paper showing its age, discoloured beige with frayed edges. The letter is dated January 27, 1979, a year before I was born, and begins (in Pop's broken written English), "Dear sun Don. Just a few words to let you now I recived your litter whas good to hear from you over their. and whas very glad what yous send me...." At the end of most pages, Pop writes "next page" or "over," signalling it's time to turn the page. Most people don't need that level of instruction and it reminds me of something I might have done as a child. He also includes a number of handwritten corrections, like repeatedly changing "off" to "of" and crossing out unnecessary words, like when he repeats himself: "you you." He even draws a tiny image of a squid over his attempt at spelling the word ("skuid"), and writes a few extra lines at the top of the last two pages: "so I say good night night" and "I well learn after a wile to write a litter." For all its imperfections, it's a perfect letter to me. Touching those words on the page is remarkable. The fact that he wrote six whole pages of text is even more astonishing; and there are more letters where this one came from. To think, Pop broke the literacy barrier that held him and so many like him back—men and women who built this fishing nation with their own hands and hard work, without reading and writing skills, but skills just the same.

There's so much of Pop in these pages—the syntax, the shape of the letters on the page, the texture of the paper. All of this, beyond Pop's handwriting and spelling, that reveals to me the place, the period, and the person. He paints a picture of a way of life. Pop writes about the "very hard frost" that winter in Little Bay East and how he had already burned through five bags of coal and a cord of wood by the new year. He writes about his water supply, threatened by a worrisome-looking dam, and of his fiftieth year of fishing, he writes:

I cross off my samlon licences and I had a call from a girl what works with the fisherys she said mr thornhill do you foget to mark in your samlon licences. I said I dinte want nether one. but you she said if you dont get one this year you would get one nixt year she said. so any way when I recived my dory number I got a samlon licences too but I got my net gone I dont worry about because it too much dirt gone around now better to try to gig a few codfish.

Pop's words capture one scene after another of the outport lifestyle. As a sixty-six-year-old man, he would have been semi-retired, but as a fisher, he never gave up. His words about jigging a few cod come across as nonchalant, given what was brewing in the background cod fishery.

Meanwhile, across the island, Mom, Dad (both thirty-one), and my sisters (six and one) were living in Summerside on the south shore, surrounded by fishing communities. What Summerside had that Little Bay East didn't was closer proximity to a city. In about twenty minutes, they could drive to Corner Brook, the largest city in the province outside of St. John's and Mount Pearl. It's also where Mom and Dad worked, at Western Memorial Regional Hospital. The first seven years of my life were spent enjoying our glorious hillside home overlooking the forest and the sea on the north shore of the Humber River. I remember our cat, Puss. We called him Puss for the sole reason he responded to "Heeeeere, puss-puss-puss" when we bellowed. Our voices carried beyond the back stoop, past the swing set, henhouse, the wood piles, and an abandoned car. And they continued to echo through the balsam firs and black spruce, down and over the hill, where the treeline turned to slate and then pebbled beach, ending in the currents of the Humber. Once we moved to Corner Brook, it was unquestionably an upgrade amenities-wise, trading our well water for city water supply, our roadside shoulders for sidewalks and street lamps, and our unkempt wilderness for manicured lawns and parks (no abandoned cars to be seen here). We were also moving closer to family (my maternal family, the Marshalls, lived in Corner Brook) and just about everything else was too: better schools and access to doctors,

Grandfather "Pop" Thornhill and me, about two years old, February 1956.

groceries, pools, and playgrounds, and my parents' work. And yet, shortly after our move to the city, Puss disappeared. It was a lot for a seven year old. In one year, I lost Pop Thornhill, moved out of my childhood home, and my cat ran away. Around me, outport life was disappearing, but I became caught up in the excitement of new friends, a new school, and, soon, a couple of new city-wise cats, whom I'd give real names, Ebony (a black cat) and Noel (an orange tabby).

By the time I was twelve, the supper-hour news was dominated by outport fishers and plant workers. They appeared out of sorts, cursing and swearing, their rage honing the edges of their accents, making it nearly impossible for mainlanders to appreciate much of what they had to say. "Six generations down the line, passed down and he's done nothing but S-H-I-T to it," shouts one fisher featured in a July 2, 1992, video clip from CBC's *The National*. Only now do I appreciate the weight of those words. The cod fishery was wiped out that day and with it, the traditional trade of generations. The *he* the fisher is referencing is then federal fisheries minister John Crosbie. The scene is the news conference where Crosbie formally announces the moratorium on cod fishing.

By then, the days of holding Pop's hand and hearing his saltwater cowboy stories were history. The image of fishers that became the new norm—out of place on the nightly news instead of in their element aboard a fishing schooner—didn't jive with what I knew, even at twelve. What I wouldn't have given to have climbed into Pop's yellow-and-green dory and set out along the shores of Fortune Bay with him. We'd look back and squint to make out the saltbox houses and fishing sheds dotting the land, camouflaged in all that glistens. Even in summer, the cold winds would bite, while the waves would make for a bouncy ride, splattering salty seawater for tasting on licked lips. It was the kind of off-the-beaten-path experience that drew me to Little Bay East time and time again. Growing up in Corner Brook, the fisheries news coverage was all that more intangible. I was no longer a *bayman* in one of the affected outports, nor was I a *townie* where the seat of government resided, in St. John's. Instead, I was learning terms that painted a particularly unflattering picture of folks from the bay. Terms like *baywop* (the outport equivalent of *redneck*) or comments that fishers were on the *pogey* or the *dole* (collecting employment insurance), all insinuated they were *less-thans*.

Television cameras that July day captured the scene of more than a dozen fishers shouting at those on the other side of the double doors, inside the formal news conference, to "get out of the way." Angry fishers in ball caps, nylon jackets, and patterned sweaters prepare to storm the room. A few of them collectively ram the doors with their shoulders—once, twice, three times—before the camera cuts to its next scene. Inside, men in suits erect a barricade, lodging a chair's legs into the handles of the double doors. The pseudo-blockade turns out to be as futile as the fishers' arguments that day. Now inside the room, there's finger-pointing and more shouting, but one prevailing theory looms large: there are too many fishers fishing too few fish and there have been for some time now.

"I'm making a decision based on the desire to ensure that the northern cod survives as a species," says Crosbie, seated at a table at the front of the room, his elbows bent and hands clasped below his chin. He's wearing his square-rimmed glasses and a grey suit, his wavy white hair combed neatly into place. Two other white men in grey suits are seated beside Crosbie. Behind them are a dark curtain and the Canadian and Newfoundland and Labrador flags—a distasteful display of patriotism if ever there was one.

That spectacular series of events was foreshadowed by the even more spectacular events of the day before. On July 1, Crosbie had taken a press trip to Bay Bulls, about thirty kilometres south of St. John's. There waiting for him were throngs of disgruntled fishers, plant workers, men, women, and even some of their children. "Are you a Newfoundlander or is Ottawa more important?" one man in the crowd calmly asks as Crosbie leans in, listening to him with his right ear. The crowd clamours all around, barely granting the politician room to walk. Crosbie, never one to back down from confrontation, gives it right back to the gatherers.

"There's no need to abuse me," Crosbie says, directing his words at another man.

"I'm not abusing you," the man replies, his voice elevated as he defends himself from the accusation. Crosbie seems out of place here, but firmly stands his ground. He's taller than most and wearing his Ottawa uniform: a navy wool coat over a dark suit, white shirt, and tie. By comparison, the man he's addressing, either a fisher or a plant worker, is sporting a bright blue nylon jacket, round-rimmed glasses, a moustache, and a navy ball cap resting on top of his mullet. The situation is getting increasingly heated and Crosbie isn't having it.

"Why are you yelling at me? I didn't take the fish from the goddamn water, so don't go abusing me," Crosbie replies in his raised voice. It's the line that will go down in history.

"Well, who took it then?" someone's voice can be heard off-screen, as the crowd erupts into taunts and jeers. They're not having any of it either.

"You and your goddamn people took it. You and your people took it," the man shouts.

"I'm trying to do what I can to help," Crosbie contends, feigning calm and turning to walk away.

"Yes, you're doing shit all. You're doing nothing. You're doing nothing. You're doing absolutely nothing," the man yells, his *nothings* sound like *nuddins*. His emphasis on the Ds drop like bombs, an indication to listeners that, in fact, everything is at stake. Crosbie walks off screen. The crowd looks disaffected—whatever eyes aren't rolling are shooting death stares.

CBC commentator and Newfoundlander himself, Rex Murphy would later call this moratorium Newfoundland and Labrador's "second biggest story since Confederation." I'm sure the older folks would have agreed with Murphy on that one, but for those of us under sixty-five, it was undoubtedly the biggest story of our lives. Unemployment rates reached a high in Newfoundland and Labrador that year of 20 per cent, the greatest in the country, where unemployment was, on average, two-fold lower at 11.2 per cent. As the largest mass layoff in Canadian history, it should have been big news for the rest of Canada too—that is, if Canadians could have understood its magnitude. The thirty to forty thousand Newfoundlanders and Labradorians who were put out of work (the majority fishers, but about one-third fish or plant workers) was the equivalent of seven hundred thousand from the Ontario workforce at that time, reported Murphy. The subject was cod in Newfoundland, but it could just as well have been pacific

A derelict schooner, *Springdale*, Newfoundland, 2018.

salmon or the forestry in British Columbia, oil in Alberta, uranium in Quebec, coal in Nova Scotia, or even automobile-manufacturing in Ontario.

The cod moratorium would shake Newfoundland and Labrador's foundation and lead to the near and certain extinction of many of its outports—the lifeblood of this fishing nation. In what would become a cod fishery graveyard, fishing sheds were boarded up, wooden dories were left to rot on beaches, and entire communities were vacated. In those days, you'd be hard pressed to find a spared pocketbook in the outports, but it's the people's collective pride that was hardest hit.

Although many saw the writing on the wall, the immediate reaction was blame. Blame the gillnets, blame the offshore foreign fleets—but mostly, blame Ottawa. Everyone hoped the cod fishing ban would be lifted in two years, as initially stated, but the harsh reality set in. The moratorium would continue indefinitely. "Rightly or wrongly, most Newfoundlanders believed that it was the federal government which was responsible for the collapse of the fishery—by granting too many licenses and increasing quotas and so on," Beaton Tulk, seventh premier of Newfoundland and Labrador, writes in his 2018 memoir, *A Man Of My Word*. "I believe likewise. But it was also believed that the stocks would recover quickly. They didn't."

Meanwhile, federal government–sponsored attempts to retrain the workforce were fraught with problems. Two of the core programs were the Northern Cod Adjustment and Rehabilitation Program (NCARP) and The Atlantic Groundfish Strategy (TAGS). In addition to offering modest financial aid, both packages required recipients to either accept early retirement packages or retrain for work in other areas. Literacy training, adult basic education, university courses, and entrepreneurial training were among the required education programs. But these courses often left trainees ill-prepared for return to work. As Heritage Newfoundland and Labrador reported:

Both NCARP and TAGS met with limited success.... Although the programs gave out-of-work fishing people a degree of financial security during difficult times, they did not adequately prepare them for work in other fields, nor did they significantly reduce the number of people dependent on the fishery.... Individuals who left high school years or even decades earlier to work in the fishery were suddenly thrust into an unfamiliar and often intimidating academic environment. Some did not complete their programs, while others found they were of no practical use to their future lives.

When it came to TAGS, more than half of those eligible participated in one or more of the programs offered. But due to budget issues, the program was forced to end early (in mid-1996), with remaining funds redirected to income support to stretch out the fund as long as possible. The income support was modest at best. Approximately twenty-eight thousand people unemployed by the moratorium were eligible for supplemented income of $225 to $406 per week based on their average unemployment insurance earnings pre-moratorium.

"The TAGS program, the feds believed, had enough funding to last until 1999. It didn't," Tulk writes. He goes on to say that it became obvious in late 1997 the funding would run out in May of the following year. At the time, Tulk was asked by then premier Clyde Wells to handle this problem—in other words, to get a program started to follow TAGS. Doing so proved especially challenging, as it became crystal clear to Tulk that many in Ottawa were disinclined to offer further aid to Newfoundland and Labrador.

"The difficulty in trying to get Ottawa's help was a feeling in certain quarters across the country, that Newfoundland was just a drag on Canada—that things weren't half as bad as we said they were," Tulk writes. The federal government would deploy the House of Commons Standing Committee on Fisheries and Oceans to travel to the province and take stock of the severity of the situation, but even then, doubt lingered. The province would eventually receive some aid, but not the $1.2 billion it sought from the federal government. Instead, it received $750 million (announced in July 1998 from then Human Resources Development Canada) to continue early retirement benefits, license buybacks, income replacement, and job-creation programs for those affected by the moratorium.

Arguably, these programs were less about creating a future than they were about expediently remedying the past. The moratorium and its associated compensation packages reopened and irritated old wounds. Remember, under the 1949 Terms of Union defining Newfoundland's relationship with Canada, the federal government gained control of the fisheries. Its primary job was to protect and encourage the fisheries. With promises like *protect* and *encourage*, how could things have gotten this bad in the cod fishery—the fishery on which this region was built? Recall that at the time of Confederation, Newfoundland was in a precarious position financially, causing the province to become immediately dependent on its new country for a bailout. In order for Newfoundland and Labrador to gain equal financial footing with its neighbouring Atlantic provinces, which were to be the yardstick for measuring the province's economic progress, Canada shelled out over $42 million in transitional grants to its newest province over twelve years.

Perhaps Newfoundland's have-not status tainted Canada's view of this province from the start. Tulk explains the measures he took to convince federal politicians of the devastation the moratorium had left in its wake, eventually resorting to handing out a few dozen copies of Toronto-born author Michael Harris's 1998 book, *Lament for an Ocean: The Collapse of the Atlantic Cod Fishery.* "It outlined, in the best way I've ever seen, how the cod stocks of Newfoundland and Labrador got destroyed," Tulk writes. Harris dubbed the cod fishery collapse the ecological disaster of the century and the political scandal of the decade. With the intensity of a forensic exercise, Harris compared the *he said–he said* (it was, after all, mostly white men involved in the debate) in news reports, policy documents, scientific papers, and other sources. There was plenty of disagreement: fishers disagreeing with fisheries and ocean scientists disagreeing amongst themselves and with unions, politicians, and other interest groups. And this doesn't begin to capture the differences of opinion between the inshore and offshore fishery or domestic and foreign fishing fleets.

But the fact that Tulk felt he had to rely on an Ontario journalist's account of what happened back home was also part of the problem. Imagine, for a moment, an issue of such great importance in Quebec or Ontario having to be explained by outsiders. To be fair, Harris had plenty of insider knowledge, having lived for a decade in Newfoundland where he worked as an editor or executive director for a variety of major television and print media outlets. But I think about the Newfoundlanders and Labradorians on the news that July day facing Crosbie on the wharf; those the next day trying to beat down the doors of the news conference; and all of those in the months and years that followed, facing the entire nation. They attempted to give voice to the voiceless, even though they were tired, beaten, and bruised—and they would be for some time to come—and their listeners were mainly deaf to their pleas or altogether unsympathetic.

In the decade that followed the moratorium, Newfoundland and Labrador's population dropped by a record 10 per cent. Outmigration wasn't a particularly new phenomenon for the province. Almost as fast as Newfoundland's population had grown—recall, in the 1800s, with the rise of the salt cod fishery, the population doubled not once, but twice—by the 1900s, the outports were shrinking in size. At that time, many outports had reached capacity—per-fisher catch rates for cod were down and there was limited land for vegetation and livestock. People in the outports left again as part of post-Confederation relocation programs, moving to more promising parts of the province—at least, in theory. Still, the magnitude of outmigration following the moratorium was like nothing the province had seen. In the years immediately following the moratorium, between 1992 and 2007, the population of Newfoundland and Labrador declined by over 70,000, from 580,109 to 509,055.

More recently, the province experienced modest population growth, from 2008 to 2016, during a time of upswing in the provincial economy. But by 2014, it had started to slow once again; and by 2017, the population was shrinking again. What's more is the population in the province is among the most rapidly aging anywhere in Canada—in 2018, the average age here was forty-six to forty-seven years old. This aging demographic is a result of several confounding factors: for example, more young people are migrating out of than emigrating to Newfoundland and Labrador. Also, birth rates are declining, from as many as 16,000 births per year in the 1950s and '60s to a historical low of 4,000 births per year in the 2000s.

Back in those character-building years immediately following the moratorium, some Newfoundlanders became more resilient and resolute, determined to stay and revive their fishing nation. It was the fortunate few who continued fishing. To do so meant assuming greater risk, both safety-wise and through capital investment (bigger boats, advanced technology, enhanced skills). This was especially the case as fishing moved from groundfish to shellfish like shrimp and crab, which also meant a move from near and inshore fishing to the deep-sea fishery. Meanwhile, many others headed elsewhere seeking education and training or careers promising a future the fishery no longer could. Alberta's oil patch became a common destination—and one that continued the legacy of seasonal work abroad, granted on land instead of at sea.

As for me, the harsh reality of where I was, who I came from, and what was becoming of our lost legacies was all around. My adolescent self was also at an age when I cared deeply about what others thought—and it seemed to me, my big brother country didn't care nearly as much as its youngest sibling needed.

The moratorium and the years of failed attempts to turn Newfoundland around influenced widespread perceptions of who we were and what we had amounted to in our collective lives. If you were a Canadian, the moratorium and its outcome undoubtedly influenced what you thought of Newfoundlanders. We were *Newfies* to many, and we came from a have-not status province; we were dependent on welfare cheques and too lazy to find steady work once the fishery collapsed. That wasn't the reality I saw. People worked hard for what they had and those who left the island for seasonal work, making sacrifices to provide for family, house, and home, continued as they always had. But when you're repeatedly told something at a young and impressionable age, you're inclined to believe it. I also couldn't see myself as having a future in the fishery, especially without Pop in the picture—and he wouldn't have wanted that for me, just as he hadn't wished it upon his sons.

The impact of all of that, particularly after Pop's death, was that I came to think of *fishermen*, *Newfoundlander*, and *Newfie* as dirty words. The signs supporting my thinking were all around me. For starters, we were largely considered laughingstocks, with "Newfie jokes" featuring a Newfoundlander—usually a fisherman from around the bay—as the butt of every joke.

I have since come to learn that the origins of the term *Newfie* were far less amusing. The first recorded public use of the term was on the radio program *The Barrelman,* in 1938. The fifteen-minute show, hosted by Joseph Smallwood, who would later become the province's first premier, aired on the Broadcasting Corporation of Newfoundland to—as the show's opening promised—make "Newfoundland better known to

Newfoundlanders." Smallwood discussed the term Newfie on air, saying he'd heard an American use it as a slur in reference to Newfoundlanders. The term gained use during the Second World War among American and Canadian military personnel stationed on the island. As one story goes, Newfoundlanders were helping to build a US naval base in Argentia, on the southwest coast of the island's Avalon Peninsula, when a number of Newfoundlanders quit their post, in turn causing an American lieutenant to call into question their work ethic. His reference to Newfies referred to the workers as lazy and useless good-for-nothings. The term was later attested in 1943 in *The American Thesaurus of Slang*, where it was listed as referring to a Newfoundland resident, seaman, fisherman, or ship. That definition was a particularly friendly one given, by then, the term was doubling for dumb, uneducated, unemployed—take your pick.

There were certainly occasions when the term was used in a harmless, elbow-in-the-side style. Like the colloquial renaming of the Canadian National Railway passenger train from the Caribou to The Newfie Bullet in 1949, when Newfoundland joined Confederation. The train's commute took some twenty-three hours from St. John's to Port aux Basques—twice the time it would later take to travel the same distance by car or bus. But post-Confederation, "Newfie jokes" became more common, told not by Newfoundlanders and Labradorians as they are today, but by Canadians and Americans to describe people from "Newfieland" as so-called numbskulls too dumb to realize their own "ineptitude and alien status" from a place "out of step with time"—this was how author Pat Byrne described it in his chapter on Newfoundland for the book *Usable Pasts: Traditions and Group Expressions in North America*.

With that kind of history, what self-respecting Newfoundlander would claim the term as their own? But over the years, that's exactly what would happen. Many in my generation are unfamiliar with the term's origins and think it has always been ours, especially given our cultural tendency to lean into self-deprecating "Newfie" humour, frequently referencing the cod fishery. Take, for example, our "screech-in" ceremonies, which involve reciting Newfoundland slang, drinking Jamaican rum, and, of course, kissing a cod. But it's also Newfoundland-based musical-comedy bands like Buddy Wasisname and the Other Fellers and sketch-comedy troupes like CODCO who helped normalize and reclaim Newfie-style humour, always in a tongue-in-cheek style. Like CODCO's *Cod on a Stick* show, billed as being about "the selling off of Newfoundland culture as if it were the latest fashion in fast food."

Old meets new: root cellar (foreground) and cruise ship in harbour, St. Anthony, Newfoundland, 2018.

Sure enough, as groundfish like cod were tanking, tourism was on an upswing. In the eight-year period of 1985 to 1993, the number of licensed tourist establishments increased by over 100 per cent (from 174 establishments with 4,226 accommodation units to 354 establishments with 6,466 units). Since then, licensed tourist establishments have increased dramatically to over 250,000 accommodation units in 2017. Even before this period, by 1984, tourism had become the province's third-largest employer, after the fishery and the construction industries. Tourism surged in the province through the 1990s, especially as the province prepared for its five-hundredth anniversary (in 1997) of John Cabot's arrival in North America. That event alone brought sixty-nine thousand visitors and over $51 million to the local economy. The trend of people coming for a good time, but not a long time would continue—making it an especially odd time to be a Newfoundlander and Labradorian. Just as locals were leaving for work, visitors were coming for play. But perhaps it showed us Newfies weren't so dumb after all, given we were able to turn our fisheries misfortune into tourism gold.

Meanwhile, for those of us born after Confederation—first-generation Canadians, given our parents were born in the Dominion of Newfoundland—our connotation of the term Newfie, with all its meanings, had certainly evolved from its sordid roots. I grew up appreciating the courage and confidence it takes to tell a joke at your own expense.

And yet, I also knew how it felt to be on the receiving end of these jokes because sometimes they were hurtful characterizations rather than playful caricatures. Like when the junior high school volleyball team from

Ontario joked that our Newfie team should stick to building our igloos. I could have laughed that one off except one of the Ontario girls, shy as she was, then quietly asked if I really did live in an igloo. On another occasion, my first day at Dalhousie University, the Nova Scotian sitting beside me announced her amazement to find me sitting beside her in both calculus and French classes. The thought of a Newfie counting beyond her own ten fingers or speaking a second language (besides Newfie) was too much for her. It would have been easier to brush off had she had even the slightest sarcastic inflection in her voice.

"You think we know fucking nothing, but we know fuck all." Dad would later share that classic one-liner they would say around the bay, perfectly capturing what I had been thinking in that moment. The thing is, us Newfoundlanders and Labradorians are not only in on the joke, we are the best ones to deliver it. So, when someone tries to turn it around to paint us as uncultured halfwits, the conversation is likely to go sideways fast. The Dalhousie student who took me for the idiot that day would go on to fail out of calculus, while I aced both courses. Not normally the vengeful type, I felt a certain self-redemption at that turn of events.

But speaking of idiots, it was around that same time that my sister Angelina (Angie), who was attending the University of New Brunswick, had a boyfriend from that province with a curious understanding of Newfie jokes. He thought Newfie was a term you used to make fun of people, as in, just any old person. It hadn't occurred to him that there might be an association between the term "Newfie" and" Newfoundlander." Fortunately, their relationship didn't last, and she met and later settled down with a proud Newfoundlander. Coincidentally, I later married a New Brunswicker, but he was living in St. John's when we met and is a first-generation Canadian (his parents emigrated to Canada from India), blessing him with a built-in sensitivity barometer.

Back in undergrad, at Dalhousie (later transferring to the University of King's College), I stayed at Newcombe Residence, part of Shirreff Hall and the last all-girls residence. Our residence mascot was, get this, a killer cod. While trying to make friends and fit in, I was reminded yet again of what separated me (granted, there were other Newfoundlanders and Labradorians among us, with whom I made fast friends). As part of our initiation week, we were blindfolded and led through an obstacle course at our brother house, Howe Hall, the all-boys residence. Wearing our green tie-dyed T-shirts sporting, what else, a killer cod, and after having rolled down Citadel Hill in the wet grass, we were made to roll in flour (like a cod fillet) and drink a spoonful of cod liver oil.

The reality of where this resolute ignorance was coming from was never lost on me. Newfoundland and Labrador has always been a place of conundrums and contradictions. Tourists cannot wait to arrive in summer, but you're liable to arrive in June to winter-like weather—what we affectionately dub *Junuary*. Our outmigration rates often trend in the unfavourable and opposite direction of our counterparts' in the rest of Canada. Comparing population growth for Canada and Newfoundland and Labrador over the last half-century shows steady growth in Canada versus what looks to be a flatlining of our province's population (which has averaged a population of 540,000 between 1971 to 2019).

Meanwhile, while the province, like Canada, has experienced patterns of up-and-down trends in unemployment rates, Newfoundland and Labrador's unemployment rate is steadily twice that of the rest of the country. Back in 1992, at the time of the cod moratorium, the unemployment rate in Newfoundland and Labrador hit a high of 20 per cent (at which time, Canada's was also at a high of 11 per cent). While the unemployment rate has steadily declined since that time for both the country and the province, Canada's unemployment rate (5.8 per cent in 2018) is still less than half that of Newfoundland and Labrador's (13.8 per cent in 2018). The minimum wage in this province is also among the lowest in the country at $11.40/hour (in 2019), which is about a dollar less than the average minimum hourly wage across the country. Our economy has also historically been busted despite (or perhaps because of) the overplayed boom-town promises of big energy and oil megaprojects.

Interestingly, we self-report good health and yet win the prize for high rates of chronic disease. I once heard a local hospital chief executive say Atlantic Canada "wins the prize for its chronic disease rates." In Newfoundland and Labrador, nearly two-thirds of the population (twelve years and older) report having at least one chronic disease and many live with two or more. But ask Newfoundlanders and Labradorians about their health and they'll tell you everything is "best kind." Statistics Canada's 2017 Canadian Community Health Survey found one in five Canadians (twelve and older) reported most days in their life were quite a bit or extremely stressful; in Newfoundland and Labrador, that ratio was closer to one in eight—the lowest of anywhere in the country.

In the same way, adult literacy levels in Newfoundland and Labrador rank among the lowest at home and abroad, and they have for decades. The province earned a "D" grade for adult literacy on the Conference Board of Canada's How Canada Performs: A Report Card. Based on the 2012 International Survey of Adult Skills, the report card deemed Newfoundland and Labrador the poorest performer among poor performers. While no province earned above a "C" and many earned a "D," Newfoundland and Labrador took home the title of "sole below-average province," with nearly 60 per cent of its adults possessing inadequate literacy skills. Data from a decade earlier (then collected through the 2003 International Adult Literacy and Life Skills Survey) show that the province scored "significantly below the national average"; data from the next previous decade (the 1994 International Adult Literacy Survey) demonstrate similarly underwhelming results.

Part of that poor literacy legacy is surely a carryover from the province's historical focus on fishing over formal education, with many having gained skills on the land and sea as opposed to the classroom. (Until 1983, secondary education in the province ended at grade eleven, and labour jobs prioritized perfecting repetitive skills like fish processing over developing critical-thinking skills, further contributing to low literacy.) Another factor is the province's greying population; as people retire from the workforce, their literacy skills invariably decline. Yet another factor may be interprovincial migration, the brain drain of young, educated professionals leaving the province for study and employment in other parts of Canada—it's one of the primary reasons for Newfoundland and Labrador's slow population growth, which reached 1 per cent between the 2011 and 2016 censuses, compared to the national average of 5 per cent.

Back in my undergraduate years—during that particularly lengthy period of out-migration from the province that continued a decade after the moratorium—I swam against the current, returning home from journalism school (or *j-school* as we King's College students affectionately referred to it) in summertime and working at local radio stations in Corner Brook. My first radio gig was at CFCB reporting news, weather, sports, and even obituaries (it was a community radio station after all). I also produced a few shows, including a regular weekend music program, a weekly buy-and-sell program called *Tradio,* and a nightly open-line talk show called *VOCM Nightline.* (VOCM stands for *Voice Of the Common Man* and you certainly gleaned that every time you listened to *Nightline* or its daytime companion show, *Openline*.) Those radio shows delivered a straight-up version of Newfoundland and Labrador culture—more than the Newfoundland and Labrador Tourism advertisements (beautiful, but too bright and shiny) ever could. CBC radio shows like *The Broadcast* (on air since 1951 and formerly called *The Fisheries Broadcast*, a telling change in its own right) and television shows like *Land and Sea* similarly offer a slice of real, down-home life. I can still hear the old *Land and Sea* theme song, "Atlantic Guardian," performed by the Royal Canadian Air Force band.

The Broadcast, as it's come to be known—the longest continuously running CBC current affairs program and one of the oldest in North America—turns seventy in 2021, but began as a fifteen-minute broadcast for marine weather forecasts and other survival information; Pop regularly tuned into the program. "There has never been a shortage of stories, even when there was as shortage of fish," said former host, Jim Wellman, during the show's sixtieth-anniversary celebrations. These shows were unique in that they have always featured Newfoundlanders and Labradorians talking to each other. I found perspectives in these shows the national and mainstream news media were unable to offer. And I worry about this today more than ever, as major conglomerates continue to buy out most community papers. A story that's published today in a community newspaper can appear in as many as two-dozen across Atlantic Canada, as if our communities and regions are one big homogenous *Atlantica*. In any case, back in j-school: I was proud to work for a station that was locally owned, delivered, and filled with local content—and I thought my early reporting chops led me to secure the job. But one of the reporters, who gave me a deservedly hard time for not knowing how to properly pronounce any professional athletes' names, later revealed why I was hired.

It didn't have anything to do with my journalism experience. First, I was a woman and they had no female on-air personalities at the time. And second, I didn't have a discernible Newfoundland accent. The second reason was particularly curious to me. Having lived on the mainland, I had grown accustomed to being asked about my accent. Friends and acquaintances would gleefully reference my manner of speech as if I'd been caught in the act of, oh I don't know, being a Newfoundlander. The real giveaway was my use of common Newfoundland phraseology. I said *hey* in place of the Canadian *eh*. I frequently referenced *b'y*, as in "what are the b'ys up to tonight?" meaning everyone, not just the boys.

I'd also respond "yes b'y" as in "I hear you" or "no b'y" as in "no," or more often to mean a sarcastic "yes." I also substituted *some* and *right* for *very,* as in "that was some good." If it was "right good," then it was all the better. Friends would tell me that my Newfoundland sarcasm and accent became more recognizable once I had a few drinks, which, in those university days, was most weekends.

The other thing that confused me about landing my first radio gig on account of my more Canadian accent was that this Newfoundland radio station only broadcast to parts of Newfoundland and Labrador. How would it benefit listeners for me to not have a local accent? (Not that there's a single accent or dialect anyway—there are hundreds.) I can only think of one instance when a listener called me up to thank me for my proper pronunciation. The caller drew my attention to the local custom to drop the "n" in The Glynmill Inn (a hotel in Corner Brook) and replace the first rounded "o" in Corner Brook with an "a" as in "Carner Brook." I am well aware that Newfoundlanders are always dropping or replacing letters and syllables, presumably in their haste to get their sentences out at a faster pace than is recognizable to anyone else. I, too, was guilty of mile-a-minute speaking, but j-school and radio taught me to at least hit every syllable and leave out the unnecessary words. Given the local disdain for the accent, at least where my job was concerned, I was encouraged to make good use of that training.

When I later moved to Ottawa, after a few years back on the island in St. John's for graduate studies, I was reacquainted with people calling out my Newfoundland accent. The "I *thought* you had an accent" or "Oh, I didn't detect the accent at first, but now I hear it" comments were frequent, but slowly petered out. I took those comments to mean I was a lesser- or other-than. I don't think that was the intended or desired effect but it's how I had grown accustomed to interpreting it. It was a likely carryover from my own coming-of-age as a Newfoundlander at a time when the fisheries collapsed, and I didn't yet see myself in the faces and voices of those representing that cause.

It was particularly challenging to interpret because I left, like so many Newfoundlanders had, in an attempt to make something of myself. Throughout undergrad, I'd had one foot out the door, spending my academic years in Halifax and my summers in Corner Brook. But now, having finished graduate studies in St. John's, I was moving away for good. My parents boasted about my move to Ottawa, with my Ottawa job and Ottawa address. Moving away, in effect, was a marker of success.

And my parents weren't alone in feeling that way. Newfoundlanders then and now still encounter a negative discourse about staying in Newfoundland and Labrador, especially the rural fishing outports.

"In order to be a success, young people often have to disconnect from rural places, or at least, that's how they feel," says Nicole Power, a professor and researcher in Memorial University of Newfoundland's Department of Sociology. Dr. Power has studied the impacts of long-term fishery closures on young people's experience and perception of fisheries employment in Newfoundland coastal communities. "If you stay in a rural place, you may be called a failure, right?" Power adds, "If you think about how people talk, they say, 'Oh yeah, so-and-so, they're doing really well, they're living in town, they've got a big house.' Those kinds of things. So, it may be that young people feel those 'signs of success' are not available to them in rural places and aren't associated with fisheries work, so I think there's real pressure to leave even if they want to stay."

And, as Dr. Power has discovered from talking to hundreds of young people across the province, many *do* want to stay, but they feel they can't because there are no jobs and they don't want to dampen the expectations of their parents or teachers. The pull of community becomes particularly strong when young adults start family planning— yearning to return to the outport-paced lifestyle where home ownership can be a reality, doors can remain unlocked, and the outdoors remains a primary source of entertainment for adults and children alike.

That deep sense of community became worldwide news on September 11, 2001, when Newfoundlanders received a dose of positive attention on the small screen amidst the most tragic of circumstances. As the events in New York City and Washington, DC, unfolded and nearly three thousand people died in a terrorist attack, Gander International Airport in central Newfoundland became the unexpected host of thirty-eight planes and their seven thousand displaced passengers and crew. The arrivals from these re-routed transatlantic flights nearly doubled the town's population, leaving locals scrambling to make urgent accommodations for the "plane people." Gander and the surrounding communities delivered. Residents opened their homes to offer their own beds. Striking bus drivers went back to work to provide ground transportation. Hospitals called in additional staff to ensure people had the medications and care they needed. Newfoundlanders and Labradorians did whatever they could to make the long layover and period of uncertainty as comfortable as possible for the unexpected guests.

"9/11 will live long in memory as a day of terror and grief," said then prime minister Jean Chrétien at the Gander airport on the first anniversary of the terrorist attacks. "But thanks to the countless acts of kindness and compassion done for those stranded visitors here in Gander and right across Canada, it will live forever in memory as a day of comfort and of healing."

That same year, 2001, employment numbers were up in Newfoundland and Labrador and all regions of the province reported employment growth. The same trend held out in the 2002–03 and 2003–04 budgets. A few years earlier, in 1999, the *Globe and Mail* reported the Rock was finally on a roll, having turned a corner economically and with out-migration slowing down.

Meanwhile, by my mid-twenties, around 2005, I was still searching for where I belonged. I remember thinking as much as I toured around Newfoundland with the Whale Stewardship Project, a non-profit out of Nova Scotia that traced lone beluga whales, separated from their St. Lawrence pods. Belugas are gregarious creatures, unaccustomed to solo travel. Given they use sonar communication, they can easily wind up in trouble, gravitating toward motor sounds and other noisy activities in working harbours. My job was to travel to the outports where the belugas had been spotted. I had waterproof, insulated gloves that reached above my shoulders, allowing me to hold an underwater camera below the frigid seawaters to capture a beluga's movements and vocalizations. If I couldn't record the beluga from the wharf, I'd find a local (often a fisher) to take me out in his dory to do so. In my downtime, I carried a small television and VCR, so I could record the sounds and actions of the belugas on behalf of an American marine biology team working with the project. I also visited local schools to offer education about how to protect the belugas while they visited our harbours. It was a great gig, but I often found myself feeling like the belugas—out of my element and catching a lot of interest from locals who knew I was on my own and not from around there.

The same feeling resurfaced when I was back in Little Bay East in the summer of 2005. That year I got the call from Dad on a Sunday in mid-August that Nan Thornhill had died. At eighty-seven she died in hospital, having been ill for some time, experiencing the general symptoms of aging that had come to a head in the days leading up to her death. As people gathered at Nan and Pop's place, or what was now my uncle John's house, there was lots of catching-up time in between the wake, funeral, and burial. I had recently started a Master of Science program at Memorial University in St. John's, opting to leave behind my short-lived journalism career. I was dating, but nowhere near marriage and kids, which seemed to be a sticking point for people in Little Bay East. I had the distinct feeling they thought I ought to be barefoot and pregnant in a kitchen (forget my career aspirations). Though not overtly stated, anything else was frowned upon for a woman *my age* (I was twenty-five). Maybe I expected too much for someone who had come from humble beginnings?

During the wake there was an open casket, and I opted not to go into Salem United Church, wanting instead to remember Nan alive. That, too, was met with mild scorn. At first, people assumed I was afraid. I should have left it at that because once I explained my rationale, people were put off by it. I was to pay my respects and that was that. I bucked the local tradition and it was yet another example of the fraying threads of what was once a strong line, connecting me to my family's outport roots.

There had been occasions before that point I'd felt like an outsider in Little Bay East. There are unpleasant realities of life in small communities. Ignorance can be a norm, be it over gender, as I had experienced, but also religion, race, and sex. Nan had always resented the fact that my two older sisters and I were baptized Catholic like the Marshall side of my family. My Protestant grandmother didn't mince words about my Roman Catholic mother. That was the major reason Mom stopped visiting Little Bay East, particularly after Pop died, because Pop had been a peacemaker while Nan was always outspoken, set in her ways and accustomed to hurting the feelings of those she loved most with her slick, biting words.

Nan had an edge to her I'd seen come out for inane things, so I could appreciate why Mom opted to keep her distance over something as giant as religion. There was the time we pulled into Nan's driveway unannounced, for example. Dad, my sister Angie, and I had driven from St. John's and would be heading back to Corner Brook in a few days. No sooner did we get into the doorway and Nan was arguing with Dad. She was "browned off" (pissed) we hadn't given her advanced warning of our visit. *The house is a state*, Nan said, unprepared for us to stay overnight. But our house was a mess, too. It was one of the traits Dad had assumed from his outport upbringing. We would joke we were the hillbillies of MacPherson Avenue, a premier location on Corner Brook's west side, overlooking the golf course. But in our basement, garage, crawl space, drawers, and closets, various doodads and whatnots blocked passage and storage spaces. Dad, the apple, had not fallen far from the tree, hoarding stuff for its rainy day uses. But the thing about hoarders was they liked to keep their messes hidden.

To hell with this, Dad snapped back. He had just given her a bag of Purity Peppermint Nobs, the ever-popular Newfoundland-made pink hard candy, as a peace offering. Unaccustomed to anyone talking back, Nan hurled the bag of candy at us as we ran back to the car. I'd always known Nan was quick to temper, but it was the first and only time it had been directed at me (or, at least, in my direction). That one time was enough. We drove all the way back to Corner Brook that day and I've never thought about Peppermint Nobs the same way again.

It was these small doses of reality that helped me understand why my father and his two brothers had left Little Bay East years before. It was a beautiful place but could be steeped in old thinking and even older traditions. Nan and Pop had never made the trip to visit us in Corner Brook, for example. Many people didn't travel off the island then and still don't. Many don't even travel across it. To a twentysomething female yearning to find herself and with an itch to travel, the thought of never leaving home seemed so backwards to me. Little Bay East was a small outport, never having had more than 140 people in the years I knew it, and its population continues to shrink. Pop and fishers or seasonal workers like him did their share of travel of course, but it was on the water, not on land. When they returned home, they were eager to stay put until the next time they would be called to cast off to sea. And then there was the expense of travel. I failed to understand then what a luxury my life had become compared to the one afforded my father. I naively chalked it up to ignorance perpetuating ignorance in the outports.

Seeing Newfoundland through the eyes of my boyfriend (and later husband) reminded me just how deep the ignorance ran. Raman and I met in St. John's as I pursued my Master of Science and he studied medicine. On one occasion at a shopping mall in Mount Pearl, a stranger walked up to Raman and said, "It's so good to see more of your kind around here. My niece married a negro." We were taken aback but managed to smile politely, knowing the comment hadn't come from a place of maliciousness. There would be countless other instances like that, giving weight to comedian-actor-writer Andy Jones's infamous comment about Newfoundland and Labrador's "galoot of a culture." True to form, when we left the island for Ottawa, we no longer heard comments like that.

By the time I was in my late twenties and living in Ottawa, Newfoundland was something of a Comeback Kid. Say what you will about the outspoken Newfoundland and Labrador Premier Danny Williams, but he was elected, in 2003, on the promise to broker better deals and capture capital from this resource-rich province to benefit its people. Williams was as accomplished as they come: a Rhodes Scholar, lawyer, entrepreneur, and self-made millionaire. It was arguably because of his leadership that, in 2013, the Conference Board of Canada dubbed Newfoundland and Labrador a "runaway leader in economic growth among Canada's provinces." Oil prices would tank the following year, resulting in an unprecedented provincial deficit followed by taxation for everything under the sun, but the boom-town period of the Williams government gave Newfoundland and Labrador a taste of what it's like to be a *have*-status province, if only briefly. Since then, history has shown us that not all that shimmers is gold, and the promise of the next big energy or oil megaproject has not yet played out in Newfoundland and Labrador's favour, least of which where the fishery is concerned.

But it was Williams who confronted Sir Paul McCartney and his then wife, Lady Heather Mills McCartney, on *Larry King Live* in 2008, too. The McCartneys were on a press tour raising awareness of what they considered an archaic, brutal, and cruel Canadian harp seal hunt. Mills McCartney notoriously referred to the hunt as "inhumane," likening the hunting of seal pups to clubbing actual human babies. Williams debunked the myth that most seals were killed by clubbing (in fact, less than 10 per cent were clubbed; the other 90 per cent were shot). He also corrected misinformation portraying Newfoundland sealers as barbarians. The appearance later garnered a retraction from Mills McCartney on her "inhumane" comment. As I watched Williams own our side of the argument that evening, I saw a new portrayal of Newfoundlanders—not as buffoons, but bright, brazen, and bold.

Back when Williams took on the job as premier with hopes to rebuild the province, over on Fogo Island a bold new build was also underway. Zita Cobb, originally from Fogo Island, had left the high-tech industry to invest back home. What many see as a luxury inn is so much more. Fogo Island Inn is a social business, funnelling wealth back into the local community in the form of employment—not just at the inn, but in its related experiences, for example, eating food cultivated on the nearby land; sleeping under quilts handcrafted locally; and touring the island to learn about one of Canada's oldest rural fishing–built cultures. On its website, Fogo Island Inn shows (through a clever "economic nutrition" label) how all of its operating surpluses are reinvested back into the community to help secure a sustainable and resilient future for the island.

Shorefast, a registered Canadian charity with the mandate to promote cultural and economic resiliency for Fogo Island, predates the inn. Established in 2006, the charitable organization supports a number of programs, from those contributing to the arts (Fogo Island Arts) to ocean preservation (New Ocean Ethic) to cod fishing (Fogo Island Fish). Given its unique model and experience, this self-described "not-just-for-profit" has garnered attention in many major travel publications and welcomed a seemingly unending queue of celebrity visitors. To me, what Shorefast and Fogo Island Inn have shown is the inherent value in what Newfoundlanders already have at their fingertips. But also, it demonstrates how sometimes it takes coming from away, or coming back from away, to see what value exists before residents can believe it for themselves.

Upholding our unique identity as Newfoundlanders—and abandoning the Newfie stereotype—was becoming the new norm in the news. Perhaps that's why I started to lean into the comments about my accent, which were becoming rarer as I spent more time in Ottawa.

I recall the fierce opposition to then New Democratic Party Leader Tom Mulcair's use of the term Newfie. Mulcair was campaigning in St. John's during the 2015 campaign lead up to the federal election when he was called out for having used the term twenty years earlier as a synonym for stupidity. Mulcair apologized as soon as the news broke and blamed his use of the slur on the heat of the moment, having made the comment out of the side of his mouth during a committee debate in Quebec's National Assembly back in 1996. *National Post* reporter Colby Cosh called the term "Canada's N-word" in a 2015 article, referencing Mulcair's faux pas.

The following year, Bob Hallett, a Newfoundland restaurateur and Great Big Sea musician, would again call into question the use of the term Newfie. As cultural ambassadors for all things Newfoundland, Great Big Sea has always publicly bucked stereotypes of the province and its people. In the lead up to St. Patrick's Day in 2016, several retailers, including Walmart, Pipers, and Only Deals Dollar Store, were selling

T-shirts with the phrase "St. Paddy's Newfie Beer Removal Service—pints, pitchers, kegs" and an image of a beer stein on it. Hallett took to Twitter to object, "Really, Walmart? We've got to get past this shit."

Hallet's band mate and Great Big Sea frontman, Alan Doyle, had recently released his first book with a second on the way. He, too, was standing up against clichés of what it means to be a Newfoundlander. Even many Newfoundland authors are guilty of just that. But Doyle avoids this in his book and music—no Newfie jokes here. To relay that Newfoundlanders are hard-working he writes, "That's the way it was in rural Newfoundland. You didn't call professionals to build you a house or put a roof on it. You called the boys, and you got a few cases of beer and you did it yourselves." Or to convey the *rough around the edges* demeanour of outport Newfoundlanders, he starts with a description of the design preference of clapboard-clad homes to showcase the rough (versus smooth) side of the lumber: "Come to think of it, that's the way most Newfoundland houses and Newfoundlanders themselves are built: rough side out." Doyle doesn't shy away from more familiar Newfoundland proof points, referencing kitchen parties and Come From Aways (a ubiquitous term for anyone not from the province), but he does so relying on description and story.

The writers of the Tony Award–winning Broadway musical *Come From Away*, about the generosity of Newfoundlanders during 9/11, also steered clear of Newfie jokes. In a 2017 media interview, Irene Sankoff and David Hein said Newfoundlanders in the production had made it clear that the term "Newfie" was not welcome. "We grew up on 'Newfie' jokes," Mr. Hein told me. "When we wrote our show it was really to honour and say thank you, so we weren't interested in using that word."

Though it helps to hear the sentiments of prominent Newfoundlanders who feel as I do, I've yet to reconcile the deep pride I feel now with the embarrassment, shame, and confusion I once lived. For a time, going back to Newfoundland was every bit as difficult as leaving because I was trying to reconcile where I belonged and who I was at a time when my home was redefining its own identify after the cod fishery collapse. It wasn't until my mid-thirties, with a strong desire to start a family, that I realized my heart was calling me back home.

I remember the day Mom called me in Ottawa with the news about Uncle John. I had bad news of my own to share. Less than a week earlier, Raman and I had learned I was pregnant. We were choked up with emotion, surprising us both. It was early in the pregnancy (just shy of eight weeks) and most would-be parents would not have had an ultrasound until weeks later. For us, though, it was the first sign we could do this—together since our mid-twenties, married at thirty, and now, at thirty-six, having our moment. To think we had made a heart. And to think we made it beat.

But that Saturday evening, I started to feel off. By Sunday, I knew something was definitely wrong. A visit to the doctor later in the week confirmed the white flickers we had seen on the ultrasound had dulled to black. Meanwhile, back in Little Bay East, John had died sometime between Saturday overnight and Sunday morning. It was a coincidence I would keep to myself until after John's funeral, knowing how difficult things already were for my parents. My father was reuniting with his brothers, one brother short.

It was during that trip that Dad and Clyde stayed on after the funeral to clear out the Thornhill house and get it ready to put up for sale. The price, set at $25,000, seemed laughable—at first because it seemed such a low price, but a year later, because we realized it might never sell. Until that point, there had been no serious offers. Another year later it did sell— for nearly half the original price—and there I was, standing outside of its chain-link fence, this time holding my seven-month old daughter, and wondering if Dad and I would ever stand in this place together again.

It takes time and courage for the person you are to meet the person you once were and the person you've yet to become. But that's what lay ahead for me, as I set out to make the biggest trip of my life across Newfoundland and Labrador in the summer of 2018, with my family by my side. Sitting at Clyde and Hattie's kitchen table, that trip had already begun with a visit to the Burin Peninsula, where this story started for me, delving into my family's roots. I had already visited the Avalon Peninsula and was next heading to the north-central coast before moving onward to the Bay of Islands and finally, north to the tip of the Northern Peninsula.

Tucked inside my bag is that 1979 letter from Pop.

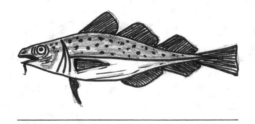

PART II. RESURGENCE

CHAPTER 4:
Comeback Cowboys

The fog lifts over the Grand Bank coastline. Like the hallway glow hitting the floor as a door creaks open, the sunlight behind the thick clouds strikes land. It's late June and my face, the only exposed part of me, smarts from the combination of the biting ocean breeze and a residual dampness in the air from the morning's rain and fog. I hold my cotton scarf to my face as I walk, gloved hands covering a red-tipped nose, and blow warm breath into my palms. It helps, but the chill persists, the way only a wet, cold wind can. I take a side street off Seaview Road, hopeful for the warmth of the more sheltered, residentially lined streets. There's no traffic or sidewalks, and because I'm trying to get my blood flowing for warmth, I pound straight down the centre of the pavement. When the odd car approaches, I step aside, wave them past, and get a wave back. This is the kind of friendliness for which Newfoundlanders and Labradorians—indeed, all Atlantic Canadians—are known. Although I've never stayed in Grand Bank before, a simple wave from locals is a kind gesture telling me I belong.

I pass Ralph Street, Blackburn Road, Warrens Lane, and Evans Street. These are likely the names of families who forged permanent roots here, atop the rocks of this place, and in the harshest of climates and geographies. They came for the promise of a simple life—a life recognized by other streets like Schooner Drive, Marine Drive, Farmers Hill Road, and even a later addition, Plant Road. Other street names are the ones you'd expect in any British-colonized, English-speaking seaside town—Main Street, Water Street, Elizabeth Avenue, Church Road, Cemetery Road.

By Newfoundland and Labrador's standards, Grand Bank is a sizeable town with its 2,500 people. Located on the southern tip of the Burin Peninsula and one of the southernmost places in the province, it's a town that can feel more down-and-out than down south. The signs are there for anyone to see. The most telling are marked "For Sale." On some streets every few houses are on the market, usually by owner. I gather the by-owner sales are because owners don't want to lose the few dollars they'll make in this bottom-dollar market.

It's not a real estate slump per se—in fact, with the introduction of new offshore oil projects to the region, the province's real estate market levelled out in 2018 after dropping for the past several years and is expected to remain stable into 2019—but it's certainly a buyer's market, and that's not confined to Grand Bank. By the time I finish my 3,500-kilometre drive across Newfoundland later this summer, I will have seen more "For Sale" signs than all other signs combined. Considering Newfoundland and Labrador's love for the roadside sign (think pitstops for fish, jam, berries, spring water, gas, local crafts, or attractions) that's saying something. Not all of Newfoundland is facing a real estate decline, however. Some places near town (St. John's) and in high-density tourist spots, like Bonavista on the northeast coast, are going for top dollar.

Even some of the buildings that have been a mainstay of downtown Grand Bank are either on the market, in disrepair, or have yet to deliver on their new owners' promises. On Water Street, I run into Arch Evans, vice chair of the Grand Bank Harbour Authority. We didn't plan to meet, but my chat with Evans is another example of how friendly people are around here. Many are willing to offer their local knowledge. He tells me about the old theatre as well as the salt-fish processing factory, both condemned. Another storefront, cluttered with junk, has become someone's storage shed. Meanwhile, the J. B. Foote & Sons Ltd. storefront, built in 1908 by fish merchant and captain John Benjamin Foote (coincidentally, also the first person in Newfoundland and Labrador to receive insulin for diabetes), and now a Registered Heritage Structure, was supposedly bought by an Ontarian who intends to turn it into an art gallery. But there's been no progress yet. In the harbour, just below Water Street, sits a vessel that's become a blight on the neighbourhood. Once owned by Clearwater Seafoods, one of the largest seafood companies in eastern Canada, after hitting rough seas, becoming damaged, and then changing ownership, it is likely destined "to die" somewhere over near St. Lawrence, says Evans. For now, it's an eyesore on the wharf.

Evans and I exchange contact information and goodbyes before I weave my way down Lower Water Street to the harbour's concrete wharf, past the eyesore. The wailing of seagulls competes with lapping water and a band saw in the distance as a couple of folks work aboard a longliner. The smell of fish comes and goes with the wind. As I try to sniff out the culprit, I spot a couple of DFO signs that read, "No fishing between these signs." I pass stacks of fishing tubs and a tractor, evidence of a recent haul. On the breakwater, I can see the Grand Bank Historic Lighthouse and, across the harbour, Grand Bank Seafoods, the processing plant owned by Clearwater.

Over the last year, Clearwater (including its Grand Bank processing plant) has been the subject of local and national news media attention relating to the $100 million-a-year Arctic surf clam fishery. That's because in fall 2017, the federal government announced a change to the allocation of its licenses for surf clams. As part of the federal government's "acts of reconciliation" with Indigenous peoples in Canada, it announced it was offering up one-quarter of the surf clam quota to new bidders. The bidders were required to be majority Canadian–owned and include an Atlantic Canadian– or Quebec-based Indigenous partner or partners in its consortium. For nearly twenty years, Clearwater Seafoods had held 100 per cent of the offshore licenses for surf clam. The company reportedly employs over 450 people in its three surf clam vessels and two surf clam processing plants—one in Glace Bay, Nova Scotia, and the other here in Grand Bank. The Grand Bank plant employs 150 full-time, year-round workers, as well as 60 workers on its ships.

In February 2018, then federal fisheries minister Dominic LeBlanc announced the 25 per cent surf clam quota would be moving from the Grand Bank (Clearwater) plant to the winning bid at the Five Nations Premium Clam Company (Premium Seafoods Group) in Arichat, Nova Scotia. Concerns over job losses and the broader economic impacts for the community of Grand Bank filled local media. No one could argue with the premise of the decision—Canada is on a journey of reconciliation with First Nations, Metis, and Inuit peoples based on recognition of rights, respect, cooperation, and partnership—but many questioned the fairness of the bidding process and its outcome.

As it turned out, the questioning was justified. When LeBlanc gave the go-ahead for the winning bid in December 2017, Five Nations had not yet secured its partners. LeBlanc let that slide, granting ministerial direction to reward the bid anyway. An investigation by the federal ethics commissioner later found that LeBlanc had a conflict of interest. LeBlanc was no longer federal fisheries minister by that time, but under the role had awarded the bid to Five Nations, which had a link to his wife's cousin. By July 2018 Ottawa had cancelled its plans to reallocate the 25 per cent share of the surf clam quota. The official word on that decision from the federal government, under newly appointed federal fisheries minister Jonathan Wilkinson, was "confidential." This was welcome news for Clearwater, which retained its share in the Arctic surf clam fishery for another two years. In 2020, the federal government says it will reopen the bidding process.

A columnist for the *Halifax Examiner*, Stephen Kimber, summarized the debacle in an article cheekily titled, "Clearwater wins. Again. Still. Always. And forever," this way: "The fisheries minister had made such a partisan, patronage-riddled cock-up of the process—start with nepotism, conflict of interest and work your way through corruption and a secrecy-shrouded bidding process—Ottawa was forced to cancel the awarding of the new license."

Clearwater is the only winner in this situation. It's a loss for reconciliation and Indigenous peoples—in the end, this has probably set the federal government's relationships back farther than when they initiated the act of reconciliation. It's also a loss for the people of Grand Bank, to know how close they came to having their livelihood pulled out from under their collective feet.

It's a close call in a place that seemingly planned ahead to avoid a situation just like this, caused by too great a dependency on a fishery at risk of closures. The Grand Bank Development Corporation was formed the year before the cod moratorium, with the mission to diversify the town's economy. But today, Grand Bank still depends heavily on the Clearwater plant and vessels. Like the old adage says, "It takes money to make money"—or in this case, it takes an economy to build an economy—and Grand Bank, like the province, remains reliant on the monies brought in by the fishing industry.

Meanwhile, the Fish, Food and Allied Workers Union (FFAW-Unifor) is the province's largest private-sector union, representing approximately fifteen thousand workers throughout the province, mostly from the fishing industry but also hospitality, brewing, metalworks, and oil industries. FFAW-Unifor released a statement in February 2018 indicating the surf clams debacle had raised serious concerns for its members. The union supported the aim of reconciliation with Indigenous peoples, but argued rural economic sustainability can and should happen simultaneously.

"I don't believe that Newfoundland and Labrador will have a real future as a fishing province until we control the quotas of fish off our shores," says Ryan Cleary, president of the Federation of Independent Sea Harvesters of Newfoundland and Labrador (FISH-NL), an organization which aims to bring alternative union representation to the province's inshore fishers. "Right now, we've got a federal administrator in Ottawa who—like what happened with surf clams—can arbitrarily give away any quotas he wants at any time. That cannot work. That cannot work in terms of us getting ahead as a fishing province."

The situation raises a fundamental point about fisheries management not only in the province but the country, says Cleary, a former reporter and former federal politician. Fisheries has been a common theme of Cleary's career—reporting fishers' stories and representing their interests. He raises the adjacency principle, the idea that those who live alongside resources should benefit most from the resource's development. Why don't fishers here—Indigenous and non-Indigenous alike—enjoy the historical and geographical benefits of living on the doorstep of the fish they depend on, he asks. Why are fishers or plant workers beholden to seemingly flash decisions made in Ottawa? According to FFAW-Unifor, "The economy of a fishing industry with no adjacency [is] no economy, at all." They say adjacency has been exercised in the fishery, citing, for example, the cases of pre-moratorium cod, post-moratorium crab, northern shrimp, mackerel, and halibut among other cases. They also cite adjacency terms in other industries such as oil and gas (as per the Atlantic Accord) and mining (the Voisey's Bay Development Agreement).

And yet, to Cleary's point, there is no legislation, policy or otherwise, firmly granting fishers the benefits of adjacency. Fishers and plant workers are beholden to Ottawa. And when we look back far enough, fishers have always been beholden to someone, harkening back to the merchant-fisher relationship.

When the French sailed more than 4,300 kilometres across the sea to get here in as early as 1640, they arrived in this harbour and called the place *Grand Banc*. It would later be settled by the English, when the 1713 Treaty of Utrecht ceded much of what is now Atlantic Canada to England. The French, banned from settling here under the treaty, populated Saint-

Pierre and Miquelon, the tiny archipelago off the southeastern shores of Newfoundland. These islands became French territory at the end of the Seven Years' War in 1763. By that time, in 1764, Grand Bank had a population of more than three hundred. There were over thirty fishing boats too, their crews having collectively cured over 457,000 kilograms of cod that same year. When Captain James Cook surveyed the south coast of Newfoundland in 1765, he visited Grand Bank and reported it having the largest fishery in Fortune Bay.

In the 150 years after its first settlers, Grand Bank's fishery operated as an inshore industry, with fishers sailing *shallops* (or sailboats, from the French *chaloupe*) and landing their catches directly in Grand Bank harbour. With the proximity to home the fishery provided, *fishing* became synonymous with *home*. Fishing was a family, community, and cultural affair. Settler families depended on merchants to advance supplies for the season (the boats, the gear, and various household goods) and, in return, the families supplied merchants with their seasonal catch.

Merchants functioned as banks, supplying the credit, but also marketed the fish to various buyers, while the families handled the production and supply. The price of a quintal (100 kilograms) of fish on the merchant's book was tied to the cost of a barrel of flour. Fishers earned a modest paycheque for their catch, while merchants ultimately cashed in on their own good fish fortune. As historian Rosemary E. Ommer said in her 1994 lecture, "One Hundred Years of Fishery Crises in Newfoundland," the merchant-family relationship "allowed families to live year-round in isolated places and the merchant to count on a stable labour force without having to pay year-long wages." It was, as Ommer points out, "an unequal deal," largely because the relationship was set up to privilege the interest of merchants versus that of the fishers and their families.

"Fishers were never calling the shots," says Dean Bavington, professor in the department of geography and author of the 2010 book *Managed Annihilation: An Unnatural History of the Newfoundland Cod Collapse.* "The island was colonized in the interest of the merchants."

The introduction of the cod jigger—likely in the 1850s—signalled a particular shift in power between fishers and merchants, says Bavington. That's because the *jigger*, a lead weight traditionally with two large hooks, was introduced as a new fishing technology by merchants so fishers could catch cod that would no longer take bait. If fishers could more reliably catch cod without having to wait until the cod were hungry, then they could pay back their debts to the merchants and the merchants would make money. This new economic model of the fishery had low tolerance for fluctuations in cod catches. It also went against the wild-fisheries model fishers were accustomed to operating.

"Fishers had learned to adopt to fluctuations in the [cod] stock by taking on land-based work and diversifying, but the [mercantile] market wanted to eliminate fluctuations to gain a return on their investment," says Bavington. Fishery science, he says, was applied in those days in order to help the investors, privileging evidence that increased profits of the merchants and corporations, with little to no respect paid to the knowledge of fishers or the health of the cod stocks. Indeed, the merchant-fisher agreement would foreshadow more raw deals for fishers and Newfoundlanders alike in the years ahead.

By the late nineteenth century, the Labrador fishery and the offshore, or Banks, fishery were picking up steam. Domestic and foreign fleets sailed to the Grand Banks, with schooners replacing shallops, and trawling replacing the handlining, trapping, and other traditional fishing techniques. Since setting a trawl still required a smaller boat, fishers created the Grand Banks dory around 1870. If you visit Grand Bank's Provincial Seamen's Museum—itself like a sailing schooner, with its triangle-shaped roof mimicking sailing masts and visible above the harbour—you can see the various model dories on display. The American dory, the French or St. Pierre dory, the Lunenburg dory and Portuguese dory—all are similar in shape and structure, made of wood, but with slightly different features in finishing and colour. Today, these dory replicas are reminders of the international fleets that once fished these

Codfish on a trawler off the Grand Banks, 1949. (Library and Archives Canada, PA-110814)

waters. England, France, Spain, Portugal, Newfoundland, Canada, Russia, and the United States, among many others, were drawn to the Banks fishery's rich source of groundfish, especially cod.

When those dories sailed the banks, Grand Bank was booming. It had a school, a doctor, a judicial system, a postal service and roads—all signs that this seaside town was coming into its own as a fishing hub. According to Ommer, in 1984, 82 per cent of Newfoundland's labour force of fifty-three thousand was in the fishery, "and that year the volume of salt cod *peaked* [emphasis Ommer's] at 1.5 million quintals, with its export value also *peaked*, at $5.5 million."

While that may have seemed the beginning of more good fortune to come, it almost certainly marked the beginning of the end. The traditional Newfoundland way of life and its fishery were already reaching their limits. Ommer writes:

Many communities were, quite simply, full up: more people were having less and less land to work with, and they were using it increasingly intensively over time. There were more acres in gardens, less in pasture, a decline in the number of animals per household and a drop in basic foodstuff production, even potatoes. The land could support no further increase in the informal (subsistence) economy which always provided a basic security for fishing communities. Only the fishery continued, in some places, to provide a rising income per household. But by 1901 it was doing so because of rising prices, for catches were, by then, falling steadily. The population statistics for the years from 1884 to 1921 show steady out-migration for all age and sex cohorts from ten to 50 years of age.

In Grand Bank, with its link to the Banks fishery, local merchants operated their own schooners and relied on residents to fish and tend the flakes as well as build and repair vessels in local shipyards. The houses merchants built were individual, land-based demonstrations of the prosperity collectively acquired at sea.

Thorndyke Bed and Breakfast could easily be mistaken for an early merchant house, but it was once owned and operated by Skipper John S. Thornhill. Born on nearby Brunette Island in 1879 to father Ambrose

Thornhill, Captain Thornhill was brother to my second great-grandfather, William Thornhill. Ambrose would later bring his family to Grand Bank. John, like his other siblings and parents, had never learned to read or write, but that didn't prevent him from captaining his own schooner by the time he was twenty-four, nor from later owning several schooners, including the *Thorndyke*, the vessel that would later inspire the name of his home. Thornhill was ambitious and worked hard, his wealth rivalling that of the town's merchants.

As one story goes, Thornhill's house is comprised of lumber from a ship he salvaged. The ship had wrecked near Saint-Pierre and Miquelon, so Thornhill towed the vessel back to Grand Bank and used the lumber to build his mansion by the sea. He also supposedly smuggled a radiation heating system back from one of his trips to Nova Scotia to avoid paying duties (just like my grandfather and the Singer sewing machine). However, Thornhill's riches likely came from his persistence: he was fishing on the Banks early and often, alongside other vessels, domestic and foreign, helping to put Grand Bank on the map as a fishing capital. Thornhills like John contributed to that reputation as much as anyone. In 1958 the well-known Captain Arch Thornhill (who skippered the ill-fated *Florence*) shared with a *Maclean's* magazine reporter that there had been as many as eleven Thornhills, all brothers or cousins, and all skippers, on the Banks only a few years previous.

In its heyday, Captain John Thornhill's home, the Thorndyke, was an architectural beauty. Next to Grand Bank's more modest saltbox homes— traditional bungalows and two-storeys, built on their slab foundations— the Thorndyke, with its three storeys, towers over its neighbours. It is exuberant, even excessive, in style and design. Although there are a half-dozen or more comparable houses on neighbouring streets—evidence of Grand Bank's prosperity in the salt cod fishery—these grand houses each stand out. Built in the Queen Anne Revival style, popular in the late nineteenth and early twentieth centuries, the Thorndyke's facade features overhanging and heavily bracketed eaves, a front-facing gable window and sunroom with large panes of glass and stained-glass trim. Its south-facing bay windows extend from the ground to the roof and, at the top of the four-sided roof, there's a widow's walk. In this house, Captain Thornhill fulfilled his childhood dream, building a castle fit for a king.

I can see the Thorndyke from the far end of the Grand Bank wharf. It's still a sight to behold, but as a guest, the house quickly turns

The Thorndyke Bed and Breakfast, a heritage structure in Grand Bank, Newfoundland, 2018.

lackluster. Recognized as a Registered Heritage Structure in 1988 and awarded a Southcott Award in 1990 for excellence in heritage restoration, the house now requires too many repairs to count. I imagine a time when the first-floor sunroom or the second-floor veranda would have made the perfect place to sit with a cup of tea to take in the ocean view and marine traffic. But when my family and I arrived for check-in, water was steadily leaking into the sunroom from multiple points in the ceiling. Despite the breach, the sunroom held the dampness like a humidifier and the cool air like a refrigerator, making it feel wetter and colder inside than out.

It didn't help that, throughout the house, most windows were sealed shut with layers of paint and foggy windowpanes were obstructing the view. Everywhere you looked—if you could get past the mishmash of decor and creaking floorboards—the plaster was cracking, the paint was peeling, and brown spots on the ceiling and corners of the rooms were evidence of persistent water leaks. My husband, daughter, and I stayed in Captain John's room, but it was dark, damp, cluttered, and otherwise uninviting. I lay there under the blankets, which also felt damp, and in my mind, I spoke to Captain John. *What do you think of what your grand home has become?*

Thornhill died in 1947. He had seen Grand Bank and the fishery evolve from its salt-fish roots to its fresh-fish future. On its cobblestone beaches, just past this Victorian home, the women and men of Grand Bank cured codfish for fleets of schooners for local trade and overseas markets. Thornhill saw the riches come to Grand Bank in the form of cod, but he certainly saw poverty around him too. We cannot mistake the prosperity of a few for that of an entire population, after all. There was never a utopian past in the outports, as much as we tend to romanticize them. Many lived in abject poverty, were functionally illiterate, and frequently went hungry. This is a point Rosemary Ommer makes in her insightful lecture: "I am not saying it was utopian, easy, a lost harmony of humanity and nature or any of those kinds of rural romantic pictures which have done us serious disservice in trying to grapple with these issues in the past. It was difficult, harsh and sometimes brought people to the brink of starvation."

Captain John's death meant he missed seeing Grand Bank's first fresh fish–processing plant, built in 1955 to serve the modern steam trawlers. Many of the men and women who were accustomed to fishing or working on the flakes began working in the plant. My Great Uncle Ches Thornhill was one such plant worker. I visited Ches's old house on Citadel Road, across from the Salvation Army church. It's a nondescript but well-maintained white two-storey with a steep gable roof and back porch, which serves as the main entry. This is where my father stayed to finish his grade eleven. By then, Ches was already working at the local fish plant, retired from his fishing days. The plant—the one I saw from the wharf—is still in operation. Owned by Grand Bank Seafoods, itself a division of Clearwater Seafoods, it processes shellfish like surf clams.

When I drove Dad by here the other day (he wasn't feeling up to making the five-minute walk from the Thorndyke), he thought this might be Ches's house. There were fewer houses back then, Dad said, and he hasn't been back to the area much since, so he couldn't be sure if this was it. But a local writer, Robert Parsons, later confirmed this was, indeed, the house.

"We all came out to see the lynx," said Parsons, recalling when Great-Uncle Ches, heavy-set man that he was, hanged a dead lynx in the front of the window of his two-storey shed, which has since been levelled. For all my time spent in Newfoundland and Labrador, I've never caught a glimpse of the wild cat, with its short body and black-tipped tail, its tufted ears and ruffs of fur on its cheeks. I could understand why the neighbourhood kids would have wanted to swing by for a look.

Dad and I would later be invited inside the house, having met the owner in his driveway while passing by. The footprint of the house hadn't changed, and Dad showed me the room where he used to stay. I was sorry Dad had missed the meeting with Parsons. He spent the days in Grand Bank mostly horizontal, in bed at the Thorndyke, feeling nauseated and complaining of pain in his jaw and right leg. I was still telling people, *Dad has good days and bad days*, but the bad days were starting to outnumber the good ones. I'm grateful Dad is here at all, spending time at meals together, even if his appetite is "touch and go." When it's a go, he eats what he likes—fish and chips and fried chicken are his go-to meals, not great from a nutritional standpoint, but we pick our battles at this stage. Mom is following suit, like she and Dad are in a competition to pack on pounds, only Dad keeps losing. He often doesn't bother with the formality of sitting at the table anymore, even if his choice of food calls for it. One time, I found him eating a chicken leg while lying down.

Dad, aren't you worried you might choke? I ask.

Well, it'll give me a head-start, he jokes.

Dad, I reply, emphasizing the *a* in protest.

You have to joke, Jennifer, because what else can you do?

He has a point. It's better to be forthcoming than to make false promises. If exploring the cod fishery collapse has taught me anything, it's that we've lost too much time wading in denial.

Back in 1958, *Maclean's* magazine reporter John Clare spent a week on the Grand Banks with Captain Arch Thornhill. Clare observed the coming together of several countries invested in the Banks fishery to form the International Commission for the Northwest Atlantic Fisheries (ICNAF). The commission would keep watch over the cod stock through research, building up "an accurate statistical picture of what is happening down in what the early operators called 'the cod meadow.'" Canada, the United Kingdom, Norway, Denmark, Iceland, Spain, Portugal, France, West Germany, and Russia formed ICNAF (which would become NAFO, the Northwest Atlantic Fisheries Organization, in 1979). Although there were (again in Clare's words) "no signs that this great natural preserve is in danger of being drained.... The day may come when it will be necessary to clamp a closed season on the Banks but it is not yet in sight."

Based on the best-available catch numbers, fishing fleets were landing more cod then than at any time in history. Nearly 1 million tonnes of cod were taken from the northwest Atlantic in 1956 alone compared with 500,000 to 700,000 tonnes caught over the ten-year period between 1930 and 1940. Among the reasons for the increased catch were the steadily improving fishing techniques and boats, but the main reason was this: a greater number of boats were fishing the Grand Banks than ever. Captain Arch revealed to Clare his worry about the increased traffic and what that meant. "By the end of the week a good catch seemed assured," wrote Clare, who tallied the total catch (a combination of flounder and cod) at about 205,000 pounds. "But this turn of events failed to remove entirely the nagging fear that Captain Thornhill shares with other skippers that the Banks will one day be fished out…. The assurances of the scientists do not allay Captain Thornhill's fears." Indeed, Captain Arch's fears would play out in real life, though he didn't live to see how bad things would become. Captain Arch died unexpectedly in 1976, a year after beginning to share his fishery stories with author Raoul Andersen.

Since the early 1500s, more than 250 million tonnes of cod are estimated to have been taken from the Northwest Atlantic—over half of that in the early to mid-twentieth century alone. The fishery remained sustainable, fisheries scientist George Rose tells us, "for 450-odd years, come weather, gear changes, and the vagaries of nature." In the foreword to Wade Kearley's 2012 book, *Here's the Catch: The Fish We Harvest From The Northwest Atlantic*, Rose writes that fish spawned, grew, fed, and survived—and the cod stocks persisted. Then, throughout the twentieth century, "overfishing, by both foreign and domestic fleets, laid waste to what remained." After the Second World War, the fishing fleets came in staggering numbers to fish what was considered, at that time, underutilized stocks. Until then, cod as a species seemed unrelenting, but these wondrous fish were no match for the even more wondrous fishing.

"It was the wild west, as all fished in a totally unregulated way in a free-for-all," Jean Pierre Andrieux writes in his book, *The Grand Banks: A Pictorial History*. As the demand for fish was growing, technology also marched on, with fish no longer able to hide as steam trawlers evolved to diesel and new radars, sounders, and gear arrived on the scene. These developments may have shown the industry's ingenuity—larger boats, quicker access to the fishing grounds, and greater catch rates—but it was too much, too fast, over too short a period, and with minimal regulation, for the codfish to have a fighting chance. In man versus nature, man often thinks he is winning. But he doesn't always realize what he's losing.

Between 1973 and 1974, all cod stocks in the Northwest Atlantic were subject to a "Total Allowable Catch" (or TAC), quota regulations set by NAFO. In theory, this was a principled idea, but in practice, the quotas were "ineffective in curbing the overexploitation, mainly because enforcement was ineffective, and catches exceeded them in many cases," writes William Henry Lear for Fisheries and Oceans Canada in the 1984 report *Atlantic Cod: Underwater World* (note: setting and enforcing of TACs in Canadian waters was Canadian responsibility). So as the cowboy culture of fishing the Northwest Atlantic heightened, so too did the concerns—it wasn't so much out of consideration for the fish, or even the fishers, but the fishery as an industry, and more specifically, the economy it supported. The question became: *Whose fish and, therefore, whose dollars are at stake?* Governments then set further limits, regulating who could fish and how close to what shores. But those limits arguably came too late and, where the Grand Banks were concerned, failed to recognize its unique geography.

On January 1, 1977, the United Nations Convention on the Law of the Sea extended the control of the fish stocks and fisheries from twelve miles to within two hundred nautical miles of North Atlantic country coasts. The "200-mile limit," as this extended jurisdiction is more commonly called, may seem a generous extension. But while the measure worked well in countries such as Iceland and Norway, it failed to consider the coastal context of the Grand Banks, where, as Rose writes, "the continental shelf extends much further than 200 miles from the shores of Newfoundland." In effect, the limits had not gone far enough to protect Canada's (and Newfoundland and Labrador's) most precious resource. What's more, domestic fishing enterprises took the new limits to mean they ought to catch as much fish as they could because if they didn't, the foreign fleets would pick up whatever they left behind. "These companies sort of took a gold rush kind of mentality, thinking they had total control over the 90-plus per cent of the entire stock," said Jim Wellman, in St. John's *The Telegram* newspaper in 2011. Wellman, managing editor of *The Navigator,* a monthly magazine for fisheries professionals in Atlantic Canada and the eastern United States, and a retired CBC broadcaster, goes on to say, "They borrowed tons of money and expanded their operations, bought new ships, modified their plans and so on, with the idea that they were going to have a lot more fish to process in the future. Five years later, a lot of these loans were coming up for renewal and interest rates in 1982 were about 20 per cent."

When I sat down with Robert "Bob" Verge, managing director of the Canadian Centre for Fisheries Innovation (CCFI, a non-profit organization owned by Memorial University and predominantly funded by the provincial government) at the Marine Institute in St. John's, he spoke about the adverse effects of the 200-mile limit in the decade leading up to the moratorium. He also filled in the gaps of that period, referencing the 1980–81 Royal Commission on the inshore fishery of Newfoundland and Labrador and the 1983 Kirby Task Force report, *Navigating Troubled Waters: A New Policy for the Atlantic Fisheries.* "The thinking at the time was that by excluding the foreign fleets we could increase our catches and have a much larger industry," Verge says. "But also, we could manage the resource, and under good Canadian management, the resource would expand. This was the beginning of what seemed to be a huge opportunity. It also happened to coincide with when the baby-boom generation was coming of age and needing jobs. So, the fishery was a way to provide jobs and income for a lot of those young people. And, of course, many of those were in rural areas so it seemed like a marriage made in heaven. The problem was that within four years in that industry that was created, it went bankrupt and had to be reworked."

Both the commission and task force supported the subsequent Fisheries Restructuring Agreement, signed by the federal government and the Provinces of Newfoundland and Labrador and Nova Scotia. "The governments...rolled the ashes of all the dead companies together," Wellman says, "and created what we used to refer to as the two super companies: one was Fisheries Products International, based in Newfoundland, and the other was National Sea Products, based in Nova Scotia." This strategy didn't work because people focused on the industry to catch the cod, yet paid inadequate attention to the cod stock itself. Verge says it took until about 1987 before the realization hit: the cod stock was failing. And we know now that it had been failing for some time. "But, of course, they didn't cut [the TAC] as much as they should have," Verge says.

To say that everyone realized the stocks were failing is a fair statement. And yet, the cod moratorium that followed five years later would send shock waves across the province, having a more devastating blow than the Burin Peninsula's 1929 tsunami. "What was shocking was the idea of a moratorium," Verge says. "I mean, people by then were accustomed to the idea we had been overfishing, the stocks were in bad shape and quotas needed to be cut. But I remember in early 1992, there were signs things were not going well. When the penny dropped for me it was probably in February of '92 when Fisheries Products International had boats fishing in the winter northern cod fishery. That was a fishery geared primarily to serving the market for fish during the Lent season in the US and it was well known the fish came together at that time of year in a spawning aggregation, so you could maintain very high catch rates even if the stock were smaller as long as you could find the stock." But that season Fisheries Products International, with all of its high-tech equipment, power, and capacity, couldn't find the cod. "Boy, if they can't do it this time of year on the spawning stock, then we're in trouble," Verge says, recalling his own reaction at the time.

All this turned the Grand Banks cod fishery into "a thin shadow of its once great majesty," Jean Pierre Andrieux writes in his pictorial history of the Grand Banks. Within less than two decades of the UN extensions, nearly forty years of overfishing, and poorer productivity in the cod stocks, waters once teeming with cod grew quiet and empty. A fish that thrived for more than half a century was nearly gone within decades. That outcome, the collapse of the cod stocks and closure of the fishery, undid all of the scientific models. And it undid the people and their spirits, too.

"To say that politicians, industry and science were caught off guard would be an understatement," writes George Rose. Jim Wellman told *The Telegram* (St. John's) it was a "disaster of biblical proportions." And biblical it was. The northern cod stock was of tremendous importance, not solely to the province, but to the country and world. In the late 1980s and early '90s, cod was on life support—and it has carried on in that precarious state for the better part of twenty-five years with minimal evidence of sustained improvement.

"Despite the fact that the moratorium was initially announced in 1992, there were some initial expectations, maybe not well grounded in biology, that the stock might even improve within a couple of years," says Dr. Sherrylynn Rowe. An expert in fisheries ecology and science with a focus on cod, particularly northern cod, she studies aspects of behaviour, life history, and population dynamics. "Well, that clearly didn't happen," she continues. "And even within scientific circles, there had been a lot of debate about whether or not it could even recover."

A look at the cod collapse by the numbers shows precisely how this disaster played out, as well as its more recent recovery. Fisheries and Oceans (2018) summarized the decline over the period of the late 1960s to early 1990s: Catches of Northern cod in Newfoundland and Labrador reached a peak of over 800,000 tonnes (t) in 1968, but then declined steadily until stabilizing around 240,000 t throughout the 1980s. In the early 1990s (pre-moratorium), cod catches declined rapidly to under 180,000 t in 1991 and less than 40,000 t in early 1992.

In *Managed Annihilation*, Dean Bavington points out the correlation between the rising cod catches and the onset of factory freezer stern trawlers after the Second World War. This observation, he says, was made by fisheries biologists Jeffrey Hutchings and Ransom Myers, who observed trawlers were catching cod off of Newfoundland from Britain (1954), the Soviet Union (1956), West Germany (1957), and others, "leading to almost a tripling of reported cod landings over the twelve-year period from 1956 to 1968."

Fisheries scientists George Rose and Sherrylynn Rowe detailed the cod collapse and its potential comeback in exceptional detail in their 2015 and 2018 *Canadian Journal of Fisheries and Aquatic Sciences* papers. Relying on estimates of cod biomass, the total mass of cod in a given region (in this case, the southern Bonavista Corridor, on the northeast coast of Newfoundland), over two decades, they show cod biomass peaked at 450,000 tonnes (t) in 1990 and then plummeted to 100,000t in 1992 (there were no recordings of biomass in 1994). Nearly a decade later, the stocks appeared to grow, slowly but surely: 5000t in 2003; 17,000 t in 2007; 75,000 t in 2008; 120,000t in 2012; 238,000 t in 2014. The scientists found that not only were there more cod, but the fish were larger, too (lengthwise), a signal of health in the stock. While scientists warned these numbers did not indicate a full recovery—2014 levels were still just above half of the pre-collapse peak levels from 1990—they did suggest a full recovery may be possible.

The Rowe and Rose 2018 paper then expanded the range, examining cod biomass from the Bonavista Corridor further north to the Notre Dame and Hawke Channels, which extend north toward the southern shore of Labrador. While the Bonavista Corridor aggregations had declined from their 2014 levels, the Notre Dame and Hawke Channels aggregations had increased by proportionally the same amount. When the sum of the biomass across all of these areas is pooled, it totals 302,000t, consistent with continued growth at about 30 per cent (as the scientists predicted and had seen in the Bonavista Corridor over the 2007–14 period). This finding is also consistent with an earlier redistribution of cod from the inshore to offshore. Rose's earlier work had suggested cod in the area of Smith Sound, the largest extant spawning biomass of northern cod between 1995 and 2006, had dispersed offshore into the adjacent Bonavista Corridor.

I spoke directly with Dr. Rowe to understand more of what she and Rose observed in their studies. First, I needed to know why the intense focus on these specific regions. "As the stock collapsed in the late eighties and early nineties," Rowe explains, "there was a real shift in distribution of the fish from being, at one time, quite widespread throughout eastern Newfoundland and southern Labrador to a situation whereby the remaining fish were primarily holed up in this area that we refer to as the 'Bonavista Corridor.' And indeed, the lion's share of what's been found in the offshore area over the intervening years since the moratorium has primarily been focused in this relatively small offshore area." When the scientists undertook their 2015 survey, they found an abundance of cod not only in the southern Bonavista Corridor but extending north through the Notre Dame Channel and into the Hawke Channel off of Labrador. What Rowe and Rose argued then, is the cod from the first region redistributed (that's science-speak for swam) to these other regions.

The second thing I wanted to understand is what was responsible for this remarkable growth in the cod stock. The short-form answer: Mother Nature handed down favourable environmental conditions for capelin, in turn helping cod. The "Northern Cod Comeback" (the title of Rowe and Rose's 2015 paper) highlighted these two main factors: capelin stock, a primary food source for cod, increased over the same period the cod began bouncing back; and ocean temperatures warmed (a result of global warming, which, in this case, created a more hospitable environment for the cod stock, at least for now).

As Rowe explains, "frugal management" may have also positively contributed to growth of the stock over that period. Fisheries and Oceans uses what it calls a "precautionary approach framework," which, in the case of cod, means keeping quotas low and basing those quotas not only on how the cod are doing, but also how the species cod depend on (like capelin) are doing. In theory, this approach sounds like good common sense. In practice, that common sense hasn't always played out.

"For northern cod right now, we still don't have a plan," Rowe says. She continues:

> There's no clear statement of what we're trying to get out of this resource or the fishery and as a result, decisions are being taken from one year to the next in a fairly ad hoc manner with no basis for people from the outside to question because sadly we still have no plan. In the absence of a plan, if you went out and talked to people within the industry, in various non-governmental groups, conservation bodies, and so on, quite consistently across the board you'd get people saying, 'Yeah, we'd like northern cod to recover. We'd like to have a sustainable, fully rebuilt fishery moving forward.' For me, it's difficult to see whereby the decisions that have been taken in the last couple of years are really

*consistent with those hopes or expectations. We need to know what
we're trying to achieve so we can hold decision-makers accountable
when needed. It doesn't matter if it's cod or anything else. If there's no
plan, how can you ever achieve any reasonable expectations or targets?*

Rowe and Rose urged the Canadian government in a 2017 letter in
the journal *Nature* (the gold standard of peer-reviewed scientific research
journals) not to act on proposals to ramp up the northern cod fishery
along Newfoundland and Labrador's east coast. They argued that despite
all of the positive indications they raised in their 2015 study, the cod stock
was "still well below historical norms." But DFO had already allowed
the northern cod quota to more than double, from 4,000t in 2015 to
10,000t in 2016 and 13,000t in 2017. This was without having a long-term
stock-rebuilding plan in place and without, at the time, an annual stock
assessment. Rowe and Rose (2017) continued to write that despite the
advice of the Canadian parliamentary fisheries committee for annual
assessments, the available data indicated—based on lower inshore catch
rates and smaller increases in surveyed biomass—the cod's comeback
may have stalled.

Finally, in 2018, DFO made the decision to undertake a full assessment
of northern cod annually. But the March 2018 assessment showed
worrisome findings: a 30 per cent decline in cod's spawning stock biomass,
which is expected to continue into the next full assessment (expected
from DFO in March 2019, though, as of August 2019, the results of the
latest assessment have not yet been released). Meanwhile, the reason
for the spawning stock decline, DFO reports, is "natural mortality,"
which, according to Rowe, is a catch-all, accounting for anything above
fishery landings. "It includes things like bona fide natural processes
like predation, starvation, and disease, all of which could be expected
to be on the rise under deteriorating environmental conditions," Rowe
explains. "But it potentially also includes things like unreported catch or
illegal discarding, which could also potentially be at play here."

Rowe's hunch seems probable as the latest report on world fisheries
from the UN's Food and Agriculture Organization claims one-third of all
fish stocks in the world were fished at biologically unsustainable levels
in 2015, up from one-tenth in 1974. A 2019 paper in the journal *Fisheries
Research* by George Rose and Carl Walters argues DFO likely under-
attributed the role unreported catches (or over-fishing) played in the

early 1990s collapse of the cod stock and over-accounted for the effects of natural mortality. In the paper, "The state of Canada's iconic Northern cod: A second opinion," Rose and Walters write: "The inference that fishing has had little impact on stock growth has likely influenced recent management measures to allow increased removals despite the stock being well below the most recently determined precautionary lower limit for spawning stock biomass (ca. 800,000 t)."

It reminds me of a quote from Wade Kearley, whose 2012 book, *Here's the Catch*, captures the fish of the northwest Atlantic in precise detail: "If we can dedicate our efforts to understanding where and how the different species live and what they need to be healthy—and if fisheries' regulators can place protecting the fish ahead of protecting the fishery—then we will become better custodians and still be able to benefit from the harvesting of this amazing resource. And really, what other choice do we have?"

Kearley is right: what other choice is there or has there ever been but to make protecting the fish our first priority? In the Northwest Atlantic, groundfish and shellfish projections are poor across the board when compared to each species' peak-year performance. All stocks for fish and shellfish are down—even phytoplankton, the food source of the ocean's smallest fish.

"In 1990, fish landings in Canada totalled 1,598,281 metric tonnes. In 2016, they were 831,980 tonnes, just 52.1% of the 1990 total," writes Bob Verge of the Canadian Centre for Fisheries Innovation in his July 2018 article "Making Do With Less" for *The Navigator* magazine. These figures represent Atlantic and Pacific coast fisheries, with Atlantic landings having experienced the greatest decrease (50 per cent decrease compared to the Pacific's nearly 40 per cent decline). Examining the landings on the Atlantic coast shows groundfish (like cod) and pelagic species (like capelin) have been hardest hit, while shellfish landings increased over that period: Those 1990 landings included "791,246 tonnes of groundfish, 560,238 tonnes of pelagic species, and 246,796 tonnes of shellfish. The 2016 totals included 206,247 tonnes of groundfish, 216,718 tonnes of pelagic species, and 409,016 tonnes of shellfish." But, as Verge points out, the 2016 figures for shellfish actually demonstrate a sharp decline from when shellfish landings peaked, in 2004, at 491,880 tonnes. Lobster was the only shellfish species to actually increase over that period, while northern shrimp, snow crab, and scallops all saw declines compared to previous peak-year performances.

And yet, despite all of that bad news, Dr. Sherrylynn Rowe holds out hope for the future of northern cod. She started studying northern cod shortly after it had collapsed. Then, it became clear the stocks may never recover. But then, with the work she and George Rose completed from 2006–07 onwards, they started to see "pretty clear evidence that indeed finally there was cause for optimism." Rowe explains:

> I guess I'm a lot more optimistic now than I was maybe ten years ago, because there was a lot of debate, uncertainty, and downright doubt about whether northern cod would ever recover, whether it could ever recover. And I guess what I've seen over the last ten years, I'm now of the opinion that if we give the stock a chance, it will indeed rebound. Maybe not exactly to the levels that we saw back in the 1960s when we had these absolute massive levels of removals, but it could certainly grow to a much greater level than what we've seen of late, and support a viable fishing industry within this province. Whether or not we can continue to fish while recovery is taking place, I guess there's also some discussion around that.

In Rose's foreword to *Here's the Catch*, he claims that three problems will face the northwest Atlantic in the coming decades: continuing exploitation by Canadian and foreign fishing fleets, climate change, and the lingering ghost effects of poor past management. We can do something about current overfishing—and we are mandated to do so under UN and national conventions—he says. Meanwhile, climate change will be harder to deal with and the ghosts of past management will continue to have their effect. Rose also mentions the pressures attributable to foreign fisheries on the Grand Banks and seal herds that have grown to unparalleled levels at a time when fish stocks are at their lowest.

Many point to seal predation of cod as inhibiting a greater cod comeback. The Committee on the Status of Endangered Wildlife in Canada (COSEWIC), in its 2010 assessment of the northern cod stock, included growing harp seal populations as one of more than a half-dozen factors associated with the cod collapse. The committee's assessment report found the collapse to be so dire, they designated cod as "endangered." This independent committee of wildlife experts and scientists focuses on at-risk species in the country, which they organize into five categories: not at risk, special concern, threatened, endangered, and extirpated. That means cod has been designated just shy of total collapse.

Regarding the threat of seals as the major factor, Dr. Rowe rejects the idea, as do DFO scientists. Seals could very well be playing a significant role in cod population dynamics, but the present evidence does not suggest that they are the primary driver. If seals did contribute to the decreased cod stock originally, she explains, then why haven't their numbers suffered over the same time frame? Rowe admits the science is "tangly," however. There is evidence to suggest grey seals in the Gulf of St. Lawrence are impeding the cod stock's recovery there, she says, but based on the analyses for northern cod in particular, there's no compelling evidence to support a direct link between large-scale changes in cod biomass over the decades and harp seal population size (even if there are some 7 million of them, and growing).

Two things are certain: there are many root causes, and there will need to be many coordinated solutions if cod are to ever experience a true comeback. But there is hope. As Rowe says, "Even some of the most collapsed stocks in the world are indeed capable of recovery."

A 2003 political cartoon in the then weekly St. John's newspaper, *The Express*, by cartoonist Peter Pickersgill shows a codfish with spectacles peering at a fisher under his microscope and saying, "Properly managed, this species can make a complete recovery." With the benefit of hindsight a decade after the cod moratorium, the cartoon captured the evolved nature of the debate: having failed to control cod, governments moved on to further attempts at controlling fishers.

Perhaps one of the reasons attempts to "control" cod has failed is because past attempts were primarily motivated by monetizing the catch versus preserving the health of the stock. Growing the cod stock represents its own challenges, as does recruiting and retaining new fishers in the workforce. Indeed, the face of the fishery is changing. Still primarily male-dominated, there are fewer people employed in this sector, fishers are aging, and the challenges to entering the fishery are greater than ever before.

In 1992 fishing accounted for 20 per cent of all employment in Newfoundland and Labrador; this industry now employs less than 3 per cent of the province's workforce. According to the *Government of Newfoundland and Labrador Economic Review 2018*, the seafood sector employed about 16,620 people from over four hundred, mostly rural communities in 2017. The overall economic value of landings has increased since the moratorium although the total volume of fish harvested has decreased by 40 per cent over the last twenty years (1991–2011). As a result, fewer people work in processing plants and on fishing vessels than before the moratorium. In 1989 the fishery employed about 37,665 seasonal workers and the pre-moratorium cod market brought in approximately $500 million annually (not accounting for inflation). By 1990 the total landed value of fish in the province was $277 million, of which cod accounted for $134 million (48 per cent). Nearly twenty years later, in 2009, the total landed value of fish in the province was $517 million, of which cod accounted for $15.2 million (less than 3 per cent) and by 2010, the number of those employed in the fishery had shrunk by 44 per cent, to 21,140.

Fast-forward to today and the total value of fish and seafood production predicted for 2018 was expected to exceed $1 billion for the fourth consecutive year—the value was $1.2 billion in 2017, with the US and China accounting for nearly 70 per cent of exports (52 and 16 per cent respectively) and the remainder exported to the UK, Japan, and Hong Kong. While Newfoundland and Labrador produces eight types of seafood—shrimp, snow crab, shellfish, pelagic (like capelin), groundfish (like cod), Atlantic salmon, mussels, and others—its primary exports are shellfish, pelagic, and groundfish. Meanwhile, new fishery opportunities, like fish-farming salmon and *smolt*, or young salmon, are estimated to be worth an additional $500 million annually. That's even with groundfish landings and associated landed value expected to decrease in 2018 compared to 2017, with landings of approximately 45,000 tonnes and landed value of $119 million.

Not only are there fewer people employed in fishing these days, but the workforce is aging too. In 1999 approximately 20 per cent of registered fish harvesters were under the age of thirty compared with 9 per cent in 2009. And over that same timeframe, the proportion of fish harvesters over the age of fifty-five grew from 12 per cent (2004) to 24 per cent (2009). A more recent figure suggests in 2019 almost one-third (32 per cent) of fish harvesters in the province will reach age fifty-four or older.

One contributing factor is certainly the overall aging population; Newfoundland and Labrador's population, as with the rest of Atlantic

Canada, is aging faster than the rest of the country. In Canada, in 2018, the average age is forty to forty-one, while in Atlantic Canada it's forty-five and in Newfoundland and Labrador it's forty-six to forty-seven years old. But another factor is that it's increasingly difficult for the younger generation to get involved in the fishing industry. There's a great deal of risk, capital, education, and time involved in trying to break into a fishing career, let alone the expense of owning and operating one's own fishing enterprise.

One individual bent on making a go of it as an independent owner-operator fisher is Rachel Durnford. The sound of the whirring band saw I heard earlier when I approached Grand Bank harbour came from Durnford's longliner. Except for the old eyesore parked near the entrance of the marina, hers is the largest vessel docked. The *Brittany Wave* stands out alongside the smaller fishing boats and pleasure-crafts not just in size but beauty. It is gleaming. Not a scratch on her strikingly coloured turquoise-blue hull with white trim. On the bow, there's a tastefully painted set of Canadian and Newfoundland and Labrador flags, flanking a crested "B," with the ship's name spelled out in bold red cursive. The wires and antennae above the wheelhouse tell me the ship has all the high-tech navigational and fish-finding gear any fisher could need. As I approach the buzzing band saw, I spot Durnford on the wharf. By her movements—head down, chopping on a flat surface—I think she is splitting fish. But I know that can't be right. There's no scent of fish in the air on this end of the wharf and the gulls are still hanging out down by the lighthouse. Durnford's shiny dark brown hair is tied back into a practical low pony and she's wearing a burgundy hoodie over a purple V-neck. I can now see she's involved in renovation work, tearing strips of fibreglass and walking back and forth between the wharf and her vessel. Onboard the *Brittany Wave* is her husband, Ross Durnford, working at the band saw.

We exchange hellos and I learn the pair are married. Ross and Rachel? I think of making a joke about *Friends* but decide against it. Instead, I say, "Can I ask what you're up to?"

"Doing some repairs to the boat," she offers, "getting her ready."

"Do you fish together?" I ask Rachel, but Ross pipes in.

"Oh no, this is her boat. She's the skipper."

"The skipper?" I reply, the enthusiasm in my voice clearly audible.

Rachel replies with an inhaled "Yep," replacing the Y with an H in a form of agreement and acknowledgement Newfoundlanders tend to offer.

"That's awesome. So nice to meet you." Ross and Rachel exchange a glance that tells me I'm not the first to respond this way. While women have always been involved in the fishery—consider the crucial role they played tending the flakes on the beaches—they have always made up the minority of workers. A 2019 statistic suggests women comprise about one-fifth (23 per cent) of professional fish harvesters in the province.

"I'm a fisherman," Durnford says, her voice trailing into laughter, as she shares another consideration for women in this field. "I just say it—*fisherman*. It doesn't bother me. Some people say, 'Oh, there she is, the fisherman. Oh no, wait. *Fisherwoman*.' And, one time, I said, 'No, b'y, don't correct me.' I'm an independent woman but I won't fight over what they're going to name me."

Durnford bought her boat earlier this year. At the time, it did not have an adequate bathroom, a necessary fix for trips of three or more days at sea. That work was now complete but there were still "odds and ends that had to be done." Among them: painting, prepping, and hooking up the fishing gear as well as making up the table for dressing fish. "Just a whole lot of little small jobs that end up being one big job," she laughs. This year, she's planning to fish primarily halibut, sea cucumbers (which is a relatively exclusive fishery with a limited season, quotas, and entry into restricted waterways), and scallops. She brings four to five crewmembers with her,

The *Brittany Wave* schooner, owned by Rachel Durnford, Grand Bank Harbour, Newfoundland, 2018.

depending on the job. I ask how she became involved in the fishery, and she explains she began at age fifteen, in 1997, fishing with her then boyfriend and now husband, Ross, and his father.

"Being a young girl, of course, I didn't want to leave my boyfriend for five minutes," Durnford says. "So I used to go out on the boat with them and I enjoyed it. I loved it. And that year between grade eleven and twelve, I fished with them pretty much the whole summer." Once she finished high school, she returned to summer fishing again. Durnford attended university for a year but says it wasn't for her. Her parents worked in the fish plant for a short stint, but moved on to other professions: her father became a civil engineer and her mother a licensed practical nurse. She recalls her grandmother speaking of tending flakes on the beaches in Grand Bank.

"Being young and not really having a game plan knowing exactly what I wanted to do, I just fell into what I loved doing. That was fishing," she says. Falling into fishing makes it sound easier than it is. Besides the cost of education and training, new fishers need hands-on mentorship to make a go of it in this industry, and acquiring a new vessel or enterprise can cost anywhere from $250,000 to $1 million, not to mention the regular upkeep that comes with maintaining a seafaring vessel and the fishing gear. Staying current on gear types, techniques, and technologies requires continuing education and investment. It all adds up.

These days, fishing makes up 100 per cent of the Durnfords' household income. And given Rachel skippers her own vessel while Ross works jointly with his father and uncle, and each has their own crew, life would appear to be good. But salaries in the fishery can range widely season to season for a variety of reasons—all of which are beyond a fisher's control. A 2015 report in the *Globe and Mail* claimed crewmembers often earn day rates of $200–250 or enter into a crew agreement, earning a share (anywhere from 5 to 20 per cent) of the vessel's seasonal earnings. Entreprise owners/operators could net several hundred thousand dollars per year, but have high operational costs, including paying their crew, vessel and gear upkeep, purchasing their licenses, and more.

Having had the experience of working aboard a vessel and witnessing the ins and outs of what it entails, Durnford wanted to strike out on her own. She secured her first lobster license in 2011. "It's a new venture for me. I'm pretty excited about it and nervous at the same time. But I enjoy it and I like being able to do it myself," she says about skippering her own vessel. "Like I said to Ross, 'We don't know what the future holds and if I sit back and do what some women do—just go work with their husbands and let them handle the boat and run their boats or whatever—then I could find myself in a situation where something could happen to you and then what am I going to do?'"

One of the most harrowing parts of the job is the beaucratic stuff that happens before the boat is even in the water. Of course, the beaucracy is necessary, explains Durnford, but it can sometimes get out of hand and cost her from getting out on the water. "There's definitely a lot of rules and regulations," she says. "I know why we have a lot of them—there's a lot of people trying to bend the rules and whatnot—but there's a lot of rules and regulations that just make no sense." She gives an example: "If I'm ready to go sea cucumbering today, [DFO] tells me they need to inspect my gear, inspect the boat, and make sure what I say I'm doing is true. Then, when that's done, it's going to be five to seven business days for a piece of paper to go through saying I can go fishing, and then probably two days after that before DFO has it on my file so I can go print off my conditions, which allows me to go."

Fishing in Pop's day often entailed trips of weeks or months at sea, but the majority of fishers like Durnford start their day at dawn or earlier to set their gear, then return later the same day for the fish harvest. Any given day is limited by the weather, availability of resources (having an at-the-ready vessel and crew as well as open season dates), and paperwork. The amount of paperwork required today would leave fishers like my grandfather out in the cold. Among the various required documentation are:

• a personal commercial fishing license and fisheries licenses for which species may be caught, how much, where, using what gear, and over what period (Fisheries and Oceans Canada)

• emergency and safety certifications for crew as well as a boat license to operate in the Canadian commercial fishery (Transport Canada)

• professional radio operator certifications (Industry Canada)

• first aid training.

Those operating larger vessels require fishing-master designation, available from various post-secondary institutions such as the Fisheries and Marine Institute of Memorial University in Newfoundland.

The job also brings physical challenges. As Durnford says, "There's a lot of hard work and lots of pulls, tears, strains, and backaches." Not to mention the danger. Like other fishers, Durnford has been involved in accidents that range from bad to worse. Hooks in fingers are common injuries. One particularly "nasty hook" sent Ross to hospital for emergency surgery, which turned out to be a blessing in disguise: "I was in the Burin Hospital with [Ross] when we had a phone call," Dunford recalls. "His father, out on the same trip that we would have been on together, was on the way in and lost the boat. The boat sunk." Fortunately, everyone survived, but the risk of going overboard is always present. Durnford recalls one particularly life-threatening experience when a crewmember fell in the fish hold of the boat. It took the crew more than an hour to get him out due to the weather conditions. By the time they did haul him in, he was hypothermic. It would take another two hours to get to shore, where an ambulance and five trucks filled with anxious relatives and friends awaited their return. On another occasion, out fishing cod on the Saint-Pierre Bank, a fish pan slid across the deck, causing Durnford to stumble backward. "I squealed," Durnford says, "and when I did, my husband turned around with his hand and grabbed me at the same time. Just caught me as I'm going over the rail. Out there in the pitch dark, if I'd gone over, I mean they wouldn't have had a chance to find me."

Such close calls haven't deterred Durnford, who is dogged and determined to live this life. She knows her safety measures and protocols and will use them when and if she needs them. And she doesn't dwell on what can go wrong because most days, fishing is a joy. "It's an exciting job. No two ways about it. You're going to work every day and it's never the same day twice," she says, laughing.

Durnford is also motivated by the scrappy go-get-'em attitude it takes to be a fisher. She started fishing five years after the cod moratorium, entering the industry at a time when fishers began diversifying from cod to snow crab to lobster to scallops. Now, as all landings are down from their historical levels, fishing a range of species remains common. "Everybody branched out," says Durnford, "Rather than stick to the one fish, we all kind of diversified and went off making all our seasons work for different species."

If she had to do it all over again, Durnford says she would; she'd even encourage her younger self to follow the same career path. The Durnfords have even taken their son and daughter out fishing, too, saying it builds character. And yet, like other fishers I have talked to, who love their careers and wouldn't have it any other way, they say it's not a career path they want for their children. "I don't think it's a job that we want to see our own kids doing, and it's hard to explain why because me and my husband are making a great living at it. I don't know if it's because it's hard work, maybe, dirty work. Perhaps we'd like to see them doing something that we feel is probably a little bit better. I'm not sure exactly the reason why there, but, yeah."

But the couple's son, in particular, may see the joy in fishing that drew his parents to the field. "We went out the other day after halibut," Durnford says, her son having joined her crew for that trip, "and we had a halibut come up to the rail [of the boat] that was 250 pound[s]. [My son's] face lit up—he thought it was unbelievable. We got the fish on board and had some pictures took, and we texted them to his dad. When we come home that night—I think we landed around midnight—he went in and woke his dad up and came out and sat down and talked and talked and talked and told his tale about the halibut."

"Until this week, when the lobster fishery ended, there was no room for pleasure crafts." Arch Evans of the Grand Bank Harbour Authority had said this to me back on Water Street, referencing the vessels docked at the wharf. For all the signs telling me Grand Bank has its challenges, I've begun to see its bright spots. With the sun now fully risen, the locals are weathering this cool day far better than I am, still bundled up in my jacket and scarf. No doubt they are eager to feel the sun on their faces and clean up the last remnants of winter. Two young mothers wearing capri pants and short-sleeved shirts are pushing strollers past the Seaman's Museum. Over there, a groundskeeper is cleaning the Fisherman's Memorial, readying the monument for its annual Canada Day reopening. Another man stops me on the street, having seen me earlier with my infant daughter, to tell me there will be activities for families and children in the park by the school on July 1. The scent of freshly cut grass fills the air. A few teenage boys bike past while a school bus drops off a girl, maybe seven years old. She runs wildly down the hill to where an older woman, perhaps her grandmother, is putting clothes out on the line. A couple of neighbours are talking over their fences as one of them mends his wooden pickets, likely broken from the weight of the season's snow. There are plenty of homes up for sale, but people here have a better shot of owning their own home at all, compared to the rest of Canada. Down on Water Street, there's a steady stream of people coming in and out of Sharon's Nook, a café, restaurant, and gift shop that's like an oasis on this street of closed and condemned storefronts. The stream of people tells me there's the local will, if only these other business owners can find their way.

I wander the area and before I know it, the sun is beginning to set. I think about the people who regularly gather here by the harbour to share stories of the good old fishing days: days on the trawlers, draggers, and coastal steamers, or stories about working in the fish plants along the coast. It's become a common practice to get together here before sundown and share a yarn or two. All of this, the continued efforts to rebuild this place, the people, the continuation of telling stories amongst friends, are precisely the signs of hope I hoped I would find. As I walk back to the Thorndyke, I brush away the tear rolling down my cheek. I take a deep breath and smile.

Thank you, Grand Bank.

CHAPTER 5:
Cod Fishery Refresh

The *Newfoundland Mariner*, built in 1992, had long since proven itself a capable seafaring vessel. It boasted a travel log spanning the entire northwest Atlantic, in and around Newfoundland and Labrador to the North Atlantic between Baffin Island and Greenland. The captain/owner and crew—comprised of the captain's right-hand, the mate, an engineer, and three deckhands—were also highly capable. Each of the men, born and bred here, had spent the better part of their lifetimes aboard fishing vessels of one kind or another. So had their families. It's what they did.

Weather conditions were expected to be on their side for their upcoming trip. But given the ice, they would take it slow and steady. Temperatures hovered around zero degrees Celsius, winds breezed between 20 and 25 knots (37–46 kph), and the waves dispersed ocean spray, forming whitecaps. That morning, the *Newfoundland Mariner* was embarking on a sea of white—it wasn't the white foam crests but the ice floes in particular that created the polar scene. Recently freed from the cold North Atlantic and Arctic seas, the pack ice was heading south, along the coast of Labrador to the northern coastline of Newfoundland. Navigating pack ice is expected this time of year, typically beginning in April and continuing into the summer months, sometimes as late as July. And so, when the *Newfoundland Mariner* and her crew set out from Triton on the northeast coast of Newfoundland on May 8, 2017, this should have been like any other late-spring fishing trip.

When I finally meet Brad Watkins, the captain/owner of that vessel just over a year later, it's to hear more about this trip. The meeting almost doesn't happen because Watkins tells me he recently quit fishing, at least for the foreseeable future. He hasn't stepped foot on a boat since that trip last season and now worries he's no longer a useful source to me. I assure him he is, although admittedly, his news confounds me. This is the man who, a year ago, on July 4, 2017, CBC Newfoundland reported as "determined to be at the vanguard of the reimagined cod business." Yet, this is also the first I'm hearing of his career change. How does a fourth-generation fisher with thirty years of experience, first as a crewmember, then working his way up as an enterprise-owner, quit the only career he's ever known? Watkins tells me he still considers himself a fisherman, but he's neither harvesting fish nor owns an enterprise at the moment. He's still involved in the fishery, however. He serves on the provincial Fisheries Advisory Council and the Canadian Centre for Fisheries Innovation (CCFI) board. Formerly, he served on the federal advisory committee to the chair of the Standing Senate Committee on Fisheries and Oceans and the Newfoundland and Labrador Independent Fish Harvesters' Association as vice-chair.

Today, Watkins is seated opposite me at a picnic table outside of his RV trailer, parked on Indian River, just west of Springdale in central Newfoundland. Watkins is like an outdoor-enthusiast version of Mr. Clean. He has the same broad shoulders and folded arms, smart grin, beaming blue eyes, and, of course, the clean-shaven bald head. He's dressed in a fitted T-shirt with the phrases "Always Outside" and "Adventure in the outdoors" printed on it. Tattooed on Watkins's right forearm is a tall ship, a reminder of his paternal grandfather who owned fishing schooners, he says. On his left forearm is an anchor with

A derelict stage, Springdale, Newfoundland, 2018.

the names of his two children—"my anchor in life," Watkins explains. Then, on his right-hand middle finger, a chunky silver skull-and-crossbones ring. "My ancestors were supposed to have been pirates," Watkins tells me when I ask him about the ring later. "I don't know, but the romance of the story is intriguing to me. A life at sea chasing treasures is basically what I did with fishing. Do the unthinkable, face challenges, be a leader was what I enjoyed. Outside the box is how I fished. Risky but exciting."

Inland, far from the wharf where we had planned to meet aboard the *Newfoundland Mariner*, Watkins shows me he's still a risk-taker. He risked everything to be at the forefront of the cod fishery—a risk that didn't go as planned. Now we're at the site of his latest risky venture—a land-based operation—an RV park and resort. Around us, construction workers are clearing the grounds, shifting timbers, building structures, all to make way for the "Blue Canoe Family RV Park," which will open in summer 2019. Watkins is embarking on his latest enterprise, a sixty-seven-acre lot with plans for one hundred full-service RV sites, with his fiancée, Joy. He can't get his words out fast enough, listing the number of amenities in the works—golf greens and a driving range, horseshoe pits, coffee shop and convenience store, a gazebo, and a timber-built entertainment building. They'll name the roads after local animals and, if they get government approval, put in a swimming pool, too. I can hear the jingle in my head, "Mr. Clean, Mr. Clean..." as Watkins takes me through his ideas for this giant patch of Newfoundland's wilderness. What looks like a pile of dirt to me has a bright future to Watkins.

I understand why he's invested in his vision. Newfoundland and Labrador Tourism is reporting a strong outlook for the industry, showing no signs of letting up. For the last several years, more than 500,000 non-resident visitors have travelled here annually, in effect doubling the population of the province over the summer months. Watkins's resort is located directly off the Trans-Canada Highway, the main thoroughfare between central and eastern Newfoundland and Gros Morne National Park, located about 200 kilometres northwest. Gros Morne alone welcomed 240,000 visitors in 2017. Finding accommodations outside of the park and larger city centres can be a challenge. Then there's the potential for local visitors, too. It's expensive to travel out of province. That, combined with the province's economy being in a serious slump, makes a staycation the preferred option for Newfoundlanders and Labradorians.

As the river trickles behind us, I turn the conversation back to fishing. This area is known for salmon, which may entice Watkins's future campers and patrons. They may want to participate in the province's recreational groundfish fishery too, setting out from nearby Springdale or King's Point. But Watkins hasn't even thought of fishing. He needed a clean break from it, he says, his Mr. Clean grin vanishing. He hesitates with his words now, too. I interpret this to mean he has some residual anxiety about the topic. "It was a hard time, very hard. I don't even know how to put it into words, to tell you the truth." As I broach the reasons for his tentativeness, he says, "I'll try to explain the best I can."

To understand we have to go back two more years before the May 2017 fishing trip on the *Newfoundland Mariner*. That's when, on September 22, 2015, a 68-foot fishing vessel, the *Atlantic Charger*, an enterprise Watkins also owned, sank to the bottom of Frobisher Bay off of Baffin Island, Nunavut. All nine crewmembers survived, rescued from their life raft after wearing their immersion suits for nearly twelve hours in formidable weather conditions and after several failed rescued attempts, before a Danish fishing trawler pulled them aboard to safety.

Watkins stayed at home that trip, and followed the harrowing ordeal from a hotel room. As the vessel's owner, he sometimes stayed home to take care of business on shore. In this case, he was lining up the vessel's retrofit. The *Atlantic Charger* was considered state-of-the-art at the time, causing a buzz amongst Newfoundland and Labrador's fishing industry players when it was launched in 2013. That's because the one-of-a-kind

Brad Watkins at Blue Canoe Family RV Park, his latest venture since leaving the fishery, west of Springdale, Newfoundland, 2018.

vessel was one of the largest of its class. Watkins had it built locally at a cost of $2.5 million to service a year-round fishery. It was painted a striking black with red-stripe accents and its bow featured a skull with two crossing curve-bladed pirate daggers, echoing Watkins's family ancestry, so it had a personality all its own, too. But Watkins had more planned for her. He was in the midst of transitioning the vessel, so they could "go at the cod," he says. For upwards of $300,000, Watkins says he would have had a newly installed hook-and-line system, which allowed harvesting groundfish like cod for quality (hooking one fish, one hook at a time on a long line of hooks) versus the old methods, such as gillnets, that target indiscriminately, capturing everything in their path and sometimes damaging the fish. This trip was to have been the last in which the crew would use gillnets in this area. Watkins had struck a deal with Baffin Fisheries, the largest fishery company in Canada's North and fully Inuit-owned, which had Greenland halibut quota in Cumberland Sound (allowing hook-and-line only) and Davis Strait (allowing gillnets). So long as Watkins could commit to Baffin Fisheries that he would have his hook-and-line gear on order from Iceland, where the move to hook-and-line fishing—and, more than that, a focus on catching cod for quality over quanitity—had already contributed to making that country's industry a world leader in cod.

"With fewer fish available to be harvested, we need to focus on obtaining more value per fish," writes Bob Verge, executive director of CCFI in his August 2018 column, "Turning Less Into More" for *The Navigator* magazine, "That is exactly what they have been doing in Iceland for some time now, with remarkable results. By improving raw material quality, developing high-value markets, and making use of by-products that were once considered to be waste, the Icelanders have been steadily increasing the output value they get per fish."

Cod is Iceland's biggest fish export, supplying much of the British demand for fresh and frozen cod (about 16 per cent of the country's cod exports), as well as Spain (12 per cent), western and southern European markets, and other markets worldwide. As a result, Iceland has one of the most profitable fishing industries in the world, hauling in more than $1 billion (converted to CAD) annually. To put the importance of cod in perspective, in 2017, Iceland's catch was valued at $1.17 billion CAD, with cod contributing $518 million CAD. That's even as the country has cut its cod landings. Between the 1950s and '80s, Iceland's annual cod catch varied between approximately 200,000 to 300,000 tonnes (t), with an increase to approximately 450,000 t in the early 1980s and a steady decline back to about 250,000 t in 2016. Over a similar timeframe, cod landings in Newfoundland and Labrador dropped from approximately 250,000 t annually up to the 1970s, to a high of 800,000 t in the 1980s to less than 20,000t in 2016—and that's where cod landings here have hovered for more than two decades. Of Newfoundland and Labrador's $777 million fishery earnings in 2017, cod contributed about $28 million. Most of that cod is exported to the United States (about 44 per cent), followed by the United Kingdom (30 per cent).

Overall then, Iceland has 10 times the cod landings of Newfoundland and Labrador and 18.5 times the earnings for its cod catch. It's not only tonnage contributing to that difference in value (though it certainly is a major factor), it's also, to Bob Verge's point, that Iceland is making the most use of its cod. Iceland focuses on cod fillets over fish sticks, and then uses all of the other parts of the fish—using whatever it can for food (including pet food) and the rest for various skincare, pharmaceutical, and other goods. "The old business model that once helped Newfoundland and Labrador dominate the global fish trade was based on high volumes of frozen, lower-quality cod, sold en masse to the markets in what was called 'cod block,' to put things like fish sticks on kids' plates around the world," reporter Sarah Smellie wrote in a July 4, 2017, CBC article comparing Iceland's and Newfoundland and Labrador's cod fisheries.

While it's difficult to make the most of a commodity with insufficient access and availability, the Icelandic approach offers lessons for Newfoundland on how to do more with less. Comparing earnings and employment, fleets and plants makes this case:

• Earnings and employment: While Iceland's $1.923 billion (2015) fishery employed 4,000 licensed inshore fishers (not including crewmembers) in 2014, reports Smellie in that same article, Newfoundland and Labrador's $862.5 million (2015) fishery employed 3,400 licensed inshore fishers (again, not including crewmembers) that same year (2014).

• Fleets and plants: In 2014 Iceland had about 2,000 small-size (less than 15-metre) vessels, and 52 larger vessels, while Newfoundland and Labrador had more than three times as many, at about 6,614 (the majority which were of the smaller variety, about 6,578, and the remainder, about 39, of the larger type). Iceland's fleet is up slightly from 2001 (1,872 smaller vessels and 60 trawlers); while Newfoundland and Labrador's numbers are decreasing (8,712 vessels total). Meanwhile, both Iceland and NL

(Previous page) Father (Don) Thornhill playing accordion, Pinchgut Lake, Newfoundland, 2018. (Scott Grant, RONiN Photography); (Above) Close-up of one of the author's oil-on-canvas landscape paintings featuring the Thornhill family home (second from left) in Little Bay East, Newfoundland.

The author jigs her first cod of the season with the Fishing for Success organization, using baited handline, off the coast of Petty Harbour, Newfoundland, 2019.

Eugene "Gene" Maloney in one of his wood sheds, Bay Bulls, Newfoundland, 2018.

Captain Wayne Maloney opts to stay ashore due to weather, Ball Bulls, Newfoundland, 2018.

April MacDonald snaps a photo from an abandoned property somewhere on the way toward Lark Harbour and past Frenchman's Cove, Newfoundland, 2018.

A child's dress and diary from an abandoned outport property, Newfoundland, 2018.

View to the Bay of Islands from the front steps of an abandoned outport property, Newfoundland, 2018.

The heritage structure locally known as Uncle Bill Pynn's House, Quirpon, Newfoundland, 2018.

View from the second level of the Roberts family fishing premises, Quirpon, Newfoundland, 2018.

Discarded codfish head at St. Anthony Seafoods, St. Anthony, Newfoundland, 2018.

View of Nobles Island and Lancy Bell Bay from Quirpon, Newfoundland, 2018.

The author, her husband, Raman Verma, and daughter, Navya Verma, ready to set out for Raman and Navya's first codfishing trip, Petty Harbour, Newfoundland, 2019.

Navya's first iceberg (though she slept through it), off Quirpon Island, Quirpon, Newfoundland, 2018.

One of the accommodations at Quirpon Lighthouse Inn, Quirpon Island, Newfoundland, 2018.

closed half their processing plants. In Iceland there were fewer than 200 plants as of 2016, a decrease of 50 per cent since the early 1990s. Over the same time period, Newfoundland and Labrador has seen a decrease from 250 to 92 plants.

Overall, there have been similar fishing industry trends in Iceland and Newfoundland and Labrador, but has this province done enough to realize the value of its fish exports—in this case, cod? In the July 2017 CBC News story, Brad Watkins put it this way: "the new cod fishery will have to be driven by the market—a tough move in a province where fisheries policy has often been calculated by political considerations, like trying to maintain as many jobs in as many places as possible."

Cutting jobs is always easier said than done—and the cuts in Newfoundland and Labrador's fishery already run deep. The moratorium hit employment in the fishery hard: dropping from over 24,500 people in the fishing industry overall to 5,400 from 1987 to 2017. Since the moratorium, there have been repeated calls for more cuts. In 2010–11, the province rejected an independent report calling for a more than 50 percent reduction in the number of inshore fishing enterprises (it called for cuts to more than 70 percent of the businesses on the west coast, northeast coast, and Labrador alone) and the closure of 30 per cent of its crab and shrimp plants.

Another factor to consider in securing higher-value catch is the favouring of fishing methods that preserve the quality of the fish. Generally, hooks and lines tend to harvest higher quality cod than trawls and seines, which in turn harvest higher quality than gillnets. In Newfoundland and Labrador, the gear of choice for cod fishing remains gillnets. There is some movement toward more sustainable methods such as hooks and lines or cod traps. Here, the Atlantic Fisheries Fund, a Canadian federal and provincial financial contribution program, supports fishers in adopting sustainable technologies and gear types like autoline—the same kind of gear Watkins had on order from Iceland.

Back in September 2015, Watkins was thankful to have one gillnet quota in Baffin Bay, since trips like this one were critical to pay down his investment and line up capital for more of the same. With so much at stake, Watkins stayed in daily contact with his captain, Byron Oxford, an experienced skipper in his mid-forties, via satellite phone and email. Watkins felt the tight line of communication was the next best thing to skippering the vessel himself. "I had a really good captain," says Watkins.

"He always kept in touch with me and he didn't make no rash decisions on his own. He'd always call me first."

Before the incident that would risk the lives of all involved, the *Atlantic Charger* was precisely where it should have been, fishing off of Greenland and Baffin Island in the Davis Strait. There were no neighbouring vessels and that was the point—the *Atlantic Charger* could sail where few vessels could because of her size and capabilities. That's why Watkins was able to strike a deal with Baffin Fisheries to catch some of their 200-tonne (t) quota of turbot, also called Greenland halibut. On September 21, 2015, the crew had over 60t of turbot in the vessel's hold and was en route to deliver it to Pangnirtung on Baffin Island, Nunavut.

Although it was September, the sea ice in Hudson Bay was packed and the *Atlantic Charger* was no match for it. Declaring a stalemate with the ice at the mouth of the bay, Captain Oxford called Watkins in the wee hours that morning to consult him on the vessel's next move. Watkins then contacted the Canadian Coast Guard in Nunavut to request the vessel be accompanied by icebreaker into Pangnirtung so the crew could deliver their catch as planned. Although the Coast Guard is commonly tasked with aiding in navigation and icebreaking, they declined to assist, saying the seaway wasn't navigable due to the ice conditions. In consultation with Watkins, Captain Oxford made plans to move the vessel due south—the only direction the vessel could travel at that point—toward Resolution Island and, ultimately, back to Newfoundland.

But there was a storm brewing in that direction, in the Labrador Sea, south of the vessel's location. Captain Oxford reasoned he would find safe harbour close to Resolution Island, where the weather was calling to be fine. Should the storm head north, he would already be in the shelter of land. It was a precautionary move. "We were watching the forecast, Watkins recalls. "There wasn't supposed to be any wind where they were to. It was supposed to have been 15 to 20 knots [28–37 kph] of southwest wind." But Captain Oxford reported to Watkins the winds were picking up and there was snowfall, too. *We're getting the crew to tie some stuff on, batten down.* That's what Watkins remembers Captain Oxford telling him in that last conversation before the ordeal that next morning. *Just keep in touch with me and keep heading toward the Labrador coast. You got to run out of that wind,* Watkins recalls replying, thinking if the *Atlantic Charger* did encounter the storm, it would only be in passing. Neither he nor Captain Oxford imagined the weather would turn from dicey to deadly within the next few hours.

Around 8 o'clock that morning, about an hour after Watkins last chatted with the captain, the crewmember on watch notified Captain Oxford of an alarm sounding in the wheelhouse. On these high-tech vessels, alarms sound for different sections of the boat. This alarm indicated water in the storage compartment, accessible through a hatch, in the stern of the vessel. The alert activated an automatic pump to pump out the water, which consequently shut off the alarm. But within fifteen to twenty minutes, the same alarm sounded again. Visual inspection confirmed there was no water in that area. Seemingly under control, Captain Oxford turned his attention to the weather conditions.

Gale-force winds had picked up and ocean spray limited visibility, churning out waves that toppled, tumbled, and rolled all over the *Atlantic Charger*. Even for this most capable vessel, a goliath built for year-round navigation and weather, it would only take a couple of rogue waves to inflict irreparable damage. The vessel survived the first wave that washed over her, but with the second brutal wave, the railing at the stern remained submerged by a few feet and wasn't recovering. As the boat was listing, the crew gathered in the wheelhouse, some still wearing their pyjamas, having awoken to their crewmates' calls. It was agreed they would put on their immersion suits. In a last-ditch effort, the crew started offloading items like fishing nets, as well as stored items like bait and groceries, hoping to reduce the vessel's weight and try to help her recover. Captain Oxford, meanwhile, issued a mayday and contacted Coast Guard and Search and Rescue. With the vessel still listing, the captain made the tough decision to move his crew to a life raft. Once the raft was launched, the men jumped into the ocean, swimming to the raft one by one, with Captain Oxford going last. It was now midday on September 22 and the weather was not backing down.

Meanwhile, Watkins, who was on the road at the time, received a call from Coast Guard he was not anticipating. As the registered owner of the boat, the Coast Guard apprised Watkins of the situation: they were no longer able to communicate with the *Atlantic Charger*, so they were contacting neighbouring vessels and lining up aircraft surveillance to monitor the situation as best they could. Preoccupied with the safety of his crew and vessel, Watkins drove the 50 kilometres to the nearest hotel, Sinbad's in Gander, where he could sit with the phone and manage as best he could from shore. Watkins called his parents in Cottlesville and asked them to meet him at the hotel. He was preparing for the worst and knew he'd need their support.

Meanwhile, miles out to sea in Frobisher Bay, the nine crewmen battled snow squalls, high winds, and rough seas from their life raft. They could see the *Atlantic Charger* still partially submerged in the sub-zero waters in the distance. Eventually, they lost sight of her. Then they waited, thinking a helicopter was likely on its way (it wasn't), and waved and shot a flare to the fixed-wing aircraft that spotted them at 5 P.M. that day.

After pacing for a couple of hours in his hotel room, Watkins finally received news the men were alive. It gave him hope. He knew the men weren't yet out of danger, but at least he had enough information to alert the families. "I had to tell them the boat has gone down, but the crew are safe in the life raft. Coast Guard is working to try to get them out.... Of course, anything can happen on the water. So, it was very bad news to give the families, but at least there was a positive sign to it." Watkins made and answered calls to and from Coast Guard, family members, and the media for hours after getting the initial word out to families. He never left the hotel room, his parents by his side offering emotional support, especially in between those difficult phone conversations. Meanwhile, the crew continued to slosh around Frobisher Bay in a life raft that was taking on water, requiring the men to continuously bail. To say they were exhausted would be an understatement, but they held onto a shred of hope—they had made it this far.

As Watkins recounts this man-versus-nature story in excruciating detail, my left hand (the one not madly scribbling notes) grips the picnic table bench. The risk of someone dying on this job is extremely high and the evidence shows it. In a data project with Statistics Canada, the Association of Workers' Compensation Boards of Canada, and the Institute for Work & Health, the *Globe and Mail* reported fishing as the deadliest job in Canada between 2011 and 2015. Other sources have cited fishing as the third leading cause of employment-related death in the country (between 1996 and 2005)—with fishing responsible for 1 death for every 2,800 fishers, after deaths in mining (1 in 2,000) and forestry (1 in 2,300). Between 2004 and 2018, the average number of fishing-related fatalities reported in Canada annually is about 9. This past year, 2018, was particularly deadly, with the Transportation Safety Board reporting 17 deaths in fisheries-related incidents in Canada; employee fatigue was listed as a major factor. Unquestionably, fishers face the unexpected elements of nature on open waters, far away from any medical aid, gambling their lives with the hopes of a hefty catch and payday. In a 2012 Transportation Safety Board of Canada report, the highest cause of death in the fishing industry was reportedly drowning, followed by falling overboard.

At this point in Watkin's retelling, the crew of the *Atlantic Charger* was still at risk of those fates. Between 7 and 8 P.M., the night shrouded in darkness, the Canadian icebreaking freighter MV *Arctic* made several failed attempts to rescue the crew. First, they threw the men a rope ladder; then, they extended their gangway (a raised platform), but with the waves causing the life raft to seesaw between 40 feet below the freighter to up beside her rails, these attempts were extremely dangerous. In the end, the *Arctic* threw the men a new lift raft. That alone was a godsend, as it gave the men a dry raft, food, and, most importantly, a radio, which meant Captain Oxford could communicate with the rescuers.

The Danish trawler *Paaimut* arrived about an hour later. The crew shot another flare, giving the *Paaimut* a location in the night sky. It was enough for the Zodiac the *Paaimut* deployed to locate the raft. Two at a time, and three for the last group of crewmen, they were hoisted aboard the trawler to safety. By midnight, the crew were calling their families themselves. They were shaken up by the experience, but at least they were safe. Still, it would take them another four days to return home.

Watkins still laments the rescue attempts that day, pinning the ultimate blame on the decision of Coast Guard: "If the Coast Guard had taken us into Pangnirtung, the boat would still be afloat today," he says.

The details of that shipwreck spelled big news in local, national, and international media. It was also profiled at length in a four-part series by Jim Wellman in *The Navigator* in 2016 and in 2018 became one of the subjects of Wellman's book *Challengers of the Sea*.

"Is there anything you would add to those accounts?" I ask Watkins, appreciating the depth Wellman went into to capture the ordeal.

"I haven't read it," Watkins says, sounding exasperated. "I started to read it and I put it down. I just, I don't know. Maybe I'll read it one of these days. I still find it a bit hard to go back now and listen to the captain, what he went through and it's just—yeah. I haven't read it."

"So, it kind of hits you?" I ask, cautiously probing. The conversation is taking a toll on Watkins. He's taking deep breaths between his responses now.

"Yep, because it was my full life's dream. It was everything I worked for. I clawed my way up and it wasn't easy. I took a lot of big risks in business to get there. Then, as soon as I got it working right and doing what I needed it to do, what I wanted it to do, it got taken away. So, when I read about it, I re-live that day of getting the phone call that the boat was sunk and they didn't know if the crew was gone down with the boat. I re-live that and find it very difficult."

The nightmare of that event haunted Watkins for nearly a year afterwards. He was still making payments and paying interest on a vessel submerged some 400 feet underwater, as he worked with his insurance company to recoup his sunken costs and had no new money coming in. The bank wouldn't give Watkins another loan, given he hadn't yet made good on the massive loan he already had in his name for his enterprise. "My business was stopped in its tracks," Watkins says. "I didn't have a boat to run. I couldn't fish." In fact, it would be the first year in thirty years, since he had taken up fishing as a boy, that Watkins didn't go fishing at all. "I've fished all my life," he tells me. "Ever since Dad would let me crawl aboard the boat." Watkins laughs, offering a reprieve from the tension. "I started with cod traps when I was probably eight, nine, ten years old, fishing with my dad in the summertime.... I was thirteen the first year I went and fished all summer down Makkovik on the Labrador Coast. And [I fished] every year after that."

Between 2015 and 2016, while he wasn't fishing, Watkins lost all of his business contacts, which made acquiring the *Newfoundland Mariner* all the more difficult. "I'm going to say damn-near impossible, but I did [it]," he says. In the years leading up to acquiring the *Atlantic Charger*, Watkins made a lot of road trips, spent a lot of nights in hotels, and even visited other countries—Denmark, Iceland, Norway—to put together his plans for a state-of-the-art offshore fishing enterprise back home in Newfoundland. He believed then, and still believes now, that this province and Canada can once again lead the market in groundfish like cod. Sure, you can buy cod from Costco in St. John's—frozen cod fillets from Russia ($8.48 a pound) and Norway ($10.02 a pound) or fresh cod fillets from Iceland ($10.43 a pound). Alternatively, you can buy local— either from a local restaurant selling a meal of local cod; or for about $3.50-4.00 a pound directly from your neighbourhood commercial fish harvester. Watkins envisions a day when Newfoundlanders will buy fresh seafood, including cod, that way again.

When Watkins was scoping his latest enterprise, the newest fisheries research touted cautious optimism about cod's recovery—buoyed by the 2015 Rose and Rowe October article. The sub-headline to a CBC News story that fall read: "Scientist says too early to resume fishery, but says planning should get underway." The paper reported northern cod had rebounded to stock levels not seen in two decades. Their findings showed the "comeback" had started in 2006–2007, fifteen years after the cod collapse, when cod saw a steep decline (from 1990–1994). Rose and Rowe, as you'll recall, noted that not only was there greater abundance of cod, but the size of the cod had increased as well, boding well for the overall condition of the stock. This gave Watkins more reason than ever to get back out on the water and lead a comeback of his own. But how was it, with cod still under moratorium since 1992, that fishers like Watkins could fish for cod while DFO cited the species' stock as still being in the critical zone?

That's because DFO operates a "stewardship" cod fishery, as the commercial cod fishery is now called, a limited seasonal fishery with gear restrictions on the amount and type of gear used and close monitoring of landings to ensure compliance but also to help monitor the recovery of the cod stocks. The Total Allowable Catch, or TAC, remains low, having built up to about 20,000 tonnes for cod annually. But as the history goes, there was no commercial inshore cod fishery between 1993 and 1997. Any cod landings during that period came exclusively from bycatch, the recreational (food) fishery, and surveys (carried out by DFO, starting in 1995). Landings from 1998 to 2002 came from a limited commercial inshore fishery restricted to fixed gear (traps/pots, gillnets and longline/setline equipment) and small vessels (shorter than 65 feet). The commercial and recreational fisheries were subsequently closed in April 2003 in response to what was called a "mortality event" for the cod stock in Smith Sound, Trinity Bay. In 2004–2005, DFO reported substantial bycatch of cod (over 600 tonnes) taken in the inshore fishery. By 2006, DFO reopened the inshore cod commercial and recreational fisheries, and those fisheries continue (from 2007) to present day.

In the commercial fishery, licensed fishers are allocated a fixed annual catch allowance. The previous multi-year management plan (2013–15) for the stewardship fishery was an individual quota (IQ) based plan, whereby each fisher was permitted an annual allowance of 2.3 tonnes (or 5,000 pounds). DFO changed the management approach in 2016 from an IQ to weekly landing limits per fisher (2,000 pounds from August 15 to September 4, then 3,000 pounds from September 4 to December 16), and removed the requirement that fish could be caught only within the fisher's home bay. The recreational fishery was also extended in 2016, with fishers allowed to fish on weekends, including the Canada Day and Labour Day holidays, in addition to the two-week season in summer and fall. This was an increase of 14 days from 2015 to 2016 (124 days total). Recreational fishers were permitted a maximum catch of five fish per day per person, or fifteen fish per boat per trip when three or more people were fishing together.

Of the cod harvested in Newfoundland and Labrador, the majority comes from the stewardship/commercial fishery, with the recreational fishery and other causes contributing minority shares. Estimates from DFO presented to a House of Commons Standing Committee on Fisheries and Oceans focused on a portion of the inshore fishery from 2016. Of the harvest levels at the time, which totalled 13,500 tonnes, the commercial fishery took home 10,525 tonnes (comprising about 80 per cent) followed by the recreational fishery (2000 t; 15 per cent share) followed by everything else—cod quality and science projects (750 t; 5.5 per cent); bycatch (175 t; 1.2 per cent); and by Indigenous communities for food, social, and ceremonial purposes (50 t; 0.3 per cent). The share of reported landings in 2017 were similar: 12,707 t from the stewardship fishery, 173 t in the sentinel surveys, 102 t taken as bycatch for Canadian and non-Canadian fleets, but excluded recreational removals. In terms of cod landings outside the 200 nautical mile limit by non-Canadian fleet, the Scientific Council of NAFO reported these were 300 t or less over the period from 2000 to 2017 (41 t in 2017).

While the commercial fishery represents the highest share of cod catches, those landings remain significantly lower than those of pre-moratorium days. The prices for cod are also lower in comparison. In Newfoundland and Labrador, a Standing Fish Price Setting Panel sets cod and other seafood prices as per legislation under the 2006 Fishing Industry Collective Bargaining Act. The Fish Panel, as it's often referred to, came into existence in 2006 to facilitate collective bargaining on fish sales. For the last two seasons (2017–18 and 2018–19), the range in pricing has been as low as $0.20 a pound (Grade C) to $0.38-0.40 a pound (Grade B) to as high as $0.70–0.83 a pound (Grade A). (Fall yields better market value given the better condition of cod, so the higher pricing range reflects that time of year, as well as cod with tongues and cheeks intact.) The grading scheme is based on what's colloquially called the *cod quality program*, a quality-grading program that came into effect in Newfoundland and Labrador in 2000 to as a joint industry/government effort "to improve the quality of [the province's] commercial fisheries, such as cod, and to further promote the province as a world leader in the production of top quality seafood products."

"Northern cod is the best-tasting cod, but fishermen are getting 63 cents a pound," says Ryan Cleary, president of FISH-NL. "A lot of fishermen, they don't want to say this, but the average price was $0.63 a pound. In '92, they were getting a $1.20 a pound. Our total cod catch last year [2017] was 20,000 tonnes. But a lot of fishermen will tell you—they won't say this on the record; they won't say it to the media—but they'd rather fucking spit on a codfish than catch it."

Cod scientist Dr. Sherrylynn Rowe, of the aforementioned Rose and Rowe report, similarly wonders why anyone would go the trouble to fish cod for those prices. "For Grade A cod in this province, fishermen are only getting 83 cents a pound," she says. "When you look at what this resource is worth, I'm almost astonished that we're taking it out of the water for that price. I think it's more valuable. I think the fishermen deserve to make more than they're making, but a lot of changes need to occur for that to happen, and, personally, I think that would be a much more productive thing to pursue than just focusing on taking more fish at this particular point in time."

To garner the higher-value market price requires a higher-quality product. And it's one Fogo Island Fish, a program supported by Shorefast, is showing is possible. Anthony (Tony) Cobb is the co-founder of Fogo Island Inn (along with his sister, CEO and founder, Zita Cobb; and brother, cofounder Allan Cobb) and president of Fogo Island Fish. Through Fogo Island Fish, Cobb and the co-op of fishers he works with are leading a "water to table" (specifically a water to restaurant table) movement. Their focus is sustainably caught cod—predominantly handline-caught or using cod pots—that is harvested, processed, and shipped directly from Fogo Island to restaurants, most of which are in Ontario. "The cornerstone of what Fogo Island Fish does is we pay more than double the market rates for fish, directly to the harvester," says Cobb. "Every pound of fish is processed in our community so as to maintain those local jobs, which are so important to our local economy." Cobb worked with Fogo Island inshore fishers to develop the business model for Fogo Island Fish. Together, they knew there was an opportunity to yield greater value from the market and needed to figure out how to do it. According to Cobb, that's precisely what the people of Fogo Island do best: they work together and figure it out.

In what's become known locally as the "Fogo Process," island residents let a National Film Board (NFB) documentary crew follow them in 1967 when faced with the difficult decision of government-sponsored resettlement. It was during that time fishers formed the Fogo Island Co-operative Society Limited, a community-based enterprise. The NFB covered the island's transformative journey, which, in turn, helped convince government not to relocate the people of Fogo Island. Now, after more than fifty years in business, the Co-op and island, along with Fogo Island Fish, continues that economic evolution.

As Cobb explains: "A pound of cod in a local grocery store or anywhere in the country, including St. John's, it's $12, $13, or $14 on any given day of the week, and fishers were getting paid on average $0.60–64 per pound at the wharf.... Suffice to say, someone in the supply chain is doing quite well. It's just not our community." Their model flies in the face of the dominant wild-fisheries model, which operates on the premise that more is better. Cobb shares an example of factory freezer trawlers, which can catch 1 million pounds a day or 15 million in two weeks. By comparison, it would take Fogo Island Fishers a year to secure 1 million pounds, and fifteen years to catch 15 million.

"Possibly the greatest challenge will be to change the mindset—our assumptions about the industry and how it operates," writes Bob Verge, president of CCFI in an op-ed for *The Navigator*. "In effect, the industry has been organized and operated based on an assumption of abundance. During an earlier era, we had abundant fish resources and many people were able to share in the abundance. We were more concerned with catching more fish than we were with increasing the value we got from each fish. Our resources are no longer abundant. Yet our industry continues to be organized and operated based on the thinking of that bygone era." Not only are landings down, but the workforce is shrinking too, both because workers are aging out of the industry and recruitment is becoming more and more difficult. There are fewer active fishing vessels, writes Verge, so finding crewmembers is particularly challenging. That's a point Tony Cobb relates to: in 2008, he says, Fogo Island had 247 fishers. But by 2017, that number had shrunk to just 87.

"We now have to start planning for a period of scarcity," Verge writes. "Our resources will be scarcer than they were and we will have to make do with less. It will require adjustments."

This is precisely the idea Brad Watkins, who serves on the board of Verge's organization, CCFI, had in mind. With lower catches, he knew the only way forward would entail capturing the highest market value of the catch. And with fewer people to rely on for his crew, he wanted to increase output value per person. To get things re-started and back on track, Watkins reached out to fishing companies like Quinlan Brothers Ltd., a third-generation family business based out of St. John's, that still believed in his vision and had quota they needed to fulfill. And in turn these companies knew if Watkins could follow through on his earlier plans with another vessel, then they would both benefit. If Watkins could retrofit a new vessel with autoline or hook-and-line gear the way he had planned to do with the *Atlantic Charger*, it would be the only vessel of its kind in the province that could spend the lengthy periods of time up North, bringing back fresh catch. A few years ago, Watkins had already demonstrated his bold plans could work. While other enterprises were selling frozen turbot to Greenland, Watkins was pioneering a market for fresh turbot back at home in Newfoundland. *It can't be done*, Robin Quinlan, vice president of Quinlan Brothers Ltd., said to Watkins at the time. But in his life and career, when people told Watkins something couldn't be done, he became all the more determined. Years ago, Watkins had harvested fresh Greenland halibut. Today there are about a half-dozen boats following his lead. It's that perseverance that convinced Quinlan to go out on a limb for Watkins the next time around.

In May 2017 Watkins was back at it again, this time skippering his newly acquired vessel, the *Newfoundland Mariner*, having regained some of his business partnerships. The crew was heading out for its inaugural trip of the 2017 snow crab season. Because of the decrease in snow crab biomass, DFO had recently cut the overall catch quota for the upcoming season by 22 per cent. It was shellfish like shrimp and crab that pulled those who chose to stay in the fishery post-moratorium out of dire straits and into prosperity. As cod stocks flatlined commercially, shellfish became the heart of a recovering fishery. Watkins's father was one of those fishers: ready for that move from groundfish to shellfish, having already started to diversify his harvesting efforts before the cod moratorium hit.

At a time when the cod fishery collapse forced tens of thousands of Newfoundlanders and Labradorians out of the industry for good, Brad Watkins was just getting started. (Tackling a mess that others wanted out of only adds to his Mr. Clean persona, I think.) In 1992, when he was eighteen and freshly graduated from high school, he remembers people laughed at him because he had written, "fisherman with a 65-footer" as his career aspiration in his yearbook profile. Common wisdom would say the industry was already dead in the water. This is further evidenced by "The fishery went away." a 2014 paper by Nicole Power and colleagues published in *Ecology and Society*: "Most young people have grown up in a context of fisheries and processing plant closures, rural depopulation and outmigration." "Nobody was supposed to be saying they wanted to be a fisherman," Watkins recalls. "You had to say you wanted to go be a game warden, or a doctor, or teacher, or something." But he wanted to take risks, just like his father and grandfather had, as a fisher who owned his own enterprise. After the cod moratorium, Watkins reaped the rewards of that first big risk.

In the last few decades, there have been fewer jobs in the fishery. The reasons vary, from plant closures to fewer fishing enterprises to increased costs for enterprise-ownership to more stringent measures in the profession that restrict fish harvester membership (particularly, lengthy education and mentorship requirements). Harvesting and processing have experienced reductions of 35.2 and 50.8 per cent, respectively, between 1989 and 2010. And yet, in some communities, the fishing boats remain the economic hub of the outports—granted one that's under threat of extinction, as the workforce ages and new recruits are disinclined to pick up from where their predecessors left off.

The dangers of the job are another disincentive—and one the industry has never fully accommodated, says Power. At the time of the cod moratorium, the move to a different fishery—the deep-sea fishery for shellfish—imposed greater risks for fishers. "For the first time, we have licenses being given to fish harvesters who've never fished crab and they had to transform their boats and take on new technologies," Power adds, "so we did see a spike in increase in accidents and injuries and deaths in that time period."

Power was part of a research team looking into some of these issues at the time. What she saw, and continues to see today, is a lot of blame directed toward fish harvesters for taking unnecessary risks on the job. But harvesters don't pick their season dates and they face a number of requirements—for example, on the size and length of their vessel. It's true that more fishers ought to take the precautionary measure of wearing a lifejacket, but the key point, according to Power, is when there are changes in the fishery and fisheries regulations, there ought to be greater supports extended to fishers to prepare and implement the new protocols.

None of this was on Watkins mind when, at the ripe age of eighteen, he set out as a fisher. He had income on the brain. "When the moratorium come, that's when, I want to call it, the riches came to Newfoundland from the fishery," Watkins says. "The fishery was a very poor industry when the codfish went, [but then] the shellfish flourished and boomed." Now, twenty-five years on, total landings for shellfish—including, until recently, lobster—are declining. In fact, total landings across all species is down. And yet, the value of those landings is up. Take snow crab, for example: while landings were expected to decrease even further in 2018 with the new 2017 quota reductions, prices were up, and significantly so—from an average price of $2.98 per pound in 2016 to $4.39 per pound in 2017.

As Captain Watkins and his crew set out in May 2017 in the 60-foot, 211 gross-tonne *Newfoundland Mariner*, with its storage capacity of 50,000 pounds, they had high hopes for a lucrative run. And it needed to be. This was the vessel's maiden voyage following a major retrofit. Although she had a fresh slick of paint, resurfaced deck, and new pumps, the steel vessel's most important renovations were its newly installed hook-and-line system, its live aquatic Refrigerated Seawater System (RSW), and slurry ice machine for fresh or frozen storage. These substantive additions meant the crew could stay at sea as long as necessary to fill their stores, and bring home catch that looks and tastes as fresh as the day it was caught.

Given the time taken for the refitting, the *Newfoundland Mariner* was late getting started for the season. Undeterred by this, her crew planned on taking their time on account of the ice floes. They would set out from Triton, fish offshore for as long as it took, then sail back through The Narrows into St. John's Harbour.

For eight days offshore, the crew dealt with pack ice and messy sleet snow, says Watkins. Setting and hauling in crab traps is difficult work at the best of times, but it's especially back-breaking work in this kind of weather. It was lonely, too. There were no other vessels in their area. These fishing grounds may as well have been private. By May 16, the *Newfoundland Mariner* had 44,000 pounds of live snow crab in its tanks. With another 6,000 pounds, they would meet their vessel's capacity and head home. Exhausted and with the end in sight, Captain Watkins made the call to pack things in for the night. With south winds at 25 knots [46 kph], conditions were fine. They'd take a much-needed rest for three or four hours, then get back to their harvest in the morning.

"We laid down for a nap and next thing I knew, there was alarms going off," Watkins says. At around 12:30 A.M. on May 17, Captain Watkins and some of the crew awoke to alarms indicating a problem on deck. "As soon as I hit the deck, I knew that we were flooding from the inside," Watkins remembers. "There's no way water will get in from the outside. It had to be from the inside, so I knew it was the RSW hatches."

We're taking on water. That's the wake-up call those who were still sleeping likely heard from those on deck. *We've got to get out to save the boat,* was another call to action. So, with their lounge pants and pyjamas on, that's what they did. There wasn't even time to put on shoes or boots. Watkins was already on deck with "naked feet," he says, but he hadn't yet noticed. He was too revved up with adrenaline from the developing situation.

It was Watkins who quickly reasoned it must have been a faulty seal on one of the hatches that was letting the water run out of the RSW tanks, which were filled with water to keep the crab fresh. What ought to have happened next is that the automated pumps would start to pump out the water on the deck. But the deck was flooded, and the pumps weren't working. Watkins saw the problem: the pumps were partially plugged with bait that had spilled out of its container on the deck. By now, the boat was listing, and to Watkins's horror, the water running off from the RSW tanks was pouring into the main fish hold and into the engine room. Quick thinking led Watkins to turn off the RSW pump to stop the flow of water on the deck. Meanwhile, the crew started working on the pumps, trying to get them running. Since the main pumps were not working, they tried the emergency pump, but it, too, didn't work. They tried the gas fire pump; it didn't work either. "This was all brand new pumps, all brand new gear," says Watkins. "It was just like Murphy's Law. Every pump we grabbed on to, something happened to it."

Watkins then moved to the engine room, using a bucket to bail out the water. This room was his priority: he knew if it became too wet, then the vessel could lose its generators and power. The crew, meanwhile, continued bailing water off the deck, also using buckets. How was it possible that with all of this new, tested, top-of-the-line equipment, their bailout of the situation depended on buckets? Things had turned decidedly desperate.

Watkins knew he had to get the water off the deck. If the boat took on too much water on her surface, even a slight wind could cause her to easily roll, become over-weighted on one side, and start to sink. Watkins remembered that's precisely what had happened to the *Melina and Keith II*—a longliner that capsized in September 2016 off the northeast coast of Newfoundland. As the crew of the *Melina and Keith II* hauled in their turbot nets, waves washed over the deck. The water pumps that were supposed to pump any excess water off the deck were unable to keep up with the incoming flow. The vessel, loaded with fish, further weighed the vessel down. With water on its deck, one rogue wave caused the boat to roll. The boat stayed out and eventually rolled over completely, never recovering. In that case, only the captain had his immersion suit on. The eight crewmembers weren't even wearing lifejackets. Four men drowned, while the other four were rescued by another fishing vessel, deployed at the request of Canadian Coast Guard. "That story came in my mind right away," Watkins says. "I knew with a dry-deck boat, the only way to get the water off the deck was with pumps. And unfortunately, every pump that we had failed."

Watkins still can't believe his misfortune that day. Every piece of new equipment had been tested and retested before the trip. The crew had even run safety drills that spring before leaving the wharf. But Watkins tells me you can't be prepared for every situation. When something happens, you need to rely on your common sense, your knowledge, and your experience at sea to take over. In this case, he remembers thinking: *You're taking on water. You've got to stop it. Now, you got to get the water out before she gets too big of a list and is not recoverable.*

Perhaps the biggest safety measure Watkins didn't take, but which the situation certainly called for, was issuing a mayday. "We just jumped into survival mode to get the water out of her so she wouldn't capsize," he tells me. "I didn't contact anyone. That's something I realized I didn't do after the fact but adrenaline kicked in and I just fought to save the boat and crew. If I had tried to contact Coast Guard maybe I would have lost the boat due to the fact I wasn't there to get all the pumps going and directing the crew. I don't really know. Protocol was to send mayday, but I didn't. But we saved the boat and crew."

Someway, somehow, efforts to bail out the water and regain control of the situation on the *Newfoundland Mariner* worked that day. Watkins managed to get the engine room fairly dry and the crew got the boat to a safe enough place where they could abort their hand-bailing to pick apart the pumps and figure out how to get them back up and running. Even then, their harrowing journey wasn't over. The vessel would later lose its power steering, forcing crewmembers to cobble back to port in St. John's on manual steering. Their health was compromised, too, having tackled the situation without wearing proper clothing. "I can remember after we got her safe, that we knew we weren't going to roll over, I went to walk in and I guess the adrenaline come off and I couldn't walk the steps," Watkins says. "My feet were frozen and numb, and we had a couple of crew that had the same situation. So, the rest of that night we just stayed where we were to, and the crew went to bunk and I stayed up and it was kind of an eye-opener again, just after this first trip, [like] after we lost the *Atlantic Charger*."

In the midst of all this Brad Watkins, whom the media had dubbed the future of Newfoundland's cod fishery, decided he needed to step back from the industry. "I realized then that night that I was done," Watkins says. "All the stress of losing the *Atlantic Charger* was clouding my judgment at sea. The feeling of it was like, 'Why is this happening to me?'" Watkins would finish out the 2017 season skippering, but he knew then he needed a break from fishing and would sell out his enterprise by the end of the season. And yet, sitting at the picnic table, excavators digging out Watkins's next big enterprise, he's not ready to let go of the fisherman title. Looking at him, I am reminded again of how much he looks like Mr. Clean. Could you imagine Mr. Clean giving up on a stubborn stain? Don't think so.

That's the thought running through my head as I drive back to Corner Brook. But there's more stacked against fishers like Brad Watkins than the near misses we've discussed today. Working in the fishery requires extensive education, capital investment, certification, and licensure. Without family know-how and assets, starting one's own enterprise can be near impossible. Fishers also must contend with ongoing threats beyond their control such as the fluctuations of available fish, weather changes (in a brand-new world given the ongoing effects of climate change), vessel and gear upgrades, and recruitment and training of crewmembers. On par with the dangers out in the ocean are the politics on land, too.

Federally, Fisheries and Oceans Canada holds responsibility for controlling (or, in the words of the Terms of Union, "protecting" and "encouraging") the fisheries across the country. A 2003 Royal Commission on the management of Newfoundland and Labrador's fishery reported the federal government held, arguably, too great an authority. In the words of the report's authors, David Vardy and Eric Dunne, the federally dominated management system was a product of a sequence of historical decisions:

> [T]he Canadian fisheries system has developed from one that did not focus much on management of fishing activities in the first 105 years of Confederation, except for some coastal fisheries and freshwater species. The post-World War II years to the early 1970s were a period of modernization, development and expansion. In

the early 1970s, attention turned more to conservation and direct management of fishing activities. From a relatively laissez-faire system has developed a complex of management arrangements that now focus on stock conservation and the social/economic state of those engaged in the harvesting sector. The latter is reflected in the many measures and special policies that now exist to control or reduce fishing capacity and protect the resource. The system for management of the fishery is anachronistic in many ways, particularly the enormous discretionary power that is vested in the minister, with respect to the establishment of quotas, fishery allocations and licences.

Partly in response to the perception the federal fisheries minister was ignoring scientific advice in management of groundfish, an arms-length body called the Fisheries Resource Conservation Council (FRCC), comprising industry and institutional experts, was struck in 1993. The FRCC's role, while it existed (DFO would cut its funding in October 2011), was to provide public advice to the federal fisheries minister on groundfish management, for example, regarding Total Allowable Catch levels. In their Royal Commission, Vardy and Dunne (2003) called for a further devolution of power that would see Newfoundland and Labrador take on more joint decision-making with the federal government to manage the fishery resources adjacent to the province.

"The FRCC was a response to the failure of DFO to listen to fishing people," says Dean Bavington, a cod fisheries management researcher. "This was a way in which fishing people could give their perspective on the stock assessment. But [decisions were] still based on the scientific stock assessment." In other words, Bavington says, the FRCC brought fishers to the table, but government still didn't listen to them. He says he heard fishers saying, "We have to think about *how* we're fishing, not just *how many* fish we're taking." Fishers, as far as Bavington could tell, wanted to inform fisheries management decisions in the interest of the fish, but fishers' knowledge and experience ranked below that of researchers' expertise, which, in turn, ranked below what was best for private industry and public sector/government, who were motivated by the market. "I was trying also to uncover the politics that when you frame something as a scientific or a management issue, then you erase all these politics," Bavington says. "Fisheries science, right from the beginning, is applied to helping out investors, basically. [The science supported] merchants and corporations, as opposed to trying to respect the knowledge of the fishers."

In today's fishery, fishers are dependent on a variety of associations to amplify their experience and concerns. Brad Watkins is a member of the Fisheries Advisory Council in Newfoundland and Labrador. The council, which is funded by the Newfoundland and Labrador government, has broad representation from fishers, processors, aquaculture representatives, and researchers alongside federal government and the general public. It provides input and guidance for growing the fishery—for example, fisher succession planning and recruitment. Fishers may voice their issues through their union representation, which is in the midst of its own provincial sea change. In January 2019, the Supreme Court of Canada ruled in favour of recognizing the newly formed Federation of Independent Sea Harvesters of Newfoundland and Labrador (FISH-NL). Fishers in the province now have the choice of union representation through the Fish, Food and Allied Workers Union (FFAW-Unifor) or FISH-NL. Amidst the legal battles in FISH-NL's pursuit to gain status as a union, the two unions have carried out a lot of what, to a layperson, may appear to be mud-slinging. But for those listening, the accusations (on both sides) point to long-standing questions about the priority granted to the fishery and fishers in this province. FISH-NL says FFAW-Unifor has more proximal relationships to the big processors and companies, the federal government, and the oil and gas industry than those they supposedly represent: the inshore fishermen. These are among the reasons Ryan Cleary, as the leader of FISH-NL, wants to bring focused representation to inshore fishers. Granted, some fishers told me they worry the complaints directed at FFAW-Unifor would only transfer to FISH-NL in due course, given how politically laden the fishery is in this country. They also worry that decisions like the aforementioned situation with surf clams are out of their control based on how the fishery is managed now. Cleary says decisions like the surf clam debacle are wholly political and he wants to see inshore fishers take their power back and have their interests properly represented.

On one of the occasions I spoke with Cleary, he reminded me of something former Newfoundland and Labrador premier Danny Williams used to say: if Newfoundland and Labrador wants to become a master of its own destiny, then it needs to regain control of its resources. One way of doing so, says Cleary, is to reopen the discussion on adjacency in the federal Fisheries Act. He also suggests the examination of every commercial seafood stock in the province: find out where it's going and how to secure higher value markets for inshore fishers. It's a premise that harkens back to Brad Watkins's story—and the future of wild fisheries in this province, I'm convinced, depends on it.

Back in Corner Brook, Dad is making swift work on an accordion repair. It's his new*ish* hobby, but one he picked up out of necessity. "I wanted a few good accordions for myself, so I went through a lot of trials and errors," Dad says. Accordions can run into the thousands of dollars, so my father, a penny-pincher with an ear for music and a knack for repairs, set out to build the best accordion a Newfoundlander could ever want. (The button accordion is practically the unofficial instrument of Newfoundland and Labrador—right up there with the fiddle.)

"It's all about the physics of sound, my dear. There are a few fine tricks to it, but it's all mathematics." Dad's comment comes in response to my asking if he can teach me to make the tedious repairs. He's unconvinced, knowing math and physics were never favourite subjects of mine. Dad is working on the reed plates of a 1930s button accordion, dipping the reeds into epoxy, then nestling each plate into its slot in the wooden reed plate of the accordion. I inspect the desk where Dad works—it's a state. My old basement bedroom, where he keeps the accordions-in-waiting (he estimates there are anywhere between thirty and fifty) is even worse. I try to get a count, but there are boxes, bits, and pieces everywhere. The room is assembled like an investigation into an exploded cargo plane filled only with accordions. Being neither an accordion enthusiast nor a disaster-scene investigator, I can't get a handle on what's what. This level of haphazardness is not confined to Dad's desk and my old bedroom. In cupboards and closets all over the house, things are stuffed into every available space. The basement and garage, in particular, are to be entered at one's own risk. (The garage having already spontaneously caught fire a few years back.) I don't bother going in those places now, especially not with my young daughter, Navya, and I leave most cabinet doors closed, my urge to tidy being too great. Both my mother and father ignore the severity of the situation—and, in fact, continue to exacerbate it. My mother buys new trinkets like the old ones need company. And my father salvages things the rest of us have thrown in the garbage.

As I look at the piles on Dad's desk, I admit to myself it's a kind of order in its disorderly way. But I also realize this is Dad's way of having brought the outport into the city. He still wants the doodads at his fingertips, so he'll have *just the thing* when the situation calls for it. Major parts of the house, in effect, have become his shed.

As my father's health worsens, I notice the accordion repairs have become a barometer for how he's feeling, too. On bad days, this can all be written off as some big mess. But on good days, like today, Dad busies himself with repairs, breathing life back into old squeezeboxes, bringing purpose to these piles and his own life, too.

Dad picks up another restored 1930s model to show me his handiwork. It's bright, shiny, and red and, when played, is layered in sound. I should be paying attention to Dad's instruction, but instead I stare. His arms are thinner than mine. His eyes are glassy. He wears a flat cap reminding me of Pop, his thin, white hairs curling around his ears. Unlike Pop, I notice that Dad's hair is thinning from the chemo. Usually by this time in the evening, Dad tires easily. But this—the sounds of a squeezebox—livens him up. As he spreads his thin arms, air fills the bellows. His chest puffs up too. Then, with what biceps he has, he squeezes the bellows together, the pent-up air whooshing over the reeds, allowing those rich tone-on-tone sounds. Dad's lips are pursed, his foot thumping along. It's taking him to another place and he's taking me with him. It's a place I'd like to stay, especially knowing I won't have this luxury much longer.

Fishers, I know, would often take their instruments to sea, their music providing relief from the manual labour. They played in their communities and homes, too—stages, sheds, wharves, and kitchens often doubling as mini-concert halls for family and friends when the occasion called for it, and even when it didn't. It's just what people did, and sometimes still do. And so, I find myself thinking about my father's hobby and how it links him to the fishing outports. Like our family's connection to the fishery, this, too, is a part of how Newfoundland and Labrador expresses itself on the world stage. In my family, accordion playing is in danger of not passing down the family line.

"Dad," I say, "show me that tune again, will you?"

Dad nods, carrying on playing.

CHAPTER 6:
The Nautical Naturalist

Anyone who go to sea for fun would go to hell for pastime. That warning is scrawled in black marker on a piece of scrap wood nailed to the wall of one of Eugene "Gene" Maloney's woodsheds in his backyard. Like many Newfoundlanders, especially the self-respecting outport kind, Gene has multiple sheds—three, in fact—but based on the materials stacked outside, he could do with another.

Gene is an eighty-six-year-old retired fisher, boat-builder, and father of five living in Bay Bulls, on the Avalon Peninsula in eastern Newfoundland and Labrador. He's a stocky man, as sturdy as the wooden boats he builds. He's dressed in his daily uniform: sawdust-covered navy work pants, a blue-and-white plaid flannel shirt, a dark grey vest, navy flannel jacket, and black ball cap and sneakers. His cap displays the Portuguese flag which, though not at all related, hearkens back to the time when Portuguese buyers would visit Gene to buy his salt cod. They could barely speak English but knew a good product when they tasted it.

"My old man was really meticulous about drying the fish," Wayne Maloney, one of Gene's sons, tells me about his father's first passion. "To dry a fish, you can't leave it in the sun too long because it'll cook, it'll bake. You can't have it in the rain because it'll wash off all the salt. You've got to be watching." When I first met Wayne in the winter of 2017, he was finishing work on a boat of his own. But this one was of the model variety, a wall-hanging to mark the hundredth anniversary of the 1918 sinking of the *Florizel*, a passenger liner that met its sudden and catastrophic end at the southern tip of the peninsula here. Using driftwood collected from a stretch of secluded beach on the opposite side of the peninsula on Placentia Bay, Wayne was piecing the wall-hanging together on a plank of plywood like a puzzle, gluing and nailing each stick into an intricate, interlocking pattern. "This is island life, man, you've got to do it all," Wayne says, his voice trailing into laughter as it often does. His smile softens his square jawline and gathers wrinkles around his eyes. Those kind blue eyes are normally hidden behind polarized sunglasses and Wayne keeps his thick, salt-and-pepper hair trimmed neatly with matching scruff. You'll often find him wearing his company's zip-up fleece vest over a long-sleeve T-shirt and jeans, ready to go.

You've got to do it all is a perfect snapshot of Wayne's personality and an accurate depiction of his lifestyle, too. Ask him how he's doing and his response is always the same: "best kind." During tourism season, late spring to early fall, he operates marine excursions, setting out to sea in a boat, that he built, with small groups of tourists, photographers, and scientists. Wayne lives a different kind of saltwater cowboy life than that of his predecessors—all fishers, sealers, and boat-builders like his father, Gene— but he's a saltwater cowboy just the same. This time of year, during the winter off-season, Wayne occupies his time by putting his artistic genes to work. He calls this his "me time," and he loves art projects, mostly painting local scenes and ocean wildlife in watercolours and acrylics. His tastes are eclectic as they are varied: a painted puffin's head on a mussel shell, a wooden puppet Mummer, a saltbox house garbage bin, and a watercolour scene of dancing fairies in the forest are some recent examples.

Back in Gene's woodshed the following summer, I see where Wayne gets his artistic influence. This is the first pitstop of my tour across the island and it's one I'm particularly excited about—getting a glimpse of boat-building and whales is high on my priority list. Here, outside of Gene's shed, the fisher-turned-boat-builder has his cap pulled down over his eyes, the beak acting like blinders, so he can focus on his woodworking without distraction. Being a gentleman, he's agreed to lift his cap so I can snap a decent photo, and he has taken a seat, so we can have a chat. Gene is sitting in the chair he built, in the doorway of one of the sheds he built, filled with rustic furniture and garden decor he built. His house, which he also built, stands atop a hill overlooking the harbour, where he built his fifty-year-long fishing career. From this vantage point, Gene can see his old fishing site, now home to son Wayne's whale and birdwatching tour company, Captain Wayne's Marine Excursions. Wayne's the only one in the family working on the water these days—it's been over a quarter of a century since Gene left his beloved fishing career behind. And yet, the memories of those fishing days still run deep for the Maloney family.

"I had flakes over there, had one, two, three, three flakes," Gene says, pointing in the general vicinity, north and down over the hill. "And boy, we had wire flakes everywhere because we had fish on them over and over. Ninety per cent of our catch, we salted. We'd come in with a load of fish. My father would come and then the kids would come and they'd cut out the tongues and tend the tables." Cod don't actually have tongues, of course, but these are the fleshy, muscly bits in the cod's throat. Kids at the time could earn some extra bucks cutting and selling this much sought-after part of the fish, what Newfoundlanders consider a delicacy best pan-fried.

Gene followed in the footsteps of his father, father-in-law, grandfathers, grandmothers, and likely ancestors further down the line, all of whom worked in the fishery. Born in 1932, Eugene Maloney started fishing at eleven years old, foregoing, as many did, a classroom education for a land- and sea-based one. Over his career, he fished for just about everything: "Codfish, capelin, herring, mackerel, squid, lobster, you name it, everything, whatever swam," he says.

Gene operated on a tight schedule in those days. Salmon was the primary spring fishery, starting around February. Then there'd be some crossover, fishing salmon in the mornings and cod each afternoon. He'd close the season by late October, fishing cod. The days were long, but the bounty was great. Gene remembers those days filling his boat when they "couldn't get another one in her." "My old man used to leave here at two thirty in the morning" Wayne says. The speedboats forced fishers like Gene to head out early to the fishing grounds in those days. The speedboats could travel twice and sometimes three times as fast as diesel engine boats like Gene's. What's more, some of the men in speedboats would steal your salmon right out from under you if they arrived at your net first, Gene tells me. You could easily spot the salmon in the net, popping their heads out on the surface. "So, it's easy to go right by the net, jab a hook, and take the salmon," Wayne explains. But the way to beat them was to head out before daylight. The guys in the speedboats were really fast, but had to wait for daylight in order to see where they were going.

"My old man and them, they started getting up earlier and earlier," Wayne says, "they'd mosey on out the bay nice and easy and take their time while the guys who were in the speedboats were still in bed."

"Why not confront the other guys?" I ask.

"If there's something going wrong, somebody's stealing your catch," Wayne explains. "Rather than confront them [you say], 'Well, I'm going to have to get up a little earlier.' And it's as simple as that."

"It's no odds," is Gene's reaction to my question. The phrase is a twist on the Newfoundland saying "what odds," meaning *it doesn't matter* or *it makes no difference*. Dealing with situations calmly, without aggression or hostility, is a common trait of Newfoundlanders—despite what the cod moratorium news stories show. This pacifist attitude shows itself in spades when Gene tells me he preferred putting in the extra hours to confronting the guys stealing his catch. It just meant Gene had to be more watchful than usual, explains Wayne. "You got to be so observant, honest to God," Wayne says. "You're watching the weather, you're watching the guys who are stealing your fish, you're watching seagulls stealing your salt fish, you know? [Fishers like Dad] always had to figure out how to do it better, you know? That's what makes him so smart. I'm telling you. They deal with it day in, day out, and they had to contend with it until they figure out a way of winning." Another way Gene would get ahead was by processing the cod himself; it was more profitable than delivering his catch directly to one of the local fish plants. Gene had what he calls his "own little mini-factory" at his fishing stage, where he would split and salt his cod. For Gene, "winning" ultimately meant being able to consistently provide for his family. Doing what he loved was a bonus.

The bonuses ended for Gene on July 2, 1992, when the federal government called a moratorium on northern cod. Already in his sixties by then, Gene took the government buyout, opting for early retirement. Nothing had a sense of permanence in those days—least of which the moratorium. "The government told people in 1992, the cod moratorium would be a short-lived thing," writes Beaton Tulk, former premier of Newfoundland and Labrador, in his memoir. "It's hard to understand why they did that, perhaps to try and dampen the reality of it all." "They were hard, I guarantee you that," Gene says, referencing those initial post-moratorium days and weeks. "I built a boat. She's in Petty Harbour now. A guy got her, 27-footer, 9-foot wide, 54-inches deep. I got at that and I built it to pass the time. Anyway, then another guy wanted one, this feller wanted one. Next thing, it exploded. I was a lifetime building boats, but I wasn't intending to go at it like that."

Gene knew one thing: he was getting out of the fishery. But he would give his eldest son, Ken, a chance to keep the family legacy alive. Gene gave Ken his crab license, the same one that had been passed down to him by his own father, and a new boat he'd built himself. Ken had spent time working with his father and was planning to make a go of it by diversifying, like other Newfoundlanders and Labradorians of the time, from cod, which had tanked, to crab, which was flourishing and paid well. But it wouldn't take long before Ken, too, got out of the fishery, selling the crab license.

"I told him not to forget me," Gene says, a quiet reference to the investment he'd made in Ken's fishing career. This is a topic rarely discussed by the Maloneys, both then and now. The pride of men in those days was supplying for your family, Wayne says. Gene would turn out to be one of the lucky ones: a carpenter with a workspace and growing demand for his woodworking skills.

But all around Gene, the moratorium had pulled the plug on a way of life, driving other, less fortunate ones to drown their depression and sorrows in the bottle. Some even took their own lives. But the Maloneys don't want to get into all that (even though they brought it up). This, I understand. The stigma of suicide has an even more pronounced ring of shame around it in rural communities, perhaps because more than abandoning one's own life and family, those who choose suicide leave their communities behind, too. But what choice did people have, Gene asks; it's not like people had a nest egg they could lean on until things got better. "When you're a fisherman you live from the last catch," Wayne says. "You are always in debt. You never have money."

I ask Gene where he was exactly that day when Fisheries Minister John Crosbie walked along the wharf in Bay Bulls. Although more than twenty-five years ago, that July 1, 1992, day always feels more proximal here because it happened down over the road, no more than a couple of minutes' drive from Gene's shed. Gene's response is immediate. He mutters a curse word (the only one I'd hear him say) in reference to Crosbie. He tells me he'd been out that Wednesday morning setting cod traps. It was Canada Day, so while most Canadians were enjoying summer barbeques and other festivities with family and friends, throngs of disgruntled fishers, plant workers, and community members gathered down on the wharf in Bay Bulls. Meanwhile, Gene and his three-man crew returned home at about 11 A.M. for dinner. When Gene walked in his front door, his wife looked at him, puzzlingly.

What are you at? she asked.

We're going back out to heave out a trap, Gene replied.

Eugene "Gene" Maloney in one of his woodsheds, Bay Bulls, Newfoundland, 2018.

Don't you know the fishery is closed? she asked.

"I didn't know," Gene says, looking at me now. As he says those three words, his voice raises an octave, as though the surprise is hitting him anew. It would take Gene and his crew the better part of the next four days to haul all of their cod fishing gear ashore. And then, "just like that," he tells me, "that was the end of it."

But it certainly wasn't the end of the cod, he says. "There was lots of fish, but [the moratorium] was all politics," Gene says. "I spent fifty years going in and out of [this harbour]. I got out of bed every morning between half past three and quarter to four. Rain, fog, no odds, I had to go; that was my living. And when they closed it down, it's hard to describe, you know?" Gene doesn't go on explaining. Instead he pauses, holds his breath, and presses his eyelids for a slow blink, as if to let his heart break another time.

Imagine having your livelihood yanked out from under you. All your pride, all your life, everything you've ever known. You can't recall spending days and weeks, certainly not this time of year, on land. But there you are, with all your gear ready but no place to go and no use for it. Leave it to Gene, a true Newfoundlander, to make light of even the grimmest situations. "I never knew we had a lawn until 1993," he says, raising his eyebrows to see if his punchline has landed. That was the first summer everyone stayed home, so everything on land got a lot more attention. The houses and properties looked immaculate, with all the lawns mowed and fences painted. The excitement of the fishery was gone, and boredom was setting in better than any grass fertilizer. Fishing had its risks, Gene says, but it had its rewards too.

I've spent the last couple of days driving up and down the north and south shore of Bay Bulls, as well as down the Avalon Peninsula, driving in and out of similar fishing communities, all the way down to Renews-Cappahayden and back again, trying to picture the fishing scenes Gene had described. In the days before the cod fishery collapse, people gathered at their fishing spots and community wharves, local fish plants buzzed with activity, and fishing vessels, seagulls, and children circled the harbours. "On this road now, from here up to the other end of the road down there to the church, if there are a half-a-dozen kids now, that's it," Gene says. "But there's a house down there used to be a busload of kids come out of it, fourteen or fifteen, or something."

I can't tell if he's exaggerating, the way Newfoundlanders tend to do, but I don't doubt him. The demographic has changed here and it's still changing; the population is aging and out-migration is happening faster than in most parts of Canada, and shows no signs of slowing. The demise of the fishery is certainly a contributing factor, having exacerbated the exodus that started long before. It's not that people don't want to stay; it's that many can't, mainly due to a lack of steady employment. It's also part of the rhetoric we all hear, as Newfoundlanders, that to make something of yourself means moving away. While I'd like to say that's changing, sociologist Nicole Power's work shows that sentiment is still alive.

As Nicole Power's findings remind us, one of the markers of success for a young person from rural Newfoundlander and Labrador is moving away. She also found, from speaking to young people in rural areas of the province, that many want to stay or return home, especially once they settle down—because they want the lifestyle they had growing up for their own children. But the realities of unemployment make that choice untenable. Based on Statistics Canada's May 2019 Labour Force Survey, the latest unemployment rate in Canada was 5.4 per cent, while Newfoundland and Labrador's rate was more than double that at 12.4 per cent.

Meanwhile, up and down this peninsula, I see tangible evidence of a lasting fishery. There are vessels, dories, fish plants, and wharves. But those structures pale in comparison to what might have been, had approaches to rework the wild fisheries model followed the Icelandic approach. Wild fisheries models have largely been built on the premise of an abundant supply, but when scarcity became the new reality, a refocus from volume to value and quality could have pivoted Newfoundland and Labrador's fishery into a more prosperous future. Here, the undeniable marks of the fisheries' collapse stand out, like the greying wooden bones of abandoned stages and boats, broken wharves and gear. Worse still, are the places where the bones have vanished altogether: quieted, childless roads ending at rock and sea, where not so much as a gull squawks.

I had attempted to walk along the same path that Crosbie took the day before he announced the cod fishery closure. I sized up the angles and backgrounds from television news footage, looking past the men and women, fishers, and plant workers, holding their picket signs and looking for answers, crowding around Crosbie. But when I tried to overlay the past images with present realities, the challenge was too great. It wasn't the emotional toll—although that hit me too—it was the sheer difference in the port itself.

Bay Bulls has undergone a major transformation in the last twenty-five-plus years. For starters, there's some fourteen acres of rock-fill waterfront that was built nearly a decade after the moratorium. It's a marine terminal that services cargo ships and the offshore oil and gas industry. It's common to see large vessels docked here undergoing repairs or collecting supplies to transport to the rigs in the Grand Banks oil fields—the same proximity to the Grand Banks that helped establish Bay Bulls as a premier fishing community. This town, like others around here, including new developments built for this purpose, has become a "bedroom community" for those working in St. John's but in need of more affordable housing outside of the city. Meanwhile, the local families who once ruled the fishery now dominate the tourism industry here.

"All over Bay Bulls, people were tangled up some way in the fishery," Gene says. "Everything is gone to tours now and the oil rigs. She's turned right reverse. Some of the tour companies were big fishermen. The Gatherall's [Puffin and Whale Watch] were big fishermen. There was a fish plant owned by O'Brien's [Boat Tours], there was another one in Witless Bay, there was three in Petty Harbour and they closed. Once I goes, there's one more man down there. He's eighty-eight, somewhere around there. I'm the only one on this street now that was involved out there. All this is going to be lost."

The fishery has clearly lost its stronghold here—and when people like Gene are no longer around to recount *the days when*, it may well be lost to communal memory too. It seems the death blow that Crosbie delivered that day had its desired effect; granted, many would argue the offshore oil activity (with its seismic activity) hasn't helped the fishery either. FISH-NL president Ryan Cleary goes so far as to say big oil is a major reason there's no northern cod plan at all. His argument goes something like this: if we get overly concerned about the fish, then we'll have to face facts about the role oil exploration plays in disturbing the marine ecosystem and undermining the growth of the fish stocks. I can appreciate where Cleary (and others I spoke to, but not willing to go on record about it) are coming from with the idea. Certainly, there's reason to believe big oil has a big influence around here. As Newfoundland and Labrador claws its way out of economic dire straits, it's oil production that is helping make it happen. With higher offshore oil production in 2018, Newfoundland and Labrador expects to once again regain its short-lived title of one of the front-of-the-pack economies across Canada. Recently, the provincial government announced expanding its offshore gas platforms to one hundred new exploration wells by 2030—that's up from thirty-five completed platforms with two in progress as of 2017. The Bay du Nord deepwater production plant is expected to create "11,000 person years of employment" and raise an estimated $10.9 billion in capital within twenty years, when the first oil is pumped (estimated in 2025). For a province with a recovering economy and where the unemployment rate is among the highest in the country, this is, for many, welcome news.

But previous attempts to ramp up oil and gas in the province haven't been exactly smooth. Take the SeaRose FPSO (floating production, storage, and offloading vessel) platform, for example: Husky Energy reported a flow line connecter failed in late 2018, spilling 250,000 litres of oil into the Atlantic Ocean. The company is responsible for implementing its own internal and environmental safety plans, approved by the Canada-NL Offshore Petroleum Board, an arms-length entity that reports to ministers of Natural Resources both federally and provincially. Decisions of the board, referred to in legislation as "Fundamental Decisions," are referred to government for approval or rejection. The board will only intervene when it deems an investigation is necessary and won't actually enforce a company's internal safety plan. This means operator transparency is paramount, especially as the Bay du Nord project entails drilling ten times deeper than SeaRose.

Residents might question the ramping up of oil-related projects on the Atlantic coast when this is far from the reality on Canada's Pacific coast, and elsewhere. In 1972, for example, off of the coast of British Columbia, the federal government put a moratorium on oil and gas exploration amidst rising public fears of oil spills and other environmental effects. That moratorium also restricted crude-oil tanker traffic, in part to restrict Alaskan oil tankers from making passage along the BC coast, which is a main route for trade and cruise ships, too. More recently, in 2017, the Government of Canada introduced Bill C-48, the proposed Oil Tanker Moratorium Act, in parliament. The act backs up the national Oceans Protection Plan adopted in November 2016 and aims to "improve marine safety and responsible shipping; protect Canada's marine environment; and create new partnerships with Indigenous and coastal communities."

One has to ask: why wouldn't the Atlantic coast receive the same level of protection?

Meanwhile, back in Bay Bulls, as Gene tells me how his coastal fishing community has gone to the oil rigs and tour boats, I come to learn he's helped the tourism industry by doing what he does best: retrofitting some of the boats. "The first tour boat O'Brien's had, I rigged her up, put seats around her," he says. "*Rob and Rand*, she was called, a longliner. That was over thirty years ago."

Bay Bulls offers a perfect location for marine tourism, situated as it is within a few kilometres of the Witless Bay Ecological Reserve, a collection of four islands—Gull, Green, Great, and Pee Pee—home to North America's largest Atlantic puffin colony. Hundreds of thousands of pairs of puffins—Newfoundland and Labrador's official bird—nest here from late spring through summer. The islands are also the nesting grounds for hundreds of thousands of Leach's storm-petrels and thousands of black-legged kittiwakes and common murres (commonly known as turres). The sea here is home to various whale species too—humpback, minke, finback, and the occasional orca, along with dolphins, sunfish, and sharks.

Wayne Maloney spent twenty-five of his thirty years in the tourism industry working for one of the big local tour boat companies. Having left the island after high school to study marine design architecture, he returned to take up skippering. He put his architectural skills to work for the company, too, helping design its fleet. His background in marine system designs and experience as captain meant he knew the comforts tourists wanted. The boats offered heat, shelter, a restroom, and had all of the necessary safety infrastructure too. But over the years, differences in opinion—predominantly over the company's growth model and safety protocol, says Wayne—led him to branch off on his own.

The big company started out by converting a longliner into a tour boat. By 1990, they had bought two brand new fibreglass boats, which Wayne had helped design. But the company often pushed the boundaries of safety just the same, says Wayne, testing the limits of how many people they could take out at a time. What started as twenty-eight people aboard a single tour boat became forty-eight, then sixty-eight, and finally nearly a hundred. "We'd have ninety-eight people aboard, [and we'd be] biting our fingernails," he says. For the company, he says, it was a numbers game. On one occasion, Wayne arrived at work to find seasick passengers disembarking the previous tour. He remembers a pair of ladies, white as ghosts and having lost their strength. He walked each one up the dock to a place they could sit and recover on the hill.

That's the only cure for seasickness—land, he laughed.

I feel like kissing the land, one of the ladies had said.

Here you are. Now you're safe, Wayne replied, before turning back down the hill to board the boat for the next tour. On the dock, he observed his boss telling four elderly ladies it was a great day to go on a tour. But passengers from the previous trip were saying the sea was crazy rough.

No, no, it's a great day for a tour, his boss kept insisting, before leaving Wayne with the four ladies.

"That was the kind of risks they would take," says Wayne, who reluctantly captained the tour that day—and yes, passengers became sick. "It became all about the money."

Maloney recalls the anxiety of those days. Parents holding their kids over the rails; some even refusing to make their child wear a life jacket. He tried to impress upon the company's owners they needed more safety protocol and certified crew, but they thought business was good as it was—and to their credit, there have been no reported safety breaches. As captain, Wayne shouldered the responsibility of passenger safety, and while that number of passengers was and is Canadian Coast Guard approved, it became a constant stressor for Wayne, who no longer wanted any part of it. The big company owners would go on to become rich, while Maloney one day decided to go his own separate way, earning a decent living for himself.

I'm going on my own, Wayne had later gone to his father and said, knowing he would need to start small and still manage to compete in what had, by that time, become a big industry.

You're kind of late, Gene had replied, but he was supportive of his son.

Get in and get moving. Don't listen to anyone—anyone—telling you you can't do this. There's no such thing as 'no' with me. All ahead.

So that's what Wayne did, building his 30-foot boat the way he wanted, to accommodate small tour groups. His father helped him cut some of the materials for the boat's keel and stem, but Wayne pieced it together himself, foregoing wood-plank finishing for a fibreglass bottom. That choice meant a more demanding and costly boat-building process, but it also meant less maintenance in the long run.

Gene's words of encouragement to his son at that time ran in deep contrast to what his own father had told him when he set out to craft his first boat in 1954. "My father told me I couldn't do it," Gene remembers. Gene was twenty-two at the time and had fished for eleven years already. His father was an easygoing man, but "wasn't too fond of much work," just enough to get by on, not wanting any prosperity. So, when Gene raised the idea with his father of building his own boat, he remembers the conversation going something like this.

You know nothing about it, his father said.

What did the first one know? How did he figure it out? Gene replied and, in that moment, resolved he would figure it out for himself. *I'm going to fool you on that one, old man. I'm going to build a boat,* he had thought, but never said anything of the kind to his father. "I went in the woods and I cut the materials. And I went down to an old man down there in Gunridge to get information. Tom Pack was his name. He could take an arse out of a cat and put it in a dog—he was that good. He wouldn't give you no time. Every minute was planned with Tom, he had something to do. And I told him what I wanted, and he looked at me and he hauled off his cap."

Sonny, go home and use that. That's more than to keep your ears apart, Pack had said, pointing to his head.

Thank you, Skipper Tom, Maloney replied. He returned home and got to work on his first boat. Sixty years later, he's still at the trade and has built every kind of wooden boat there is.

Captain Wayne's tour boat dips and bobs in the Atlantic, while the hamlet of Bay Bulls pops in and out of view above sea level. The sky is bleached by the sun and the ocean glistens with the kind of darting light that makes you squint, even with your sunglasses on. The voices of the half-dozen passengers are muffled by the wind, but somehow we hear that unmistakable *poof* of air expelled at the water's surface. Cameras click furiously in anticipation of what lies beneath the blowhole. Then,

Captain Wayne Maloney sets out for a whale- and birdwatching excursion, Bay Bulls, Newfoundland, 2018.

another *poof*. It's a mother and calf, and the mother is feeling especially friendly, allowing the calf to come between her and the boat. I can see flashes of turquoise as their stocky bodies reach the surface, then exposing their eponymous humps. These ocean giants were once whaled to near extinction, but today passengers watch them from an appropriate distance, taking only photographs, otherwise leaving the friendly giants be. Wayne Maloney, or Captain Wayne, as he's called in these circumstances, has delivered again.

A fluked tail emerges as the whale dives below the surface, but I miss the shot. There are two professional photographers on the boat—they get it. So too does "citizen scientist" Deborah (Debbie) Young. I met Debbie yesterday, while standing by with her and Wayne to hear the marine forecast. It had been bad news: northeast winds gusting to 80 kph.

"Not fit for man or beast" when the winds blow northeast, Wayne had told me before. For sailing conditions, westerly winds are best, as winds blowing offshore make calm coastlines. To get up close and personal with the birds at the Witless Bay Ecological Reserve, especially, requires calm weather. Wayne likes to bring his boat in close to the rockfaces—not close enough to touch, but almost. The bigger tour boats can't offer that experience. "The wind is our concern," says Wayne, looking out from the windows at Debbie's place at the end of the north shore of Bay Bulls atop the hill overlooking the Spout, a popular salmon-fishing grounds. "And the bigger sea, like you can see, it's safety concerns. I'm not desperate to bring somebody out there today. You know what I mean?"

I do know what he means and I'm happy to wait out the storm. Gene had told me the day before how he used to head out no matter what the marine forecast was reporting—even on a day with northeast winds, he'd find a safe window and head out. It's so engrained in his psyche, even a quarter of a century later, he still wakes up thinking about it. "I come out of the house in the dark and 90 per cent of the time I came home in the dark," Gene said, recalling his fishing days. "That's all we knew, right? I woke this morning, I wake every morning between 3:00 and 3:30 [A.M.]. Every single morning, I'll wake. Today, I looked out and blowing up from the northeast and rain, lots of things, and I said, 'Thanks be to God, I don't got to go.'"

In Wayne's industry, fair-weather sailing is best. Overnight, the northeast winds died down to 30–50 kilometres an hour, then turned southwest around 40–60 kilometres an hour. Today, the water is a bit choppy, but Wayne handles these seas with ease. Meanwhile, I continue my conversation with Debbie. "What's a citizen scientist?" I ask. She tells me she's spent over thirty years documenting humpback whales up and down North America's coastlines and Iceland, predominantly on her own dime. She had read about the humpback whale pods that frequent this region and started visiting the province in 1999 to see for herself. She loved it so much, she bought a place here, sight unseen, thanks to a particularly strong American dollar. She now considers Bay Bulls her second home. Her first home (and where she winters with her husband) is a small city outside of Chicago—or what she's become used to Newfoundlanders calling *Chicargo*. "It's just such a special place." Debbie says, her enthusiasm for this province visceral. She has the passion of a Jane Goodall, and even resembles Goodall, too—same long white hair, but with wire-framed glasses. "You've got the birds, you've got Gull Island, you've got *National Geographic* right there. Everything is right here. You don't have to go 10 miles offshore."

Wayne and Debbie are neighbours turned friends and colleagues. They have a friendly work exchange going: Wayne uses Debbie's garage for his various woodworking activities and, in return, Debbie joins Wayne on his excursions, keeping a detailed photo log of the marine life they encounter. They've worked together for fifteen years, creating a whale identification catalogue, which now includes a staggering one thousand whales or more. Debbie shares the information with an online community of citizen scientists and academics. Together, they swap information on the migratory patterns of the whales.

Today's mother humpback is one Debbie has photographed before. A whale's fluke is like their fingerprint. By comparing today's fluke photo to those in the catalogue, Debbie spots the match.

"Who spots the whale first, usually?" I ask.

"Are you joking? He can see a whale from—" Debbie begins.

"Miles, miles," Wayne pipes in.

"It's amazing, how far he can see a whale," Debbie adds.

On this two-and-a-half-hour tour, I see Wayne constantly scanning the horizon for birds and whales. We head out around the south shore of Bay Bulls, where Wayne speeds up to the locations that deliver, "locking in" there so the passengers can get comfortable with their sea legs and pull out their cameras. The giant sea stacks on the south shore, big rock fingers reaching out from the deep black and blue, are a geological sight to behold. There are caves and reefs, too—evidence of the innards of an earth pushed out from nature's centuries-old construction process. Then there's Gull Island, where the birds are crammed into rockface nooks and crannies nesting among the grasses. You can focus in on one pair cooing to one another and another in a seemingly heated discussion. The panoply of hundreds of thousands of birds cooing, cawing, screeching, and shrieking is only outmatched by their smell. I'm thankful for the westerly winds, blowing the air away from the coast and our nostrils too. "Is that a penguin?" a British passenger asks. *And we're the Newfies*, I think to myself. Wayne corrects her: it's a common murre, dressed nicely in a black and white tuxedo, so a natural mistake. He's *that* kind.

As we leave the sheltered area of the islands for open sea, Wayne's whale watching kicks in to high gear. From a distance, you're looking for ocean signals, he tells me. When whales surface or dive, they leave a disturbance on the water, concentric circles that expand outwards, before disappearing. It's their footprint. Then, if it's foggy, you're relying on your sense of smell.

"Smell?" I ask.

"No kidding, you can smell their breath," Wayne says, "they're exhaling 2,000 litres of air."

Adds Debbie, "Minke whales stink, we call them stinky minkes." The fog has a way of trapping in the sound too. "You've heard of *Gorillas in the Mist*—humpbacks in the mist are funny too because you close your eyes and you're sitting in the middle of the bay and you heighten your sense of hearing," says Debbie.

"Right, and just listen," Wayne adds.

But on today's clear day, Wayne spots an incoming eagle, heading straight for Island Cove, where there are thousands of penguin imposters tucked into crevices and stacked along ledges. The approaching eagle causes them all to take flight, dispersing in an attempt to confuse or disorient the eagle. We lose sight of what happens, as the mother and calf pay us another visit. As more cameras click, Wayne draws my attention back to the point, past the lighthouse on the cove of the north shore, where Gene used to spend his days fishing. It's one of "the toughest places to fish," Wayne says. That's because when you leave the harbour, you're in the open Atlantic. "There's no shelter outside of this harbour. So, in a 30-foot boat, you need prime weather conditions to be safe. And you can't overload your boat. You got to be tough, you got to be keen, you got to be smart, and you got to watch the weather."

When it comes to a career at sea, practice brings some degree of perfection, but luck comes into play a lot of the time too. That's what comes to mind as I recall what Gene told me about navigating tricky weather in his fishing days. "People used to say to me, 'It's thick with fog. You're not going out today.' I said, 'Honey, I got a compass, I knows where I'm to.' But I said, 'The other fellers can't find me.' On a fine day, yes, no trouble. Anyone could go to fish on a fine day, but I often went forty days out here and never saw land. Forty days in the fog day after day after day, nothing, only fog. I could only see to the end of the boat. But I was happy. I would sooner be out there then in here." And yet, Gene is well aware of the risks of being "out there." He told me about one dicey situation when he went overboard.

I went with an anchor. One Saturday evening, it was thick with fog and mad rough. We were setting a net from here to there somewhere. I was on the gurdy [a hauler with a set of horizontally mounted car tires that turn hydraulically and pull up nets or ropes] hauling up the anchor, and I don't know what happened. It happened so fast. Rope come off, the gurdy went around me, and I went down. It got dark. I could see a rope, so I grabbed the rope. The anchor was hauling me down. When the anchor got on the bottom, I got the rope off me and I started to come up. And next thing, I could see the propeller

*on the boat spin because I had only just slowed the gear. Anyway,
I come up and I grabbed the rail of the boat and I got a bit of air.*

Haul me in, boy, Gene remembers calling to his fishing partner, Ray. Ray had been at the opposite end of the boat, the bow, when Gene went in, but came to the stern when he heard the commotion. *Gee, man,* his buddy had said, *where were you to?*

Despite the breezy conversation Gene claims he and his mate had that day, Wayne, then about ten years old, vividly remembers the serious scare his father had on the water that day. "I remember him coming home froze to death," recalls Wayne. "I'd say [he was] very close on hypothermic. And I remember he got a good fright that time. Well, geez, imagine you're gone under. He can't swim either. I'd say he must've been pretty close to death because my recollection is seeing him lying in bed, which felt like a hospital scene. I knew it wasn't right."

It still surprises me when I hear it; fishers who can't swim taking even greater risks with their already high-risk careers. In reality, surviving a fall into the Atlantic has little to do with one's ability to swim. Even the strongest swimmer cannot last long in those waters because of the cold, currents, and confusion that sets in under those conditions. Once you're in the water, it all comes down to chance.

As soon as Gene hit the water, panic set in. He gasped. That's the body's way of coming to terms with the frigid water. In the chaos and commotion, your arms start flailing too. You try to grab onto something, anything. And all you want to do is to get air in your lungs. A steady flow of air. But now you're hyperventilating. You're inhaling seawater. It's ice cold and yet it burns your lungs and airway. You think you're drowning. You *are* drowning. Then, someone has a hold of you. And as fast as you were in the situation, you're out of it. But not quite. There's the coughing. You cough your belly up, it seems. How much water did you take on? The days' and days' worth of coughing answers your question, though you can't give a precise amount. Too much. In bed, feeling and looking oddly out of place (*you shouldn't be here, you have a job to do*), it takes time to recover from those seconds in the water. Still, you'll go back out there and take the same risks the moment you can because that's your livelihood. That's all you know and darn it, you're good at it. So, for Gene, life carried on after the accident.

I'm sizing up Wayne's driftwood interpretation of the *Florizel* he made back in 2017. Before starting to assemble the art piece, he studied photos of the ship on his computer. Then, he sketched a mock-up on paper. For the wood, he went with his buddy, John Chidley, a former fisher who occasionally captains another tour boat in Bay Bulls. The pair drove across the Avalon Peninsula, from Bay Bulls, which faces the Atlantic Ocean, to Placentia, on Placentia Bay. There, they unloaded Wayne's 14-foot aluminum boat and rowed it along the shores southeast toward Cape Shore. The weather was unseasonably warm for February, with no snow on the ground and no ice inshore, making for clear sight lines to what Wayne calls "boneyard heaven."

"The mother lode was there," says Wayne, his *mother* sounding distinctly like *mudder* and his *there* like *dere*, but I think he's making the switch for kicks.

Wayne's photos show his weathered finds along with evidence of precisely the kind of weather that accomplished it. It's the kind of grey, dull day for which the east coast of Newfoundland is known. The colours here are dark burgundy, plum, and sage green beach stones; the hills in the background are forest green, and Wayne's light green boat floats in the foreground. Everything else from sky to sea to shore is in muted grey tones, the lightest of all being the scraps of wood. Upon closer inspection, the woods piled onshore stretch—like the beach—farther than the eye can see. This driftwood is comprised of old trees stripped of their barks, abandoned or lost wooden lobster pots, all disabled beyond use but not recognition. Everything here has met its final fate thanks to the unrelenting salt, gales, and currents of a temperamental climate. The wooden bones are locked together in a jumble that Wayne and John will work to untangle today. "I love going to the beach because everything is recyclable," Wayne says. "You see an old shed that's weathered or a boat. I love that."

I've participated in my fair share of beachcombing and this doesn't look to me like the leisurely strolls I'm accustomed to along the sheltered shores of Fortune Bay on the Burin Peninsula or the Bay of Islands on the west coast. This is serious work. Step by step, you must walk carefully to avoid slipping on the slick stones, then source the scrapped pieces that inspire artistry, untangle those pieces, and cart them back to your boat, load them aboard your boat, leaving adequate room and weight allowance so as not to sink your boat when you climb inside, and finally, you must pull the boat to shore and unload only to reload everything into the back of your truck, tying it all down securely for the one-hour highway drive home. This outing makes my former beach strolls with a salt beef pail seem especially juvenile.

SS Florizel *bound for icefields.* (The Rooms Provincial Archives)

Ironically, these are the kind of days that remind me of the absolute ease of life in outport Newfoundland. The distractions of city life aren't present here. Instead, people make their own schedules—and they make their own entertainment, too. Not everyone has an endless supply of leisure activities and pastimes like Wayne, but he suspects every outport has a couple of folks just like him. "I think it is common. I think in every community someone's doing the same thing. I'm not kidding either." The rest are *gawkers* or *rubberneckers*—though these are my words, not Wayne's. He describes to me a type of folk who go for walks and drives to see what everyone else is doing. They stop to poke around, ask, gawk, satisfy their curiosities, and then take off to rubberneck somewhere else.

After a full day of collecting driftwood, the two friends wind up deep into a bottle of rum back at Wayne's place. John spends the night, too sauced to make the hour-long drive from Bay Bulls to Renews, where he lives. The next morning, they both take a crack at their own model *Florizel.* Wayne sets up the tables and benches, starting with his band saw by cutting to size a plank of plywood for the picture's backing. "Sometimes you've got to figure out ways of cutting things that don't scare the bejesus out of you," he says. "Better than run something all the way through and have your fingers right at the very backend of the piece of wood, then you stop halfway through and flip the wood over and put the uncut side towards the blade, you know."

Using everything from a pocket knife to the scroll saw and band saw to whittle away at the pieces, Wayne cuts and positions each piece, staggering the driftwood pieces on a diagonal for the sky. Then, he constructs the boat; the bottom is a single piece of driftwood with a flat bottom and rounded bow. That design made the actual *Florizel* able to slide onto ice floes and break through them. Wayne has cut a few pieces to look like ice floes in the water too. He then uses another, single piece of thin-cut wood to make the gunwale. Then, he cuts pieces for the "Marconi shack," the communication room that would be credited for keeping most of the survivors safe during the wreckage. Wayne adds the tower and flags, the rescue boats, the railings, and the central steam stack. He finishes the piece by adding string for the towers' affixing wires, then darkens the bow waves with soot and ashes from another reclaimed board he has lying around. "It worked better for my eye," Wayne says, pointing out how he's brushed the ashes from one piece of scrap wood onto another.

Their finished products will be displayed in John's art gallery in Renews, near where the *Florizel* wrecked. The gallery itself is a repurposed property: it was once John's father-in-law's fishing stage. A fishing-stage-turned-gallery shows exactly the kind of creativity and resourcefulness I've observed in my fellow Newfoundlanders. The same is true of the driftwood *Florizel* folk art. They haven't aimed for scale models with perfect precision, proportion, and perspective, but their work is pleasing to the eye nonetheless. The story behind the models offers something for the heart and mind too. They reveal something about life in these parts, from the unfortunate *Florizel* wreckage to the day-to-day lives of folks like Wayne Maloney, who call this part of the world home.

The story of the ill-fated *Florizel* is well known in these parts. I'd come to learn the story by visiting the site on shore nearest the wreckage and the "Faces of Florizel" exhibit at the Admiralty House Communications Museum in Mount Pearl. The exhibit ran during the one-hundredth anniversary in the former wireless station–turned-museum—the same one where, coincidentally, the *Florizel*'s distress symbol was relayed.

After a long legacy at sea, the passenger liner struck a sudden and catastrophic end. There are more stories of recovery than rescue from this shipwreck, despite the readiness and willingness of those who arrived on scene to help. The *Florizel* was among the first steel ships in the world designed to navigate through ice—a necessity for year-round navigation off the coast of Newfoundland. Built in 1909, this steamship was the flagship passenger liner of the Bowring Brothers of St. John's. The ship had many noteworthy voyages. On June 11, 1912, the *Florizel* transported the *Titanic*'s last recovered victim, Steward James McGrady, to Halifax, where he was buried at Fairview Lawn Cemetery. On October 3, 1914, she transported the *First Five Hundred*—the men who volunteered as part of the 1st Newfoundland Regiment—to Europe to fight on the front lines of the First World War. Each spring, the *Florizel* transported sealers to the seal hunt, too. The vessel was even part of the rescue operation of the great 1914 Sealing Disaster.

Despite her impressive track record, the *Florizel's* voyage from St. John's Harbour on February 23, 1918, en route to Halifax and then New York City, would be her last. Just after she left harbour, the weather turned bad. Nine hours into her journey, the captain believed they had steamed southward sufficiently past Cape Race, the most southeasterly point of the Avalon Peninsula. When the ship left port, the captain ordered the vessel to steam at full speed but the chief engineer reduced the speed. With the lesser speed and gale-force winds, the *Florizel* had only travelled seventy kilometres and was still shy of Cape Race. When the captain steered west, the ship's demise was irremediable. They were heading straight for land. It was the captain's next move that would seal the fate of the *Florizel*. Mistaking the white frothing water at Horn Head for ice, which the *Florizel* could navigate through, the captain veered directly toward land and into the reef.

Renews–Cappahayden, two independent fishing towns that came together as one in the 1960s, is the closest one can get, on land, to the wreck site. Nestled on the southern shore of Newfoundland, less than 100 kilometres south of St. John's, this region has a storied history that, according to a local tourism website, "spans pirates, shipwrecks, secret midnight meetings and even a supposed visit from the *Mayflower* en route to Plymouth Rock." As one of the closest harbours to the fishing grounds of the Grand Banks, the region was first settled by migratory fishers.

Once the *Florizel* ran aground, the captain sent a distress signal which was received in Mount Pearl, the neighbouring city of St. John's. Men and boys from Renews–Cappahayden arrived on the surrounding beaches to help. With the sea as rough as it was, in the middle of a blizzard, they were helpless to mount the rescue operation. The passengers battled for their lives as the ship was repeatedly battered against the rocks over the next twenty-four hours. One can only imagine the sights and sounds of the *Florizel's* last moments. Steel, bending and scraping against rock. People trying to secure their safety. Waves crashing over the decks, sweeping many away. The waters too rough to launch the rescue boats. Of the 138 people onboard, only 44 souls survived (17 of them passengers), saved by ships that had come to their rescue once the seas had calmed.

Each of Gene's boats starts as an idea. He cuts the material for the keel, the bow, and the stem, scuttling them together into a frame. Today he's working on his seventy-second boat, a 15-foot speedboat. Hat pulled over his brow, he's sealing his boat with caulking and applying oakum to the seams. He's also taking measurements for final adjustments. Tape measure in hand, he assesses the hull at the boat's bow. He carries on measuring along the starboard side of the boat toward the stern. The stern is not yet in place; it will be the final piece to be assembled and fit. Gene then repeats the measurements along the port side. Inside the boat, also along the port side, he then adjusts a series of three clamps holding the planks to the frame. There's a thick layer of sawdust in the bottom of the boat. And one of the seats in the boat is doubling as a shelf for Gene's tools: a framing square, a hand saw, and a couple of hammers. The rest of his tools—countless saws, levels, and rulers among various bits, pieces, and doodads—are hanging on the walls, in the windowsills, and anywhere there's space. In the rafters are countless pieces of wood—some new from the hardware store, some scrap that will be put to good use at some point.

Over in the far side of Gene's shed is a wood stove with a metal wall behind it upon which Gene has scrawled in black marker what looks to be hundreds of dates, weather and otherwise noteworthy special events. (They're listed on the wall adjacent to his statement of warning mentioned previously, the one comparing going to sea with hell.) Some of the entries read: "STORM BIG SEA DEC 21 RAIN WIND 100K," "XMAS DAY 2010 RAIN 10CM," "FIRST BOAT IN 2012 JAN 29," "FIRST SNOW OCT 23," and "DEC 30 2010 FINE DAY." There's a collection of news clippings, too, some assembled as collages or glued to a piece of board. One features stages and fishing boats of fishers in the area before wind lifted the structures into the harbour and ice crushed the rest in a particularly bad storm on February 3, 1987. Another has an excerpt from Michael Harris's 1998 *Lament for an Ocean* featuring a photo of Gene unloading his catch of cod. Other clippings show lobster pots, the frame of a boat, and an ice crew preparing a strap of sealskins. The place certainly has character and outside, there's another one: Joe the seagull.

"I've had a seagull for twenty-eight years," Gene says. "The first one just hung around. Pete. He'd answer to it. 'How are you, Pete?' 'Rhum, rhum, rhum, rhum,' That's what he did. We were fishing down on the shore and he come aboard the boat crippled. A brown young gull just hopped up on the rail of the boat. And we kept feeding him scraps, whatever we had. And when it was all over in 1992, he used to come back and forth—he used to follow us in the daytime over when we'd be splitting fish. We'd give him liver or whatever. And he'd be up on the roof of the stage, and you'd hear him walking around. And when it was all over, he followed me home." Then, about three years ago, Pete disappeared. Eagles killed him, Gene figures. But two years ago, another fellow, Joe, showed up. "All last winter, he was there on the roof of the shed, and I was working away, and I fed him every morning," says Gene. "I fed him this morning—gave him some scraps and whatever I had. He'll stay now until coming on dark. Gone again. He'll be there tomorrow morning at dawn."

There's a deep joy that this place, the work, the pet gulls, gives Gene. The man simply likes to be busy, using his hands. Wayne tells me he never knows what his Dad will pull out from the rafters of his shed. "He builds things like rocking chairs, and benches, like swing benches. All of a sudden, man, the sun comes out one sunny afternoon and [Dad says], 'Yeah, I got two. Somebody wants two swing benches?' And he'll take them out of the rafters, pop them down on the floor and [say], 'Here you go.'"

Woodworking has become Gene's passion. He used to cut the timber frames for his boats in the woods, then get them made into planks at a local sawmill, but there are no more running in the area now. It used to be that you could bring ten to fifteen logs to the sawmill and they would cut five planks from each log. "There's no demand for it," Wayne says. "That was a big thing in Dad's day." Gene explains: "People say to me, 'It must be a lot of work building boats. Today there's no work. It's like fishing. Fishing is only a joke today because you push buttons, stay awake. But in my day, you hauled everything by hand. I can go up there now and start building a boat, planers and band saws, the whole works, but when I started first, you had a rip saw, you had to file that two or three times a day on old hand planes."

To get their timber, they head into St. John's to a big-box building-supply store. The demand for wooden boats is not what it used to be either. Fewer people want boats and when they do, they are going for aluminum or fibreglass ones. That's despite the fact that the price difference is significant: Gene's boats retail for about two thousand dollars, while a similar-sized fibreglass boat retails for eight to ten thousand. "It's just so much easier. A wooden boat, there's a bit of upkeep to it. It can get weathered pretty fast, so not everybody wants a wooden boat. Most guys want the fibreglass. It's like a house. They want vinyl siding on it. They don't want plank siding. They don't want to do upkeep. So yeah, when you see a wooden boat, some people shy away from them because they don't want to do it. But if you done them when you were a kid, you know that's only to put some caulking in the seam and a lick of paint and put her out on the water and away with you."

After Gene works on the stern of his boat, he'll continue to caulk the seams and make fine adjustments with his plane and clamps. Then he'll apply a few coats of paint—usually white with a dark green gunwale. The finishing touches, like adding the engine, will be up to the prospective buyer. Once she's painted, his work is done. Then, it's on to his next project.

"He will not retire," Wayne says. "Until he can't put his boots on, he will build things."

But Gene is less committal, even as he finishes his third boat this year—one that's gone to Conception Harbour; another in what Gene says is a "big house up in Tors Cove"; and then this one, his seventy-second boat, destined for Avondale. "I might never build a boat again," Gene says. "I take this one day at time. In the morning, if I feel all right, I might go in the woods. But I got enough material now to build an 18- or 20-foot speedboat. But I makes no promises and then you don't need to back it up."

I have a model dory my father made. Like Dad's refurbished accordions and Pop's wheelbarrow lessons, that dory feels like home to me. That's why Dad made it for me, a replica of a bright yellow, green-trimmed dory Pop once owned. "Tell me how you built it, Dad," I ask during one of our phone calls—me in Ottawa and Dad at home in Corner Brook. "I was actually building a cardboard dory, and I had built quite a few before, but the stern used to take on a shape that I didn't quite like," Dad begins. The dory needed to have a flat stern, but the cardboard model wouldn't hold its shape, he explains. "First, I used timbers and then the individual side pieces," he continues, referencing his switch to wood, but affixing it to the cardboard. "Then later on I [added] two bigger side-pieces and a bottom and stern. Then I would lattice the inside and follow by the same method on the outside [with wood]. When finished, it was three layers thick and the sides looked like individual boards!" Instead of finishing what he had started, Dad had another idea. He filled the cardboard dory with concrete. Once dried, he used the mould, building my model dory around it. He thought he'd use the mould again and again, but with his growing to-do list—everything from accordion repairs to chemo treatments—he never seemed to find the energy or time to make another dory.

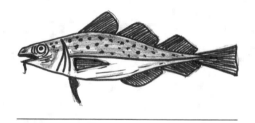

PART III. REVIVAL

CHAPTER 7:
Architectural Time Capsules

April MacDonald was a teenager the first time she photographed an abandoned house. She and her friends happened upon the derelict dwelling one evening while seeking a sheltered hangout in Meadows, near Summerside where MacDonald's family was living. Meadows is a quiet fishing town in the heart of the Bay of Islands, an inlet off the Gulf of St. Lawrence on Newfoundland's west coast. In this sleepy outport, hanging out with friends to enjoy a smoke or a few drinks was often all a teenager had for weekend enjoyment. The orange two-storey saltbox house made a perfect refuge, says MacDonald. But she knew then the abandoned property was more than what it seemed. She returned alone at daylight to document the site, camera in hand. Against a backdrop of fishing villages in decline, MacDonald saw the house as an architectural time capsule steeped in history, hinting at how people—her people— once lived.

It was a scene she identified with, given that her own family had vacated their home before she was born. The MacDonalds were resettled in the 1970s from one fishing community on Woods Island to another in Frenchman's Cove as part of the Fisheries Household Resettlement Program offered by the governments of Newfoundland and Labrador and Canada. It is estimated the provincial government encouraged some thirty thousand residents spread over 250 communities to resettle into "designated growth centres."

Those facing resettlement were "forced to confront wrenching alterations to their ways of life," Graeme Wynn writes in Dean Bavington's *Managed Annihilation*. With Newfoundland teetering on bankruptcy when it joined Canada, the new province was desperate for solutions. Shuttering communities allowed cutting and centralizing government services like health and education, which was expected to help the bottom line.

Born into a fishing family that continued to fish once resettled, MacDonald remembers frequently travelling by dory back to Woods Island with her paternal grandfather, Edward MacDonald. It was his family home that was relocated—uprooted and towed across the bay— but the MacDonalds made a return pilgrimmage to their island-off-the-island home each spring and summer. They fished the same fishing grounds, too. For MacDonald, the site of the Woods Island home holds a special significance beyond her family connection. That's because it's where she first "learned to love what was falling down around her."

The MacDonald family's resettlement story is like many others across Newfoundland and Labrador. Resettlement is as much a part of outport life in this province as the fishing that brought people here in the first place. The early twentieth-century censuses (before Newfoundland joined Canada) show outports disappearing decades before the 1950s and '60s brought formal resettlement programs to Canada's newest province. Although those programs officially ended in 1971, the practice of relocating remote communities to more accessible ones continues today. The town of Williams Harbour, an island off the southern coast of Labrador, was home to a population of thirty-four when it was relocated through a government-sponsored relocation program in November 2017. In February 2019 Little Bay Islands, an island off the north-central coast of Newfoundland with a population of seventy-one, voted unanimously, under the same program, to resettle. The ongoing roster of abandoned communities, both existing and upcoming, offers vast terrain for MacDonald and her camera to cover.

Today MacDonald lives in Corner Brook on the west coast of Newfoundland but has travelled south to Port aux Basques, north to St. Anthony, and farther north still to Labrador, along with countless stops along the way, to find and document images of resettlement. The draw in visiting these places, she says, is imagining the lives left behind amidst what's still standing.

It's a Sunday in July 2018 and I'm tagging along with MacDonald to visit an abandoned house she's visited too many times to count. We pull into the driveway, but it's so overgrown I shrink back into my seat the

April MacDonald with her family's former residence (Woods Island) in the backdrop, Frenchman's Cove, Newfoundland, 2018.

way a passenger does when they think the driver is about to get into an accident. I don't see an address and MacDonald doesn't want me to reveal it even if I had one. "I worry after I post a photo," she had said to me earlier. "Even though I don't post locations, I worry someone is going to somehow figure it out and they're going to ruin it." For MacDonald, it's important that her work preserve the integrity of the places she documents. For her, these are not abandoned properties; they are homes, and their contents are all the evidence she needs to prove it. Besides keeping her locations quiet, she takes extra precautions like delaying the release of her photographs on social media.

The property we're visiting today could easily be overlooked. It's off to the right of the main drag, somewhere on the way toward Lark Harbour and past Frenchman's Cove, just as the road bends around and over a hill. MacDonald pulls her Jeep into park and I'm taken aback by the view ahead, which feels every bit as impactful as the collision I'd anticipated. The wild plants and grasses make way to a narrowly clear-cut area, where the land appears to drop off and rolls directly across the Bay of Islands to the green hillsides of the north shore. It's a view that's in deep contrast to the house we're about to visit. Set back in the trees, hidden from the road, the house's clapboard has greyed, showing minimal evidence of its original white paint and French-blue trim. Two of the five windows are boarded up, while the other three windowpanes display dingy venetian blinds.

As I make my way out of the vehicle, the door brushes the tall grass aside creating a landing. I step down, anticipating bog, but the ground is dry. I shut the door, trapping the tips of the grass in the doorframe. With no visible path to the house, MacDonald and I lift our knees above the overgrowth, taking long steps. The subject of garter snakes comes up: about a decade ago, news reports indicated they had been introduced to western Newfoundland. *This is starting off well*, I think. I've never encountered a snake, even of this harmless variety. And I don't want to today. We reach the door, which is a couple of feet off the ground with no stairs. "The house is open or you're not getting inside," I say, querying: "You're entering, but you will not break?"

"I will not break," she confirms. "I don't want to hurt these houses at all. I won't hurt anything to get inside or while I'm in there."

The storm door is already unlatched, so we step up into the doorway. I'm following closely behind MacDonald. I see the inside door is broken— the entire strip of wood housing the doorknob has been snapped clean off the door and set in a corner. We don't need to break in because someone else already has. Inside the entry, we take quick stock of the house; MacDonald is already familiar with the details. It's a two-storey, five-bedroom, single-bath house. A central stairwell greets us upon entry, though it's a dismal hello. The stair railing is partially gone and not a single step is level. To my right is the formal living room, with a glass-knobbed French door, white wood trim against beige walls, and orange shag carpet. The matching wood coffee and end tables are all the furniture that remains. Behind the living room is the dining room with a retro stainless-steel table and chairs and a buffet-hutch with ornate carved-

April MacDonald explores an abandoned house somewhere on the way toward Lark Harbour and past Frenchman's Cove, Newfoundland, 2018.

wood cabinets. The hutch is still set with a glass decanter, matching glasses, and tray: this sight looks particularly out of place in an otherwise gutted room. Ceiling drywall litters the floor, having succumbed to persistent and pervasive water damage. The mould overwhelms my nostrils, so I take to pinching my nose and breathing from my mouth. The musty smell is likely coming from the dank blackness between the visible ceiling joists. I can see fuzzy white growth on the pages of every book piled on the dining table, too. The first book I notice is called *New Book of Knowledge Annual 1974*. It's one of a dozen or more of its kind. There are popular science and world geography textbooks, too; a collection of Harlequin romance novels and children's storybooks. There's a set of tarnished silver salt-and-pepper shakers inscribed "Canada" with a gold maple leaf, still boxed, with a matching tray. Sitting in the middle of the living room there's a rusted-out navy and white toy police wagon, the kind a toddler sits in and moves with her feet like a Flintstones vehicle.

We turn our attention to what's on the other side of the stairwell. Past a double mattress resting against the wall in the hallway is a sitting or TV room with peeling powdery blue walls and torn vinyl flooring. The simple scene of a wood-framed tube television decorated with a rectangular doily, a glass candleholder, and mirrored tray reminds me that televisions of the mid-twentieth century were more than electronics—they were furniture. In the opposite part of the room, a single child's wooden chair looks out of place, surrounded by fallen ceiling debris.

On the wall, there's a small, metal-framed painting of Jesus and the disciples at The Last Supper. On the floor is a June 1976 issue of *Chatelaine* magazine featuring a fresh-faced Queen of England in a sun hat, pearl necklace, and Jackie O–style turquoise suit jacket. The cover story is, not surprisingly, royal family–inspired: "Royal Vacationers: Where They'll Go This Summer." Another feature headline reads: "New marriage laws— how they could change your whole life."

I spot a toy lobster pot amongst a pile of empty boxes, while MacDonald picks up a copy of Freya Littledale's *The Magic Fish*. I've not heard of it, but MacDonald knows it well. "I remember this book [from] when I was kid. You should take this," she says, going against her usual practice of taking only photographs and leaving only footprints. "It's a good story. It'll be OK." I set the little blue paperback aside to take with me before I go. I'm keen to read more but am distracted by the buzzing that hasn't stopped since I walked in the front door. I bat my ear trying to brush whatever it is away, but my swatting fails and the buzzing persists.

I turn my attention to the galley-style kitchen off the sitting room. MacDonald has already made her way there. "Shoes on a table," she huffs. "Some grandmother somewhere is feeling that, so I've got to move these." MacDonald knows the place has had visitors since she was here last, only a few weeks ago. Besides the shoes, there are fresh cigarette butts and the mattress from upstairs has been dragged to this new location. I want to understand why she feels obligated to move the shoes and reset the place as she originally found it. More than that, I'm struggling to see the beauty she sees in abandoned properties like this one.

"When you're in here, what do you see?" I ask MacDonald, trying to make sense of it.

"They love the Queen. It has an identity," MacDonald offers earnestly. "I'm building a family. Piecing it together. Things they loved." I hold that thought as we head upstairs, me following MacDonald. "Oh, that's great—someone ransacked it," she says, her voice coming from the bedroom at the top of the landing. I peek inside the bedroom doorway— the room is a disaster of opened boxes, their contents strewn about the room. "I'll come back and fix it another time," MacDonald says with a sigh.

I can't imagine wanting to spend that kind of time in this house. I have the urge to be wearing full protective clothing. I'm grateful it's a bright, sunny day because the sunshine is the only light source filtering in through the cracks of the shuttered windows. The breathing conditions are deplorable; I'm forced to take shallow breaths. The buzzing sound has intensified, too. I'm standing on the landing amidst a pile of broken ceiling tiles. Here, where I have the benefit of a quick departure down a flight of stairs and out the front door, I've decided I'm not going in the bedroom. That way I can also avoid bumping into the clutter and disrupting the black mould growing on the wood-panelled walls and between the ceiling tiles.

Just as I'm convincing myself it's safer out here than in there, I wave my cellphone's flashlight into the ceiling gaps spotting something worse: a giant wasp's nest. I duck instinctively, then give MacDonald the news. "I've found the source of the buzzing," I muster, crouched outside the bedroom doorway. But she's in her own world, nonchalant. For me, the house is a living thing, attempting to fold in on itself and return to its former earthly state. MacDonald sees past the obvious signs of decay to the lives of the people who once roamed here. I put my anxieties aside to take photographs of her hunkered down, her own camera lens pointed

A child's chair in an abandoned property, Newfoundland, 2019.

at various artefacts. Although she never would have opened these boxes herself, she is, admittedly, delighted to see what's inside. It's mostly toys and children's belongings. She points out a Snoopy lunchbox, a model CN tower among various other Canada memorabilia, and an ice cream maker.

"They must have really loved their kids," MacDonald observes, showing me an old carriage filled with dolls. She's experiencing a moment in time. A moment when the children could burst in here and play with these toys. Or perhaps the mother will pick up reading her issue of *Chatelaine*. "Their kids have the greatest toys and the toys were well taken care of," MacDonald continues. "They made the beds before they left. They boxed up the toys because they thought their grandkids would be back."

One of the dolls in the carriage is a Wendy Walker doll, popular in the 1960s, '70s, and '80s. Wendy was larger than most dolls and she could close her eyelids and bend her knees. My older sister Natalie had a walking doll in the '80s and my middle sister, Angie, and I desperately wanted to play with it, but Natalie wouldn't allow it. "My nan worked extra shifts at the fish plant for literally three months to get me [and] my cousins Sarah and Jen one each. They were so expensive. Let's get you in the light," MacDonald says, turning to talk to the doll. She positions Wendy for a photograph atop the dressing table, attempting to bend her knees, but they don't cooperate. Even this supposedly indestructible plastic doll is showing signs of age.

Satisfied with her photos, MacDonald picks up a news clipping on her way out of the room. It features Miss Canada 1958, Joan Fitzpatrick of Windsor, Ontario, granting us a broader timeframe of the family's life here. We round out our tour of the upstairs, MacDonald more daring than I'm willing to be, worried I'll fall through the floorboards and ceiling rafters or disturb the wasps' nest. I manage to follow MacDonald into the bathroom, painted pink with matching coral sink, tub, and toilet, and

April MacDonald photographs an abandoned property, Newfoundland, 2018.

decorative towels folded neatly on the shelf in what MacDonald describes as "perfect nan condition." Despite the insulation falling from the ceiling, I can picture this room in its original state, with its printed floral curtains and bottle of Alberto balsam shampoo at the edge of the tub.

In another bedroom, which I also view from the doorway, there's a child-sized yellow dress in pristine condition, likely having been recently unboxed. Next to the dress is a locked diary, which MacDonald has seen before but never considered opening (and she still doesn't open it, so I don't either).

"On the one hand, you don't know the people who own this house," I say to MacDonald. She has a few leads from her father, but nothing firm, so why does she have this deep honour and reverence for this family she's never known? I continue my thought, "On the other hand, you—"

"—Probably know them more than most?" MacDonald says, finishing my sentence.

We turn to head back downstairs. Maybe it's because I'm a new mother, but the child's chair in the kitchen, the yellow dress in the bedroom, and the toy wagon and school books in the living room stand out. I take my time walking down the rickety stairs and, out of nowhere, an image of giggling children barrelling down the staircase beside me flashes in my mind. There's something haunting about being this deep into someone else's discarded belongings. I shake off the image, ducking back into the kitchen to grab *The Magic Fish*, and make a beeline for the front door. I can't wait to jump into the overgrowth, take a deep breath, and trade the buzzing for chirping. I hear a loon calling in the distance.

Once we're back in the Jeep, I'm still trying to understand why we came here, why MacDonald returns here time and time again to take photographs or to reset things as they were or why she would think things ever could be reset. I ask her how she still sees that place as a home, why she does it. "It's what I've been brought up to do" MacDonald says. "They could still come back and I'm sure they wouldn't want shoes on their table."

"You can really see how the people lived," MacDonald tells me in an interview later. "There are telltale signs if you sit on the floor of an abandoned house long enough." She has captured upwards of one hundred abandoned homes on film, and she speaks with an authority those years of experience have granted her. MacDonald launched a website in 2017 to sell prints and paper merchandise featuring her photography. Still, she's reluctant to even call herself a photographer.

"I kind of accidentally fell into it," she says.

"Okay, where's your camera right now?" I ask.

"In my Jeep outside," she laughs.

"At the ready?"

"Yes, along with a giant pair of rubber boots."

"See, that sounds like commitment to me," I reply. MacDonald laughs.

MacDonald could just as easily be considered an artist, an archivist, or sociologist. She categorizes her photography under four themes: *settings* are exteriors of abandoned houses and landscapes; *the guts* are the interiors; *what remains* are objects and textures; and *filtered* are photos edited with effects. Ask her for a self-portrait and another category comes to mind: *hidden*. In every photo MacDonald shows me of herself, her face is obstructed. In one, she wears a wool cap and sips tea from a mug, so only her sideways-glancing eyes are visible. In another, she sits atop a bale of hay, her head down as her long blonde-brunette hair conceals her face in the shade. In yet another, she peers through her lens, hiding her face behind her digital single-lens reflex camera. Once I draw MacDonald's attention to this trend, she works on getting comfortable in front of the camera lens, but her photography has nothing to do with her at all, she tells me. It's about documenting the discovery, not the discoverer. It was her daughter, Emma, eight or nine years old at the time but now sixteen, who first referred to her mother as an adventurer of sorts. Emma's grade-school class was making a Mother's Day film in which all the kids shared the reasons they loved their mothers. While other kids noted their mother's cooking (*best sandwich*) or affection (*best hugs*), Emma said, *I love my mom because she's an explorer.*

"I've never thought of what I do as exploring before, but yeah, I love that," says MacDonald, utterly driven by the find. It's a romantic idea, especially given the more pragmatic motivations behind her work. "Gas money," she says, laughing in a way that tells me she's only half-kidding. "Prices are through the roof," she adds.

It's no secret that as Newfoundland and Labrador faces an unprecedented deficit, residents have seen serious tax hikes. The same oil that inspired the Conference Board of Canada to dub the province a "runaway leader in economic growth among Canada's provinces" in 2013 upset the economy when oil prices tanked the following year. In 2016 the provincial government designed its budget to accomplish two things: cut spending by slashing public programs and services, and generate revenue through levying new taxes. Some are comparing today's economic situation in Newfoundland and Labrador to the Great Depression of the 1930s.

When it comes to photographing abandoned houses, the fiscal climate adds to MacDonald's sense of urgency: "I don't know how long [these houses will] be here, and I don't think much longer," she says. "Each budget year there's more abandoned houses, so I have lots more to take photos of, but for these [century-old] homes, there's only so many houses to go through."

MacDonald is feeling the brunt of these tough economic times. With her lightly freckled complexion and delicate frame, she could pass for a twentysomething herself at forty. She's a divorcee, co-parenting her teenage daughter, and recently in a new relationship. She holds down several jobs in addition to motherhood. She's a parent coach at Child, Youth and Family Services in the province. She also recently started an online shop, Sweet Gentle Clothing and Decor, selling upcycled women's clothing. And she sells prints of her photography online, in various shops and at the odd Sunday flea market in Corner Brook.

Before she was a Jill of these trades, MacDonald studied folklore at Memorial University's Grenfell Campus in Corner Brook. Folklore is a discipline rooted in social and cultural studies, examining how different 'folk' groups use various genres—from narrative to music to customs and beliefs to health practices to architecture and more—to assert their identities. When I ask her about her own ancestry, she immediately professes the irony of a folklorist not having deeply explored her own family's roots. And yet, what she does know explains a lot. "Everyone in my family had one of two jobs: they built boats, or they rowed them," she says. MacDonald's maternal grandfather was a carpenter, while her paternal grandfather—the one resettled from Woods Island—was a fisher. Her father and all thirteen of his living siblings also work or worked in the fishery, whereas her mother's side and her twelve siblings all took up various trades and careers. Family on both sides are predominantly from the island's west coast.

Her paternal great-grandfather lived the farthest afield. John MacDonald came from Conne River, a community on the south coast of central Newfoundland. The area is home to the Mi'kmaw band Miawpukek First Nation, where the MacDonalds lay claim to their Indigenous ancestry. At some point, the family moved to Cul de Sac West, also on Newfoundland's south coast, before settling on Woods Island. April's paternal grandfather, Edward MacDonald, was a boy when his parents moved to that island to fish.

The largest island in the Bay of Islands, Woods Island sits due north of the Lewis Hills with views to the Long Range Mountains. The Humber River flows into this bay, the waterways continuing west to the Gulf of St. Lawrence. The island is uninhabited now, granted there are dozens of cabins welcoming fair-weather (spring and summer) visitors, many descendants of those who once lived here. It's surrounded by fishing communities past and present on the bay's southern and northern shores. Catching a glimpse of Woods Island, and other abandoned communities, is possible through MacDonald's photography. Her photos show teacups at the edges of counters and tables, awaiting the return of their owners; faded floors in front of kitchen sinks and windows where women looked out longingly to the sea for a loved one's return; aging wooden houses and docks, still standing and trimmed in teal greens and marine oranges despite decades of disrepair and relentless beatings from ice, winds, salt and waves.

Last summer was the first time in over thirty years MacDonald returned to Woods Island. She was finally ready to go back, she tells me. The island is quite literally in MacDonald's backyard, just across the bay and easily accessible by boat. So, what's taken her this long? "I really loved my grandfather," MacDonald begins, her voice quivering. "I thought he was amazing." I want to probe deeper about that connection, but MacDonald begins to share the details of that last day trip home in July 2017. It was a MacDonald family reunion, so everyone visited the island for a barbeque hosted by her uncle, who has a cabin there. The family mostly stayed on "their side of the island—the Anglican side," she tells me, although she took a stroll over to the Catholic side, the side visible from Frenchman's Cove, where her grandparents moved after the resettlement. Old barriers formed on the basis of religion no longer exist, at least not for our generation, and not here, but the island has two graveyards, one for each faith group, reminders that differences once ran deep. While there, MacDonald found her Aunt Betty's grave. Betty's death came at a time when MacDonald's grandparents couldn't afford a gravestone. They planted an elderberry bush marking the grave instead. Her grandmother also planted mint. MacDonald found both plants, paying respects to the elderberry bush and gathering fresh mint with her daughter Emma to take back home. Since the MacDonalds transported their house across the bay during resettlement, the elderberry bush and mint are the only remaining physical markers of the MacDonald legacy on Woods Island. Her uncle's cabin is located on the same land as the family's one-time home but is of newer construction.

For April, the family reunion was special for several reasons. It was the first time her daughter set foot on the island of her ancestors. Her father, Reginald MacDonald, was also returning to Woods Island after a long absence. As a fisher, Reg had circled the island by dory and crab boat many times, but had never stopped to revisit the place where he was raised. Of course, the most special reason was April's own return.

Before this visit, MacDonald remembers returning to Woods Island with her grandfather. She recalls a moment with him digging mussels on the cove on the island. "I don't know how old I was. It was just a moment. I remember looking up and the sun was setting over the trees. I even remember how things smelled." That tangy smell of the sea conjures my own memories. Bathed in sunlight, skin taut from a salty ocean breeze, and the unmistakable dewy scent of the beach and sea. MacDonald describes her grandfather as calm, quiet, and reserved. He reminds me of Pop. "He's not like anyone else around me," she recalls, beginning in the present tense. "Everyone else is hyper and angry. The cod fishery kind of destroyed everything but he was just kind of done fishing. I loved being around him."

MacDonald's grandfather taught her how to fish. By then, he fished solely for food for the family. He had his favourite fishing spots throughout the Bay of Islands. Even though his catches were not what they once were, he didn't complain, says MacDonald. She would have been a young child, no more than seven, when he took her along in his orange and green dory—a dory he made himself—setting out from his backyard in Frenchman's Cove for the bay. The footprint of the dock and fishing stage are still there, though in rare use these days by her aunt and uncle, who live in the MacDonald house now. April remembers her grandfather's 1950s greaser-style hairstyle and blue-green plaid jacket. She remembers his perfect teeth, too—noteworthy given most people were not lucky enough to have such a smile, not having access to proper dental care. "He was hands down the most handsome man in Frenchman's Cove," says MacDonald. He taught her how to bait a hook and respect, of all things, the seagulls. "Seagulls saved so many sailors and fishermen from crashing on the rocks," says MacDonald. "They are like little lighthouses."

MacDonald remembers her grandfather giving her the guts left over from his fishing bait to feed the seagulls. She wonders out loud why the Atlantic puffin is the province's bird symbol when it's the seagulls that have served a more crucial role, even if just as company for generations of fishers. To many, the seagull is to Newfoundland what a pigeon is to most cities: a nuisance bird. But vouching for the seagull is MacDonald's royal right, as it were. Her grandfather used to say she was the Princess of Woods Island and would one day become Queen. It was his way of relaying the history of the Dominion of Newfoundland leaving the Queen of England to join Canada. Her grandfather's subtle lessons on history, be it Confederation, the fishery, or resettlement, are one of the things MacDonald loved most about spending time with him.

Historically, there were two resettlement programs in the province. Dr. Jeff A. Webb, professor in the Department of History at Memorial University and author of *Observing the Outports: Describing Newfoundland Culture, 1950-1980*, explained it this way to me: "The first program was intended more to save government resources and provide access to social skills and social services that just couldn't be provided to people on very remote islands. The second program was intended more as part of a package of making the fishery more modern and efficient." Predating the 1965 fisheries resettlement program was the 1954 provincially led Centralization Programme. Of the reported 1,200 outport communities at that time, nearly half had thirty or fewer families. Supplying health care, education, electricity, and transportation services for this sparse population would have amounted to economic suicide for Newfoundland and Labrador at the time. "The majority of the rural population accepted [then premier Joseph] Smallwood's promise that union with Canada would mean an end to poverty," writes George Withers, who earned his PhD working with Webb studying the topic of Newfoundland's resettlement programs. Moving out of the outports was part of Smallwood's promise of prosperity—evidenced by his call to fishers to burn their boats and flakes and alleging Newfoundland must develop or perish. The 1954 and 1965 resettlement programs assisted some communities in deciding for themselves and migrating without intervention, while others were relocated to a destination as determined by government decision.

During the first program, which ran from 1954 until the next program came into effect, Withers writes, "Many had been awakened to the benefits of industrial employment during World War II. Between 1945 and 1954 nearly 50 communities relocated voluntarily." He continues:

> In Newfoundland migrations have had a long history but rural to urban migrations have proceeded at a slower pace than in most Western states due to dependence on a staple resource. The construction of the railway, development of mines and paper mills along with military base construction drew people from coastal settlements. In the post-World War Two era the pace of migration speeded up when thousands left the shore fishery to build roads, hospitals, schools, as well as to work in the small-scale manufacturing industries established in the 1950s. For rural communities Confederation represented a chance to escape the poverty trap through a combination of wage labour and social welfare benefits that they were entitled to as Canadians.

Indeed, resettlement programs arrived as some Newfoundlanders were already leaving those outports that were floundering under the changing fishery. The inshore fishery had become "the occupation of last resort," writes Withers, and yet the dependence on the inshore fishery continued. "Even in the fisheries growth centres the fish processors needed the inshore fish to create full-time work and to maximize profits," writes Withers. "Fish plant managers realized that the inshore sector could produce a higher quality product at less cost than trawlers could supply."

Where the provincial Centralization Programme failed—it having only effectively relocated people from rural to urban centres—the federal-provincial Fisheries Household Resettlement Program offered a more fulsome attempt "to modernize and rationalize the fishery by moving people from small outports to growth poles," writes Withers. But, in part, it was the speed with which these changes happened that led many to worry it would unravel completely those elements of the province's culture that made it wholly distinct from the rest of Canada. Historian and former Memorial University president Leslie Harris asserted at the time the same changes that spanned decades in other parts of Canada were being crammed into years in Newfoundland.

"The Newfoundland government put money into the resettlement program a little like pouring gasoline onto a fire," says professor Jeff Webb. "So it caused something that had been happening naturally to happen much more quickly and with a greater degree of disruption." Without question, "[i]n Newfoundland, the word 'resettlement' evokes strong emotional sentiments decades after the program was abandoned," writes Withers. "Many people feel that a heartless government uprooted families and interrupted an idyllic lifestyle."

This wasn't entirely the case, as communities played an active role in the decision to be relocated. Communities were only resettled if a majority (80–90 per cent) of the population consented, Webb says, but questions arose such as who qualified to vote. The greatest issue, perhaps, was the sheer scale of the changes that followed a decision to resettle a community and the limited timeframe over which those changes occurred. "The failure was not in moving people out, it was the fact that the government lost control of the pace of moving," says Webb. Though he acknowledges that resettlement was an appropriate decision in most circumstances, he raises the point that there were many cases of inadequately prepared "receiving communities."

The late Dr. Parzival Copes, expert in fisheries economics and Order of Canada recipient, would have agreed. He argued resettlement failed to go far enough to encourage people to leave their rural communities, the fishery, and the province altogether. The greatest failure of resettlement, in his view, was a continued reliance on the fishery, specifically, *too many fishers catching too few fish*. Copes's views earned him quite the reputation— as Withers points out, "Memorial University's orator, Shane O'Dea, introduced Parzival Copes as the chief apologist for resettlement and the man who had tried to destroy Newfoundland's cultural soul."

If Parzival Copes tried to destroy the province's cultural soul, then perhaps April MacDonald is attempting to honour it. MacDonald tells me about another abandoned property on the Northern Peninsula in Hawke's Bay, which, together with Port au Choix, was designated a receiving community in the mid-1960s, with fishing as the main economic activity. Even here, where additional government funding targeted regional economic growth, MacDonald finds abandoned properties. A single-storey grey bungalow sits at sea level, sinking into stunted greenery in a losing battle with the elements. The weather doesn't grant vegetation much of a chance. Any trees that are standing tilt sideways, the branches lopsided as if permanently bracing against the wind. The weather and proximity to the ocean are responsible for the house's greyed wood siding too. There's no green or orange trim here.

Walking through most houses, MacDonald sees the same objects time and time again.

"They all have the same margarine tub, the same salt beef buckets, the same starburst clocks on the wall," says MacDonald. But this house was different. She was struck by its diamond-patterned curtains with their flash of orange, black, and grey, and the set of moose antlers atop a burgundy sofa cushion on the rotting wood floor. She couldn't make sense of the kitchen's orientation, facing the road instead of the water. As she sat in the living room, cautious of popping sofa springs, she spotted the view to the mouth of Torrent River.

"What could you see?" I ask.

"From that house, just the sea, just the sea. There was nothing else but sea," MacDonald responds, her voice trailing as if she's back in that place now.

"How did you happen upon it?" I ask.

"That one? Actually, I came across it while visiting another house," she says. "One of the greatest parts of doing this is that I get to see so many communities in this land. I don't just drive through; I get to stop and talk to people. It makes you fall in love with the province all over again."

Given her practice of allowing herself in (remember, she never breaks in, per se) abandoned homes, MacDonald said she's not always greeted with enthusiasm. It usually takes some quick referencing of her background to put people at ease. "I'll tell them my father's a fisherman, also my grandfather. Once they know who you are, who you came from, then they're more open to chatting."

She recalls the day she first came upon this home in Hawke's Bay. She was taking her time, snapping photos outside and planning her entry into the house. The front door was locked and the road-facing windows were boarded up. A man across the street headed in her direction and stared her down from across the road. She remembers he was "kind of gruff," his feathers clearly ruffled by her presence.

What are you doing here? he asked.

Oh, I'm just taking photos.

Who do you work for?

For the photos? I just take them because I like taking them.

Oh, I thought you worked for the government.

No sir, I don't.

The man was relieved and crossed the road to chat with MacDonald. He told her the government had deemed the property a hazardous and unsafe site and wanted to tear it down. Opposed to that, he was happy to share what he knew about the family who had once lived there. They had been gone some thirty or so years. A couple with their young daughter. *When it all dried up, they hauled off and left,* said the man, referring to the cod collapse. MacDonald distinctly remembers the phrasing because it offered such rich imagery, of fishers hauling up their gear and storming out of town. It's how MacDonald remembers the years leading up to the cod moratorium. "I feel like the dates are messed up in my head because they had the moratorium, but there was no fish before then. So the moratorium, in my mind, started way before. When you're dependent on fish for food and then there's no fish…I remember things not being well when I was a kid. I remember my grandfather not catching as much fish as he used to. That was it. As far as I knew, life in this place was over."

One of the most devastating blows of MacDonald's childhood was her grandfather's passing. Edward MacDonald died on Canada Day 1990 in long-term care, two years to the day before the cod moratorium. A few years earlier, when MacDonald was twelve, a stroke had left her grandfather unable to speak. He never returned home after that. "I remember him having the stroke because he was fine and then he wasn't," MacDonald says. That day, the family was all together playing cards; they were happy, partying, she says. The next thing she remembers is her mother being upset, crying. Her grandfather couldn't speak. He was trying, but nothing was coming out, she says. The severity of the stroke left Edward MacDonald unable to communicate. It also meant he needed indefinite institutional care. A lifetime at sea no longer able to be

Fishing stages dot the coast in Twillingate, Newfoundland, 2018.

spoken aloud, shared, passed on—it sounded to me like a moratorium of its own. For April MacDonald, by the time the cod moratorium began, the connection to her past was already fading. And it had been fading for some time, just like my own family's ties to the fishery.

During the early moratorium months and years, MacDonald remembers finding comfort in watching stories of the event on the supper-hour news with her family. She also remembers the song "She's Gone, Boys, She's Gone" by Newfoundland and Labrador singer-songwriter Wayne Bartlett. The song tells the story of the impending moratorium and the people it threatened to leave behind. For MacDonald, that song relayed what she couldn't yet put into her own words.

"I'm lucky because I can still fish and I still get to lead a life that is still very much connected to the sea," says April MacDonald. Her parents live in Summerside, where her father, Reginald, works as a fisher. While she doesn't get out in the dory with her father as much as she'd like, she does from time to time. One of those times recently became local news. "Those bigger lobsters don't seem to have as much get up and on the go in the morning as the younger ones—something like myself right now," Reg, as he's known, said to a CBC reporter in the summer of 2018. HE'S NOT SHELLFISH: N.L. FISHERMAN GETS CATCH OF LIFETIME, AND LETS IT GO read the accompanying headline. Reg had caught a lobster estimated to be between 75 and 125 years old. At granddaughter Emma's suggestion, Reg agreed to release the lobster back into the bay. April joined her father in the dory that day to commemorate the occasion, snapping the photo of her father and the lobster that would appear in the news story. It was a fitting tribute marking the anniversary of her grandfather's passing and the fishing tradition Reg MacDonald carries on a quarter of a century after the moratorium, too.

Back in Frenchman's Cove, after we've finished touring the buzzing abandoned property, MacDonald suggests we have tea at her Nan's place. It's her aunt and uncle's place now, but for MacDonald it will always be *Nan's*. The drive here is a series of sharp turns with narrow and steep sections passing hillside houses, cliffs, greenery, and creeks. *Stormrunner*, *Gulf leader*, *Glyndon Joan*, and *Miss Lee* are some of the longliners and fishing vessels docked alongside the fishing stages here. Laying upside down on a platform are a few dories, freshly painted and waiting to be flipped right side up and re-launched into the water, as has been the way around here for generations. More than a hundred years ago, a small-boat inshore fishery was the economic mainstay of the area, as fishers went to work on schooners operating from Grand Bank.

"I wonder if I'll be alive long enough to explore my childhood community as an abandoned village?" MacDonald ponders. "There's no community anymore. All the kids are gone. Now when I drive here, there's people in their fifties and sixties. Most of them still work at the fish plant or they're retired." MacDonald tells me she has two childhood communities—the one in Summerside, where her parents still live, and here, in Frenchman's Cove, where she spent time with her grandparents. Both fit her description. Meanwhile, the fish plant she's referencing is the one in Curling, which is now part of the greater Corner Brook area. The plant is owned by the Barry Group and is the same one where MacDonald's mother and paternal grandmother worked.

We pull into the driveway at *Nan's place* and show ourselves in the front door (actually, a side door, but it's the only door). It's a narrow single-storey with all the rooms located off one main hallway. It's a cozy home with childhood photographs and decals on the wall that say things like "Dance like no one is watching." We head to the kitchen, where MacDonald helps herself to the milk and teabags. She plugs the electric kettle in and grabs the teacups. On the kitchen table, there are rolled cigarettes, making us nostalgic for the past (who doesn't remember trying to roll an aunt or uncle's cigarette and getting it horribly wrong and then never being allowed to do it again?). That's when I spot Woods Island out the kitchen window, a straight shot to the middle of the bay. Every morning when

MacDonald's grandparents prepared their morning tea, they could look out this window and see their home away from home.

We set down our tea, making our way outside to the backyard. There, the air is calm, seagulls are calling, and the water gently laps the beach. There's a glare from the sun off the bay. Save for a pair of white cats pressed up against the screen of a neighbour's back window and a wandering, limping white dog, the only souls besides us here today are out in the bay. Some forty feet out, a minke whale, a solitary and usually elusive creature, surfaces. Based on his antics, we've decided it's a male. "He's showing off big time," MacDonald says. "There's his dorsal fin." This whale will interrupt our conversation another half-dozen times over the next fifteen minutes with his surfacing, but we don't mind. We're enjoying the show. "Wherever that seagull is, he'll pop up there," MacDonald wagers, pointing out the seagull I'd heard earlier. "He's having a grand ol' time," I offer, enjoying the fact that we're whale-watching from the backyard. Out here in the bay, the ocean floor drops off quickly, so whales of all kinds are a common sight. My ears follow the common sound of an outboard motor before my eyes spot another familiar sight: a small boat in the middle of the bay. A group of four are headed to Woods Island.

Macdonald's grandfather would set out fishing from this backyard; remnants of his fishing stage are still intact, but the wharf is gone. "That's where he'd clean, salt, and dry the cod," MacDonald tells me, pointing to a plank-wood landing. "And over there is the shed [where] he would keep the seal," she says. She tries the lock to see if it's open, but no such luck. "Sheds are locked, houses aren't," MacDonald says. Her words perfectly encapsulate this place. The shed holds fishing supplies and other valuable gear, so MacDonald's uncle keeps it under lock and key.

I admire a couple of homemade wood smokers, mostly used for smoked capelin, MacDonald says. The smokers have a compartment for a heat source—likely a pot filled with hot coals—then compartments to lay the capelin to smoke for a couple of hours. There are dozens of things I would have taken for junk, now repurposed. An old washer or dryer drum serves as a firepit, a half-dozen salt-meat buckets are pots for seedlings, and a dumbbell serves as an anchoring weight for a crab pot. The wood from these old wooden lobster pots will surely be put to good use if they can't be repaired first. I gather that's the same thinking behind a stack of various abandoned bits and pieces: banisters, a door, and other scrap wood along with plastic buckets and milk crates at the ready for reincarnation. But there's trash, too: a hairbrush, a tire, and rusted metal have come to die here in plain sight, their lives as useful objects lost. There's a dryer sitting out front across the street, too, but I presume that will be picked up and brought to the local dump.

"That's new," MacDonald says pointing to the bright red Fisheries and Oceans "Contaminated Fisheries Closure" sign, which indicates "Bivalve molluscs—scallop, mussel, clam" are "not safe for use as food." It's likely due to the sewage runoff here, and from neighbouring Corner Brook and Curling. That's when Mr. Minke surfaces another time. For all of the talk of smoked fish and foul smells, I'm surprised to not smell much of anything. "You don't really smell the ocean here," I say, puzzled. "You've lived here too long," MacDonald replies. I take the comment as a mark of pride, now having lived away from Newfoundland nearly as long as I've lived there.

Back at home later, I'm scanning MacDonald's photography. Her work is steeped in a nostalgia for a rural life that continues to inspire artists and aesthetes alike. It creates a draw for tourists, too, says Professor Jeff Webb, reminded of a recent trip to Fogo Island. "Tourists don't go there for the weather," he says. "They don't go there for the theme-park kind of Disney excitement. They go there because they want to immerse themselves in a community which has an old cultural tradition that the people there maintain."

Communities and their traditions are often the focus of the Government of Newfoundland and Labrador's tourism campaigns. Each slick cinematic advertisement features its own shock of colours and marvellous sounds. The visuals appear produced within an inch of the filmmakers' lives—footage that is practically perfect in every way. Often the viewer will see saltbox houses sitting precariously on burnt-orange seaside cliffs as blonde and redheaded children run wildly in their Sunday best through green grasses. Here, vibrant fishing communities teem with quiet, down-home activities. Clothing dries on a line as a man takes his dog for a stroll. A schooner passes in front of the harbour as a puffin flies silently overhead, an active port in the background. A pair of feet dangle from a dory, calmly bobbing on the endless ocean backdrop. Wooden fishing floats suspended from a wired fence dance in the wind. A humpback whale surfaces, making its distinctive blow. And a luminescent white iceberg creaks and groans in the bay. Without question, that style of marketing is drawing tourists. Newfoundland and

Labrador Tourism reports that this seasonal tourism boom has doubled the province's population every year since 2010—coincidentally, the year after the province launched its award-winning "Find Yourself" campaign. According to a recent NL Tourism survey, to "understand perceptions of Newfoundland and Labrador," is among the top reasons people visit.

The communities MacDonald focuses on offer a different visual altogether, but there's evidence they are drawing in tourists just the same. Google "abandoned Newfoundland," and one of the top hits is for a 2011 article in *The Independent*, an independent online newspaper based out of St. John's. "In the large scheme of the world, our island and our chunk of mainland are still quite 'new,'" begins the article. "But, regrettably, much of Newfoundland and Labrador has been not only found, but already lost." The article links to an interactive map displaying the towns and outports that were "founded and later deserted in our short 500 years of history." Among the abandoned towns are ones with laugh-out-loud names like Nimrod and Spread Eagle. Then, there are places that sound like they ought to be avoided, like Muddy Hole and Burnt Island. And there are welcoming ones such as Safe Harbour and Gin Cove.

The Maritime History Archive at Memorial University in St. John's has estimated that some 307 communities were abandoned between 1946 and 1975, and over 28,000 people relocated. But history professor Jeff Webb says determining the magnitude of resettlement is anyone's guess. The numbers don't come from a single source, for starters, says Webb. People were leaving outport communities on their own prior to the introduction of formal resettlement or relocation programs. Had the government not sponsored the resettlement program, many communities would likely have disappeared on their own. Comparisons between the 1911 and 1921 and the 1935 and 1945 censuses show there were already communities disappearing. Then there are the countless outports that may not even register to some as a community at all.

"To start with, what constitutes a community?" says Webb. "In some instances, it's just a very small number of families and they're moving from one place to another place only a few miles away. In other instances, there are communities that might have several dozen families that are being moved. I can't quote a number of individuals or a number of communities confidently."

Whatever the number, the legacy of resettlement is unquestionably broad. "There is a lot of nostalgia and romanticizing of rural life among people that grew up in this province, particularly people whose young childhood, in many cases, was in a remote location but then they later moved to a bigger town," says Webb. "For many of those people, they drew on the stories, songs, and imagery they remember when they were young and from the stories that have been passed on by parents, aunts and uncles, and other family members. That's been a source of inspiration and a source of raw material for many people." For some, it's not enough to be inspired by those memories; they need and continue to return to where they or their ancestors once lived, like MacDonald. "I know it is not unusual for many families to have semi-regular or regular reunions each year in the places their families came from," says Webb. "It's also not unusual for people to have gone back to the communities they came from and build summer camps. In some instances, the [resettled] community has been recreated as a summertime leisure site rather than a year-round economically productive community."

Newfoundlanders and Labradorians often talk about resettlement as if it's unique to our context, but moving people from rural to urban areas has been going on for at least a couple of hundred years all over the world. In 1971 the Province struck a new Resettlement Agreement between then federal Department of Regional Economic Expansion and Newfoundland's then Department of Community and Social Development. Today, any community—be it a municipality, local service district, and/or unincorporated area—may initiate the process by first gauging "the level of community support for relocation by undertaking an Expression of Interest by submitting ballots to the Department of Municipal Affairs and Environment for consideration." With community support formally indicated, the Department of Municipal Affairs and Environment may then formalize what is titled the Community Relocation policy. This relocation then prompts financial assistance to those who are eligible (residential and commercial property owners as well as permanent residents) and withdraws all community services (garbage collection, water and sewer, street lighting and road maintenance, ferry service, school services, health services, and hydro/electricity). Residents retain title to their land and properties, and those who wish to remain in the community must do so without government services.

With recent government-sponsored relocation examples such as Williams Harbour and Little Bay Islands, I wanted to know if reloca-tion yields savings for the province. Media reports indicate eligible homeowners in both communities received or will be eligible for up to

$270,000 per household to move. Further, the Williams Harbour resettlement reportedly cost the province $4 million. A media representative for Newfoundland and Labrador's Department of Municipal Affairs and Environment, the department responsible for the province's Community Relocation policy, said it takes twenty years to generate savings from any single community resettlement. The magnitude of those savings—and the cost-benefit analysis that produced them—were not available, despite repeated commitments from the department's media rep to provide them to me. They did, however, offer this piece of unhelpful information via email: "Once a community is relocated, the Department of Municipal Affairs and Environment has no further need to track government expenditures related to the community." A CBC News story about the planned Little Bay Islands resettlement indicates the department quoted a projected $20 million savings over twenty years. Given that relocation withdraws all municipal and provincial services from each relocated community, it's reasonable to assume costs to the province are contained at the least.

For MacDonald, it's not about the economics.

"You are very delicate the way you walk through the house," I observed out loud as we drove off together in MacDonald's Jeep, leaving behind the abandoned property on the south shore of the Bay of Islands.

"None of this is mine," she offered by way of explanation. "You've seen Frenchman's Cove; it may not have much longer. One day someone may be going through my grandparent's stuff and I hope they treat it the same way." Still, she acknowledges, "When people haul up and leave they usually don't come back." But MacDonald will be back here again in a few weeks' time, camera in hand, ready to do some tidy-up to the abandoned property we've just visited. Fall and spring are her preferred seasons for photography, allowing a profile of two views: one when everything is dying or already dead; the other when things are coming back to life. Her photos may point to lives past, but there's life in them just the same.

CHAPTER 8:
Nor'easter Nights

The community of Quirpon (a name rhyming with harpoon) is the most northerly sheltered fishing village in Newfoundland. This far north, the earth is a combination of rock and muskeg, spongy moss and marshlands. The roads here echo the nooks and crannies of tiny coves and beaches. As the coastline dips and bobs, so too do drivers and passengers. Driving can be an upset stomach waiting to happen. Fortunately, the air is brisk and fresh, a reprieve from nausea so long as you can manage a short gasp out the window before the wind gusts steal your breath away. Summer is the brief period interrupting the more severe winds of winter that bring ice and snow. The snow banks can strand people in their homes or trap children in their schools. As a result, there's an accepted isolation here, far away from St. John's—and everything else, too.

As spring comes, new visitors arrive. Some of the earliest are the polar bears. Like the weather, they too can seclude people indoors, but not before the locals snap a photo from the safety of their vehicles. The novelty of a polar bear coming to town, having arrived on the drift ice along the coast known as Iceberg Alley, never gets old. It speaks to the remoteness of this place too. *Who thinks they'll happen upon a polar bear outside of Canada's far north?* The ice is what attracts many of the human visitors here as well. In July, this place is your best bet for spotting an iceberg in Newfoundland and Labrador. But the price you pay for seeing icebergs this time of year are cool winds, damp conditions, and temperatures a few degrees lower than elsewhere on the island.

In July, when I visited with my sister and our young children, we added layers of clothing as we drove the six or so hours north from Corner Brook through Gros Morne National Park to Quirpon. *Are we there yet?* my six-year-old nephew, Ross, asked predictably within fifteen minutes of departure, and every thirty minutes thereafter. My sister Angie and I laughed it off for hours before we started asking each other the same question, taking turns in the driver's seat. The trip took us from the sunshine and lush forests and along the Humber River, past the Tablelands where the earth's mantle, once below the ocean, is visible along the horizon as an amber landscape. Standing bold and barren between evergreen hills, the Tablelands mark an ancient collision of North America and Africa. The force of that collision squeezed the ocean floor until it rose up as mountains on earth. Near here, you can stop and see a 500-million-year-old fossil of a trilobite, an extinct marine arthropod vaguely resembling a horseshoe crab. We zipped on by the fossil, knowing the kids wouldn't take kindly to stopping to see some old rock in a place filled with old rocks. "They aren't as old as the big bang, but they did hear the echo," reads a clever note referring to the rocks on the Newfoundland and Labrador Tourism website. It was one of my last searches as my cellphone lost its steady signal.

Farther along the drive is the glacier-carved Western Brook Pond fjord and its surrounding cliffs and mountains. Mantle-turned-mountains and fossilized creatures are indisputable reminders of Mother Nature's presence here. The Gulf of St. Lawrence lapping the jagged and raw shoreline offers further proof, clues of the effects of plate tectonics and ice floes. At some point, the land gives way to an incessant sea spray and wind, revealed first by the manner in which the trees grow. Abundant evergreens become stunted, forced to cling to the coast in their gnarly and stubborn way. They are called *tuckamore* trees and, though often mistaken for dead, are what hanging on for dear life looks like. No longer in the protection of sheltered forests and mountains, this coastal landscape seems almost impenetrable to any life form, even in July. The muskeg appears to be the only vegetation in parts, but lying low (when in season) are wild berries like bakeapples (also known as cloudberries), partridgeberries, blueberries, crowberries, and squashberries.

Eager to make good time with restless kids in the backseat, we pass little communities with their dashes of coloured boxes butting up against fishing stages, falling down shacks and structures, and the occasional church or lighthouse. Dashes become blurs as the rain starts, gentle at first, then hard and fast. The wipers can't keep up. I'm having a time avoiding the puddles in the thick grooves of the highway, too, all the while keeping a lookout for oncoming traffic on this single-lane highway. The odd convenience store and gas station pops up, and we load up on candies and baked goods, besides the obvious pitstop needs. We point at unique sights as we continue on our way, chomping on marshmallow candy strawberries and bananas, which, for my sister and I, tastes like our youth. There are lobster pots packed neatly on beaches, a tribute to the recent end of this year's lobster fishing season. It's also a reminder that lobster continues to do well as other shellfish and groundfish are declining. I have a strong feeling no one in my present company is thinking about that, but it's become my preoccupation.

Before long, our drive takes us away from the coast and back into the shelter of forest. We spot roadside gardens, wood piles, and intermittent signs offering fresh, seasonal produce. Root vegetables and lettuces flourish in these soils, covered by the forest. Such inland gardens could never make it near people's outport homes, pitched on the side of a cliff, exposed to the elements. Likewise, folks chop their firewood for the season and leave it to dry on the gravel pits alongside the Trans-Canada Highway. People employ the honour system here—no one bothers with anyone else's vegetables or firewood.

It's that kind of inherent small-town trust that allows people to leave their doors unlocked, too; some even leave them wide open, and they may as well. In communities like our destination of Quirpon, everyone knows what's going on in town simply by looking out their living-room windows and front doors. And that's what people do here, particularly the older folks, bound to their houses by their age rather than the weather or wildlife. Today, some are likely watching us arrive among the wave of summertime tourists.

Last year, the Viking settlement nearby, L'Anse Aux Meadows, had more than 37,000 new visitors. To put that in perspective, that's 165 times the local population (which is 224 based on the last [2016] census, which shows a 20 percent decline since the previous census). This census region covers the area between Quirpon (which has about 77 people) and L'Anse Aux Meadows, a World UNESCO Heritage Site, where Norse sailors, better known as Vikings, set up an encampment some thousand years ago. It's the only known Viking settlement in North America and was settled upon as part of the Icelandic explorer's Leif Erikson's pursuit of Vinland, the Vikings' name for coastal North America. When the Vikings first arrived, the ancestors of the Beothuk, the earliest Indigenous populations in the area, were already here. Rather than pay them respect, the Norse referred to the Indigenous people as *skrælingjar*, meaning barbarians. The Vikings would eventually abandon their camp for reasons that remain unclear. Centuries later, European exploration forced the Beothuk people inland, pushing them away from their traditional food sources such as seal, sea porpoises, and seabirds like gannets. The Beothuk are said to have starved and succumbed to disease as a result. Some historians believe French explorer Jacques Cartier met Indigenous people on Quirpon Island, amicably trading goods while he and his crew were stranded due to weather for two weeks in May–June 1534, before continuing on their course to the Gulf of St. Lawrence. While it's possible there were some peaceful relations, there were most certainly hostile and deadly ones—and those atrocities against Indigenous peoples would continue as settlers, like my own ancestors, colonized the land, laying claim to what was never ours to take.

We've arrived at the wharf in Quirpon, a place steeped in history. There was a fish plant across the way on Nobles Island, which is smack dab in the middle of Quirpon and Quirpon Island. All that remains of the plant are the wooden beams of its foundation, easily missed if not pointed out. There's also a smaller island, Salt Island, which gets its name from housing the salt that fishers used to salt their cod. All of these places are unmarked, but they don't go unnoticed, at least not by me.

My sister and I unload our kids from the car and begin adding more layers to our layers. We had already replaced our sandals, shorts, and T-shirts with sneakers, pants, and sweaters, but now we're layering on waterproof jackets, hats, mittens, and scarves. We are getting ready to set out by Zodiac to Quirpon Island, just across the harbour. I hold my daughter, now seven months old, close to my chest as the Zodiac bounces on the choppy Atlantic, the cold drizzle and salty spray stinging my face. I don't have enough hands to adjust my scarf for more protection but am grateful Navya is easily lulled to sleep by the sounds of the motor and the warmth of my arms. The entire ride is about thirty minutes before the Zodiac drops us at the foot of a narrow cliffside dock and stairs at the bottom of a hill on Cape Bauld. On the top of the hill is a century-old lightkeeper's residence—a main house and smaller one—which is where we'll spend the next two evenings.

"Well, we're here now," I say to my sister, who looks downright offended by the accommodations. The five of us are cramped into a

Visiting Quirpon Lighthouse Inn, me holding Navya Verma (left), my sister Angelina Thornhill (right) and niece Lauren Gunson and nephew Ross Gunson in background, Quirpon Island, Newfoundland, 2018.

second-floor room with low, gabled ceilings and barely enough space for two queen beds with a small nightstand squeezed in between. The room is surprisingly warm and humid, likely due to the nearby bathroom which has no window or fan. I put my daughter on the bed, admiring its handmade quilt, with leftover fabric stitched back to life in an indecisive array of colours and fabric. The only pattern is no pattern at all. Extra quilts are folded on the chest of drawers.

I'm grateful Angie and the kids have come along for this adventure. We can feel the remoteness and potential perils of this place, ruggedly beautiful as it is. The view through the hazy window is a land of mustard, rust, chartreuse, and sage. It's magical, but if you start walking in any direction, you're liable to fall off the edge of a cliff. The terrain cuts abruptly to charcoal-hued rock, wet and jagged from the blue lapis waters breaking into white caps here, there, and everywhere. We are surrounded.

The lighthouse, still in operation, is undergoing major repairs too— it's a plywood-covered eyesore, but I'm glad to see it's getting the attention it deserves. Repairs are also underway to the main house from when a polar bear attempted to break in this past spring. If we thought cell service was shoddy before, it's worse now. I find one corner of our bedroom where, by luck, my phone shows one bar of service.

I don't tell my sister this island is shrouded in myth and mystery. Telling her would be like rubbing salt in the wound. In 1508 Quirpon Island first appears on the map as the *Isle of Demons*. It was believed there were wild animals, monsters, and other demons residing here who sought to torment passing ships and vessels, especially if they were foolish enough to cross the island. A popularly told story is the one of a French noblewoman, Marguerite de La Rocque, who was marooned here in the mid-sixteenth century. She allegedly had an affair with an officer aboard her ship, en route to New France (what is now Quebec). Marguerite's uncle, the Lieutenant-Governor of New France, disapproved of this newly formed relationship and in turn abandoned his niece, her lover, and maid servant on this island. The lover and maid servant eventually died, as would a child Marguerite supposedly conceived and gave birth to while stranded. Meanwhile, Marguerite not only survived the ordeal, but later returned to her native France thanks to a rescue off the island by Basque fishermen.

Migratory fishers frequented Quirpon Harbour in the early to mid-1500s. As centuries passed, seasonal settlements by the Portuguese, French, and English gave way to year-round settlements established by the English, who claimed the land as their own. Just by the wharf, where we boarded the Zodiac, is the oldest house in the area, known locally as Uncle Bill Pynn's House, nestled in the aptly named Pynn's Cove. Built in 1892 by William Henry Pynn and Henry Bartlett, the house was constructed on the site of another house built by Pynn's grandfather, Henry Pynn, the first known Englishman to settle in Quirpon, in 1820. There once was an accompanying fishing stage and wharf with fish flakes and other buildings, all part of the Pynn family's fishing enterprise (at one point they had nine cod traps and four fishing crews). The property housed many visitors, from fishing crews—who stayed in a nearby bunkhouse, also now gone—to the Cape Bauld lighthouse keeper and his family, who overnighted during inclement weather when stranded from returning to Quirpon Island, to passerby passengers aboard coastal vessels. Quirpon's first telephone and post office were housed here, too. Behind the house is a working outdoor French (bread) oven. There are remnants of ovens like this throughout this area, artefacts of the French settlements.

The Heritage Newfoundland and Labrador website describes the Pynn house as a "well-preserved example of 19th century vernacular architecture," but from my view it looks derelict. Its high-pitched roof is one of its architectural giveaways, but the period beauty is otherwise difficult to appreciate past its aging facade: broken windows, crooked clapboard, and wounded roof. Over the house's left shoulder is a flagstaff waving the Newfoundland and Labrador flag. It was from this vantage that Uncle Bill would signal to ships in harbour, waving his own coloured flags. In 2001 the property was granted Registered Heritage Structure status (reserved for its footprint only) by the Heritage Foundation of

Known locally as Uncle Bill Pynn's House, now a registered heritage structure, nestled in the aptly named Pynn's Cove, Quirpon, Newfoundland, 2018.

Newfoundland and Labrador, but little has happened to preserve that status, or the home. There's not even a sign recognizing its significance.

At one point, Quirpon was a natural waypoint for fishing schooners travelling to Battle Harbour, Labrador, which Newfoundland and Labrador Tourism cites as both the one-time salt fish capital of the world and as unofficial capital of Labrador. Located on a small island in the Labrador Sea, this historic fishing village has been preserved by a non-profit organization, the Battle Harbour Historic Trust, earning the community National Historic District status. While there are no permanent residents in Battle Harbour (government relocation programs in the late 1960s and early 1970s resettled the residents), many people keep summer homes here and there are accommodations for visitors as well.

Back on Quirpon Island, there's nothing that speaks to the community's history. During the Second World War, the US military had an overseas Radar Unit (No. 30 RU) on Cape Bauld. It was considered an overseas detachment because Newfoundland was a British colony at the time. True to the island's storied past, military officials were sometimes sent here as a form of punishment. Bill Lloyd, an airforce meteorologist, is one such case. He was banished to No. 30 RU, which was considered "one of the more severely isolated stations," for a minor infraction—technically, for riding his bicycle while carrying his rifle, but more likely for inadvertently knocking into a higher-ranking official while doing it.

"I had no idea where Cape Bauld was," says Lloyd in a 1989 interview published in *Canadian Military Biography*. "For eighteen months I had been plotting weather information on maps and I knew the location of every Weather Station on the North American continent. Cape Bauld was not one of them." Getting there proved even more challenging. A flight to Gander, then a ride aboard the "Newfie Bullet," the railway of that time (having earned its cheeky nickname for its slow commute) to Botwood, then a boat ride to Cape Bauld. "Sighting our first iceberg was exciting for most of us but they were to become routine in the days to come," says Lloyd in the same interview. The excitement would fade as Lloyd and his stationed officers sized up their accommodations. "Our first glimpse of the station, our new home, was unnerving to say the least. Not a tree in sight. Mostly low bushes and moss growing on rocks and boulders of all shapes and sizes."

Unnerving is a good word for it. I keep all of this history—from the stranded French damsel to the American military man and all the rest—to myself, certain my sister and the kids, as ever, will adjust to their surroundings and make the best of our time here. Then, the best arrives. From our front porch, we can see and hear humpback whales. The water turns cerulean as each whale nears the surface, then takes its unmistakable puff of air, a mist of water visible even in this misty weather. As they dive, their tails create a circle that ripples outward until it disappears in the waves. We spot a few icebergs too. Later, on the Zodiac to and from Quirpon, we get up close and personal with the humpbacks, dolphins, and icebergs. One night, we spot a fishing boat netting capelin in the harbour below the lightkeeper's house. Seagulls are passing overhead and humpbacks surface at a safe distance. Over the hill, an iceberg makes its way due south. I try to imagine a scene more quintessentially Newfoundland than this, but I can't think of one. The annual *capelin roll*, as it's called when schools of capelin roll into shore to spawn, signals more good things to come. For starters, it marks what many consider the true beginning of summertime. It also draws in whales like humpbacks for a feast. Groundfish like cod feed on capelin too. So, when capelin flourish, so can cod.

I imagine all of the people who stood here and drew this connection, appreciative of the land and sea's bounty. Cod fishing, in particular, transcends time and culture. Bill Lloyd recalls it as a highlight during his time stationed here:

As fishing was a way of life in that area, a few of us naturally had to try it. We had the use of the station landing scow and an outboard motor so we scrounged some line and hooks from local fishermen and off we went to the cod "Jiggin" grounds. When we reached a spot about half a mile from shore where the locals said we should fish, Sgt. McCutcheon killed the motor and we all lowered our lines until we felt bottom then pulled back about a fathom (approximately six feet) and sat cross legged or lay flat on our stomachs and proceeded to "Jig" for cod (pull the line up and down slowly). A sudden resistance meant you had hooked something and you simply pulled the line in hand over hand and brought the fish on board. Our catch was good and we fished and shot the bull contentedly until we felt a sudden bump and turned to find we had drifted into an iceberg which was grounded. It towered up and over us and seemed to fill the whole sky. It didn't take much coaxing to get McCutcheon to start the motor and get us out of there. Our catch was enjoyed by the whole camp at supper that day.

We see small-boat fishers enjoying the same outport luxuries, likely on the same fishing grounds Lloyd describes. Fisheries and Oceans Canada (DFO) has allowed an inshore commercial and recreational fishery for northern cod here and other parts of the province since 2006. Since 2016, in the stewardship fishery (as the commercial cod fishery is now called), each licensed fisher or harvester is allowed weekly landing limits, during set weeks over the summer and fall months. For example, in 2018, harvesters were collectively allowed to harvest up to 9,500 tonnes (t), which is a 25 percent reduction over last year's total allowable catch (TAC) limits. They cannot harvest their catch in one or two trips, but must distribute it over the season, reporting their catch to DFO, which subsequently adjusts the following weeks' catch quotas and season dates, in accordance with the TAC. Meanwhile, the recreational fishery is open to everyone, tourists included, allowing a maximum of five fish per day per person or a boat limited of fifteen fish per day only over the set weekend dates, also over a summer and fall season.

Although the stewardship and recreational cod fishery allows a modest harvest, people here are happy there's a fishery at all. When the cod fishery collapsed, Quirpon was hit hard. Singer-songwriter Wayne Bartlett, born and raised in Quirpon, wrote the 1992 song "She's Gone, Boys, She's Gone," marking the end of the cod fishery before it had even been announced. That song would put Bartlett on a national stage, helping to relay the emotion many Newfoundlanders felt but couldn't articulate themselves. As a result, the song would become the unofficial anthem of the cod moratorium.

It's likely there are hundreds of songs influenced by the cod motarorium. Research by American folklorist Peter Narváez, an Honorary Research Professor in the Department of Folklore at Memorial University of Newfoundland, shows that by 1995 there were at least twenty-seven well-known songs on record. Among these are Wayne Bartlett's "She's Gone, Boys, She's Gone" (1992); Great Big Sea's "Fisherman's Lament" (1993); Bobby Evans's "Jig One on the Sly" (1994); and Fred Lee's "We all Knew 'twas Comin'" (1994). "She's Gone, Boys, She's Gone" was among the most popular and remains so. It was featured on episodes of CBC's *Land and Sea* and docu-series *Witness*. Over the last ten years, the song has garnered nearly 330,000 YouTube views. "Fisherman's Lament" by Great Big Sea is another popular one. It was on the band's debut album in 1993, reaching gold status with sales of over forty thousand. That song takes more of a political stance, as much moratorium music and art does, talking about "brave Newfoundlanders" having their lives taken away by "some government bastard."

The effects of the moratorium on arts and culture are vast with songs, plays, novels, films, artwork, and more, attempting to capture the four-hundred-year-old fishery tradition snuffed out in that moment, July 2, 1992. But creating art about the fishery extends beyond its demise to the early days of the cod fishery. One can trace the region's rich culture based on cod as far back as the sixteenth century, when fishers visited for the annual cod harvest. When people in small fishing communities had little to no disposable income, they had to make everything for themselves, from clothing, furniture, housewares, tools, and, above all, the buildings, boats, and churches in which they lived, worked, and worshipped. These kinds of physical objects mark the region's sense of place, its culture and history, as it emerged as a fishing colony.

It's why when I look at Uncle Bill Pynn's House, I want more to become of it. I want Newfoundlanders and Labradorians to refuse to let this piece of rich history vanish. What are we without our history? What will we become?

The main reason I've come to Quirpon is to sit down with local musician and writer Wayne Bartlett to discuss exactly this. In addition to learning about his music and the northern fishing village that inspired it, I've come to learn how his community has changed.

"How do anybody see their hometown change?" Bartlett says, self-reflectively, "There's always changes no matter whether it's fishery-based or whether you're working in a coal mine. Things change. But it didn't when I was a boy. Everything was pretty busy around here. There was lots of fishing and no money. But then when it changed in the eighties and nineties, there was no fish and there was still no money. That was a big difference."

Bartlett lives across the harbour in Quirpon, which, given my transportation restrictions from Quirpon Island, may as well be on the other side of the country. On top of that, the unreliable tele-communication coverage has made arranging plans by email or telephone annoying at best and impossible at worst. In my attempt to finalize plans with Bartlett, I ignore the most sensible option of all—knocking on his front door—before I boarded the Zodiac. His bed and breakfast, The Big Blow, with its red siding and white trim, is one of the first sites visible from the Trans-Canada Highway turnoff. It cannot be missed en route to the main wharf, not only because of its location, but predominantly because it's the newest structure here—bright, shiny, and new, overlooking the bay. When I finally do knock on Bartlett's door, two days after arriving to Quirpon Island, I've demonstrated my ignorance.

Bartlett's partner, Cheryl McCarron, greets me at the door of the B&B. She invites me in, as I wave goodbye to Angie, who takes the kids to the nearby Viking village. McCarron offers me a coffee as we await Bartlett. She tidies the kitchen and I make myself comfortable at a kitchen table, overlooking Quirpon Harbour and the island. I pick up the Newfoundland dictionary—a familiar sight to anyone from here, and a conversation starter for locals and visitors alike—beside the table.

"Wayne bought me that so I could talk proper English," McCarron says warmly. She grew up in Nova Scotia and later owned and operated an independent bookstore in Toronto before selling her business and moving to this part of Newfoundland. She had no family connections here but felt a connection to the land and sea just the same. She opened a coffee shop in a small cove near L'Anse Aux Meadows and met Bartlett

View from behind The Big Blow B&B overlooking the Roberts family home and fishing premises, Quirpon, Newfoundland, 2018.

through mutual friends. He was newly back to Quirpon too, with plans to build The Big Blow. Over the years, Bartlett had driven a tractor-trailer, worked in a coal mine, taken up welding and taught it at a trade school, opened his first B&B, and more. There was one season he even took a go at fishing, having built himself a boat to get started, but abandoning it after one year ("Fishing wasn't for me," he says), then went back to driving tractor-trailer. Truck-driving would eventually take him to western Canada, like so many Newfoundlanders and Labradorians, but Quirpon called him back home. When he did return, he worked on this new B&B, knocking down the family home where his father and mother had lived and died. This time, he would build a bigger and better B&B, offering visitors a luxurious accommodation in this most unexpected of places. The constant in his life, during all of that time, was his songwriting and music. The man is an established singer-songwriter with seven albums under his belt. He's also a writer, with a three-part non-fiction book series profiling the people, place, and history where he grew up, and a novel based on the same premise. (The non-fiction series is called, "Grandpa, tell me a story" and was published by League Rock Publishing, the first in the series released in 1996, while the novel, *Louder than the sea*, was published by Cormorant Books in 2003.)

McCarron hands me a recent photo album Bartlett put together. It's called "According to Dad" and the cover features a young Wayne Bartlett climbing a chair next to his father, who is smoking a pipe and holding a guitar. I flip through the pages. On one, Wayne's birth name and date is listed: "Wayne David Young, 1955–56, born to Olive Nellie Young." Then a photocopied, handwritten note: "I gave this child to Mrs. Joshua Bartlett for her own. He is gone for adoption. [signed] Nellie Young." And then a caption by Wayne [now] Bartlett): "Kinda funny now looking back…my life began on a piece of scribbler paper."

Scribbler paper—that quintessential Canadian school supply—would turn out to serve a big role in Bartlett's life.

At a later time, while talking about his songwriting, Bartlett told me, "I never had a notebook as such, just had some old paper lying around, sheets of paper or bill books or something, and I'd just write right on the back there. I suppose I must have eleven or twelve hundred there—songs I've got written on old scraps of paper that I never bothered to enter into the computer. And I've made away with a lot over the years, just silly songs. I used to put all my songs in a butterbox one time. Then when I got my first computer in '94, I put them in there, organized them."

As I flip through the photo album, it picks up with Wayne Bartlett's two kids (from his previous marriage), a son and a daughter. His daughter would be around my age. I didn't know it when we first met, but Bartlett's daughter, Angie, had died a couple of months earlier in childbirth in Halifax, Nova Scotia, also losing the child. By the time I'd return, for a second trip, a tribute had been paid to her and her son in a gathering at the local graveyard. It's a beautiful location, nestled in a cove at the edge of a hilly, grassy embankment overlooking the ocean. I consider this may have been the only way Angie and her infant son would have come back to this place permanently. Quirpon, after all, is a community with an uncertain future.

When Wayne Bartlett arrives, he sees me flipping through the photo album, and he seems put off I'm here. He shakes my hand, a firm grip and angry stare, but there's no verbal response to my hello. He's a broad-shouldered man with a trim salt-and-pepper haircut. He's wearing blue jeans and a jean-look collared shirt. I think there's paint on his pants, but I suspect these are his nice pants. (He later tells me there's paint on all of his clothing). Bartlett turns to head downstairs to tend to the wood stove. He takes the elevator he built. It's still under construction but there wouldn't be anyone else in the vicinity with an elevator in their home. Bartlett returns after some minutes, complaining about the neighbourhood cat, who he pledges to kill next time he sees it (it supposedly shit in his pathway one too many times). He then gets straight to the point wanting to know why am I here exactly.

"What qualifies you as a writer?" Bartlett asks. He doesn't wait to hear the answer. He's in the kitchen tending to something else. In my head, I'm recalling conversations from my Master of Fine Arts class at the University of King's College in Halifax. *I write because I must*, I think. *I have a story to tell. Well, my grandfather's story. My father's story too. His brothers. And mine, too. And there are other people like me. Aren't you like me? Quirpon was a fishing community, but what's become of it now?*

I don't say any of that. I'm nervous and intimidated. I don't want to mess this up any more than I already have. I play it safe.

"That's a good question," I reply casually, trying to lighten the mood. Bartlett still doesn't look at me. He's rummaging in cupboards and preparing something to eat.

"Shouldn't any good interview start with one?" Bartlett quips. My instant reaction is a burst of laughter—he has me there. I'm going to lay it out for him, my real emotion, no put-ons.

"My uncle died last year. He was the last one living in the fishing outport where my father grew up. His father, my grandfather, was the last fisher in our family. I have an infant daughter now. She's here in town with my sister and her two kids. I want her to know the Newfoundland I knew growing up." My eyes well up and it's not just because of the pressure of the situation, but there's real and raw emotion behind my words. I still get choked up and it surprises me just how much.

"Do you want jam bread?" Bartlett asks me, looking directly at me this time. I'm full, but yes, yes, I'll take this special jam bread peace offering, yes. Bartlett cuts us each a thick slice of homemade white bread, then layers on equally thick globs of homemade strawberry jam. He takes a seat across from me with jam bread for two. I talk to him more about my project, clumsily picking up the jam-bread with both hands, balancing it on my fingertips, worried I'll drop it on the plate or worse, the floor, and, with my luck, it will land jam-side down. Bartlett watches and listens. He's not talking. He's holding his jam bread in his thumb and forefinger, almost folding the bread, having perfected how to eat it. He demolishes it in four bites. Then he's up again, this time to his laptop in the living room. He wants me to keep talking, I think. So, in between bites, I do. I talk. Maybe he's checking his email or something.

"Little Bay East, you said?" Bartlett asks.

"Yes," I reply.

"Come over here. Does this look familiar?" Bartlett swivels the laptop in my direction as he clicks through the images. The photos are from about ten years ago. I don't recognize it at first. But then I see the unmistakable view across Fortune Bay. Fishing stages in the harbour. The welcome sign to Little Bay East. Pop's house.

"There, that's my grandfather's place," I say, pointing, more surprised and animated than perhaps I ought to be. But the reaction comes from the connection that's happening. First the jam bread and now the recognition of place—Pop's place, my fishing place. Bartlett knows this area. Beginning in 1988, he spent time in Little Bay East's neighbouring community of Bay L'Argent recording his albums—cassette tapes at the time. "She's Gone" was the big song that caught on. I ask Bartlett to take me back to what inspired the song.

Bartlett was overlooking Quirpon Harbour when the idea for the song came to him, he says. It was 1991 and no one knew the Canadian government would close the Newfoundland cod fishery the following July. And yet, the cod collapse was as clear as the view that day from Bartlett's living-room window.

His entire life, Bartlett watched the fishing boats come in and out of this bay. Everyone did, with their harbour views from their kitchens and coffee tables. Even the gravestones just around and over the hill have an ocean view. With the fog, you could often hear the boats before you'd see them. The *putt-putt-putt* would eventually be replaced with a *purr* as inboard motors advanced to the outboard variety. In the same way, handlining and jigging cod would eventually be replaced with cod trapping and gillnetting. Still, the results were the same. Small-boat fishermen would return to their wharves at the end of their driveways and houses with their skiffs and dories resting low in the water, weighed down by cod, often packed to the gunwales. Kids like Bartlett would meet their old man and earn a few bucks cutting out cod tongues from the discarded fish heads and selling them about town.

The harbour hummed with life in those days. Fishers splitting, drying, and salting cod on their fish flakes. Seagulls screaming for their share of the leftovers. Kids spinning in and around the wharves, gallivanting along the beaches, zipping in and out of coves, and darting up and over the hills. Dogs barking at everyone and everything and each other too. Mothers shouting for their kin to come home—it was dinner, then it would be supper, and then bedtime before long.

One of Bartlett's oldest friends, Alec Roberts, has joined us at Bartlett's place.

"You were always the leader. The instigator," remarks Roberts, referencing his and Bartlett's childhoods. Roberts is one of only two remaining inshore fishermen still working out of Quirpon Harbour. He expects he'll keep fishing cod for another few years, but then call it quits. He's not doing it for the money, he's doing it because he loves it. Being out on the water, doing what he knows, doing what he's good at—that's what he enjoys. He has two daughters who live in western Canada and neither are interested to pick up fishing where he'll leave off in a few years. Out the kitchen and living-room windows of Bartlett's B&B we can see the Roberts family's fishing stage. It's just on the other side of Noble Cove and painted in the traditional red ochre, with a pile of gillnets stacked on the wharf—a perfect backdrop for our conversation today. When Roberts "goes at the cod," as he calls it, he relies on a half-dozen gillnets and his 23-footer (his motorboat).

I'll later visit that fishing stage and meet one of Alec's brothers, Boyce Roberts. I'm familiar with Boyce because I've seen him on a CBC TV episode of *Witness* (the episode aired in 1993 and was titled after Bartlett's "She's Gone" song). About ten minutes into the hour-long episode, the narrator (Linden MacIntyre) describes how Roberts is leaving behind the bay where Jacques Cartier camped, where Vikings roamed, and where his family settled generations ago. The Cape Bauld lighthouse marks the tip of the island portion of the province, where the codfish used to run.

"Used to," the narrator repeats. But on this day of filming, there are no fish at all.

Meanwhile, back in 1986, Roberts and his crew were again featured on television (Newfoundland television, or what's called NTV), bringing in large net-loads of cod. They reported having landed 200,000 pounds the year previous; another 175,000 pounds so far in 1986 (about 3000 pounds that morning, and it was only August, with more cod fishing to come).

Episodes of *Witness* (1993, "She's Gone, Boys, She's Gone") and *Land and Sea* (1995, "Moratorium Music") are some of the many television programs capturing the loss of place and purpose felt across the province at the time of the moratorium.

"I'm the lost generation," says one fisherman, about fifty years old, on the *Witness* episode.

"We woke up and the fish were gone," another young fisherman says, feeling cheated his career ended before it started, "Well we saw it going, but the rest of Canada woke up and saw it gone. Now, we might never see it again."

The band Stuffed Squid perform their song "The Last Water Haul."

"And everybody knows what a water haul is," Syl Drover, who wrote and performs the song, says, "It's when you haul your net or cod traps or your nets in some cases, and you got nothing but water. And the emptiness of the nets and the traps, and the plant closing, the emptiness, the feeling you get inside, the emptiness you get inside."

"If you go down to the wharf now, you won't see anyone. Nobody down there," says another fisherman, "Something is dying out. That something is a way of life. A way of life, that's exactly right."

It's not completely dead yet but the end is likely near, I learn, as I talk with Alec Roberts. This year, Roberts has a cod quota of about 2,000–3,000 pounds a week. He says there are ten to twelve crews involved in cod fishing around here now (that's about forty people total). But there used to be fifty to seventy-five crews (fifteen crews in Quirpon alone, whereas he and another guy are the only ones doing it now). In terms of catch, in the four to five years pre-1992 (moratorium), Roberts tells me you might get 100,000–200,000 pounds a season (50,000 pounds in one shot, often); now, you get 25,000-30,000 pounds a season if you're lucky.

It's something. But it's not like the good old days Roberts and Bartlett remember growing up.

"Devious, I was," Bartlett says, practically giddy, remembering those days as he chats across the table from buddy Alec. Bartlett's grin wears his face. It's all I can see. When he's happy, he's thrilled. It's like his ten-year-old self may burst out of his body. That's who's telling me about the kind of make-your-own-entertainment kids like he and Alec enjoyed back as boys, when this fishing community was still a fishing community.

"We always were playing games around stages," says Bartlett. "Stick your feet up in the beams, let go your hands, and just holding on by your toes. Little things like that."

"My dad said they used to jump ice pans," I offer.

"Oh, gee, yes, that's just a common thing," says Bartlett, "All around those little coves there'd be jumping on the pans, from one pan to the next. I was always the guy who fell in the water every day, several times a day. Oh, geez, I was always taking chances."

It's difficult to imagine kids in this harbour. The majority of people here, all seventy-seven or so of them (though I'm finding that number even difficult to believe), are long retired or mostly bound to their homes by their elderly status. The same is true of the people in many of the neighbouring communities. Meanwhile, my sister's kids and my daughter are the only children I saw here during both trips, save for a teenager who visited Quirpon Island with his grandparents around the same time we were there in the summertime.

When my sister came back to get me at the B&B on that first trip, the two older kids were high on their experience of meeting actual Vikings, while Navya was doing what she did best—sleeping. My nephew Ross had figured out their tour guide was a *real* Viking (the guide was also featured as a Viking in the Parks Canada information video that started the tour and he still donned his long hair and beard). At the B&B, Bartlett was immediately warm with the kids. There was no earning of his trust required where they were concerned. Bartlett grabbed a jar full of coins and offered it to my nephew to reach in and grab a handful.

"Whatever he grabs, he can keep," Bartlett says. Ross's eyes are wide and he's smirking like he's getting away with something he knows he shouldn't be doing. Then my four-year-old niece, Lauren, gives it a go, too, not wanting to miss out on this experience that she doesn't fully understand. I remind her that coins can buy candy and Lauren instantly appreciates their value.

Children spark an energy here that's visible in Bartlett and McCarron's warmth—McCarron offered the kids snacks and, although they had already eaten, they welcomed the treats. And yet this place, with so much love of life and such deep history, could vanish if most residents get their wish for a government-sponsored resettlement package. In the last community vote, prompted by the residents a few of years ago, the town reached 88 per cent agreement in favour of resettling. That's 2 per cent shy (and likely one swing vote short) of what's required for the provincial government to formally tally the votes and, if meeting the 90 per cent cut off, pull municipal and provincial services and compensate residents, providing residents with resources to establish roots elsewhere.

But that would be another nail in this community's pre-purchased coffin, which brings us back to 1991 and Bartlett writing his "She's Gone" song.

"When I wrote it, nobody didn't have a clue that the fishery was going to close," Bartlett says, "Neither did I. So, the song was recorded and came out in America before the fishery even closed and then when it closed, [people] just jumped on it. I said, Geez, this is *the* song."

But Bartlett knew things were amiss that day back in '91. Usually when inshore fishermen came back to their wharf, having checked their traps or nets, the stern of their boat would be seated deeper in the water than when they set out, weighed down by cod, the gunwales skimming the water's surface. When Bartlett began writing the tune, he saw the boats coming back, one by one, just as they had set out: empty. This is the definition of a true water haul. Seated on a dining chair, one foot up on the coffee table, Bartlett tells me he was strumming on his acoustic guitar that day, letting the lyrics flow.

"The boats were coming in and I said, 'She's gone b'y, she's gone b'y, she's gone. Jesus. That's a catchy phrase. I might make a song of that,'" says Bartlett. He started with a few more lines, crafting the chorus:

She's gone, boys, she's gone, she's gone,
She's gone boys, she's gone;
What we didn't destroy, we allowed to die,
And now, she's gone, boys, she's gone.
She's gone, boys, she's gone, boys, she's gone.

That evening, Bartlett kept writing and before he knew it, he had a song put together. In those days, his music career was relatively new. He'd recorded his first song back in 1988, with three self-released audio tapes since. Bartlett and his band had already toured around Newfoundland three times by then, too, so his name was becoming quite familiar. It was "She's Gone, Boys, She's Gone" that gave his popularity "a little boost," as he calls it.

"Whenever you see somebody on the road, they'd look at you and say, 'She's Gone, Boys, She's Gone'—like it became a saying to them."

Fast-forward twenty-five years and what's gone somehow feels like it's back again.

"As you can see, they're an elderly crowd," Martin Hynes says. Hynes is the manager of Northern Lights Seafoods Inc., which operates a fish plant in Main Brook on the Northern Peninsula and has recently partnered with another fish plant to process northern cod. Hynes set up and manages the new cod processing line at St. Anthony Seafoods, a fish plant specializing in coldwater shrimp with distribution all over the world. The plant is co-owned by Clearwater Seafoods (75 per cent share) and St. Anthony Basin Resources Inc. (25 per cent). To Hynes' point about the demographic of the workforce, the youngest person on the fish-processing line today is in her late fifties, while the oldest is closing in on eighty. That's Juanita Elliott, seventy-seven years old in a couple of months, with the kind of boundless energy I'm enviable of at half her age. She'll be one of the last people here today, cutting out cod tongues from the leftovers—a perk of the job—to bring home.

"Yeah, there's no one from my age group here and mostly women," I shout, competing with the buzzing and whirring of equipment, which is all the louder in this wall-to-wall concrete, hanger-like echo chamber of a building at the edge of St. Anthony Harbour. This is a neighbouring building to the main shrimp-processing facility and it was empty before Hynes was called in to set up the new line in August (it's now mid-September). Things were slow at the shrimp-processing plant this year too, with many of the plant workers not receiving a call to work over June and July. There simply wasn't enough work to go around. When the cod processing started, it granted folks some hope, especially since this marked the first time northern cod was processed at St. Anthony Seafoods since the 1992 moratorium.

"There's a lot of spunk there. Trust me," Hynes shouts back in reference to the workers. He looks like he's laughing, but if he is, I can't hear it over the racket getting louder as we walk the line. Interspersed between the low, continuous thrum of motors there is a periodic, high-pitched squeal. Many of the workers are wearing noise-cancelling headphones over their hairnets. The rest of their uniform is comprised of gloves, sleeve covers, and aprons. Otherwise it's whatever comfortable attire—casual clothing like hoodies and polos over slacks and footwear—they choose.

"It does seem fun," I yell, a bit too loudly this time, trying to gauge my volume and wondering if I'm getting any of this on my audio recorder. The workers—about two dozen of them—are smiling or making small talk. Part of that may be because I'm here with a notepad, camera, and recorder, but I stick around long enough to try to blend into the background. When the smiles, laugh, and small talk continues at that point, I know it's for real.

"You'll have talk to one of our graders," Hynes says, "She'll tell you off before the day's over."

I smile, wondering what exactly he means. *She'll tell me off?* On my tour of the plant, I come to find out what Hynes is getting at: he may be the one with the office, but the culture at St. Anthony Seafoods is wholly family driven. As I finally get to interview Hynes in a quiet space, not to mention freed from my hairnet and gloves, we are repeatedly interrupted by plant workers popping into his office. Some are serious requests, others are opportunities to crack a joke or sarcastic remark—that's what Hynes was getting at.

On a good day, the plant processes upwards of 40,000–50,000 pounds of cod (with cod that can be as long as 36–40 inches, but often get 14 to 18 inches), but today was a short day. Many of the workers showed up as early as 7:30 A.M. and by noon, the day is over for most.

"We only had, I think it's 14 to 15,000 pounds today," Hynes says, "so that went through fairly quick. I was hoping another truck would come by today. If the fish is at the door, it's easily 50,000 pounds a day."

The process itself entails four major steps: landing, grading, processing, and shipping.

"A very simple process," Hynes says, smiling, but he has the experience to carry the statement. His father worked a similar role running a fish processing business in the early 1980s on the Northern Peninsula. Hynes became involved in the business just like his father, but got out of it and left the province after his father died. Hynes made a name for himself building high-end kitchens in Ontario, but when Northern Lights Seafoods called him up to take things over, he jumped back in. That was four or five months ago. Hynes lives in Plum Point and makes the one-and-a-half–hour drive to and from St. Anthony Seafoods each day. It's a slog of a drive and apparently it can be dangerous too, as evidenced by the passenger-side windshield of his truck parked outside, marred by a series of caved-in, concentric circles etched in the glass from a recent moose collision.

But the job is worth it, Hynes tells me.

"The guy on the filleting machine ran that identical filleting machine before '92," Hynes says, pointing to the 6-foot-something man standing near the beginning of the line. "We have people here that actually ran all this machinery prior to the moratorium."

To think, there are workers back at processing cod a quarter of a century after everybody thought "she" was gone. The thought makes me hopeful and yet still uncertain about the future of the cod fishery, given the state of the stocks. But the positive spirit in the room, in the entire plant, it's palpable—and that, too, instills hope.

The workers processing cod are the ones with seniority from St. Anthony Seafoods—they have the most number of years put it at the company, so had the choice of taking on the extra work before anyone else. Northern Lights brought the expertise in setting up the line and managing the overall production—from buying the fish to grading, processing, and shipping it to market. The workers come from the plant, with many of them putting their old skills to renewed use. Yet some are at this for the first time, and there are new steps in the process, like grading the cod and keeping the skin on and bone in to prove buyers are getting northern cod. This is in response to widespread findings in the global fishery that white fish is often mislabeled. One such study was published by the ocean conservatory and advocacy non-profit Oceana in 2016, showing seafood labels for white fish are often not what they say they are.

Both management and workers are motivated to be here. It's September and shrimp are finished for the season ("well, most of it," Hynes qualifies), so processing cod is putting additional money in people's pockets.

But an October 2018 news story in the St. Anthony newspaper, *The Northern Pen*, argues not everyone working at the plant reaps the same rewards. The headline reads St. Anthony Seafoods employees looking to make ends meet, telling the story of what happens to plant workers who lack the seniority to qualify for the additional cod-processing work.

"[W]orkers struggling the most were not the ones to benefit," reporter Stephen Roberts writes. "Most of the work went to those with seniority, many of whom already qualified for employment insurance (EI)."

Roberts profiled Audrey Patey, a fifty-six-year-old St. Anthony Seafoods plant worker from nearby St. Lunaire-Griquet who worked 27 hours, grossing $450 this season—not nearly enough to get her near the 420 hours needed to qualify for EI. And yet, all around Newfoundland and Labrador are people who are worse off than Patey. In 1992, the then provincial department of fisheries reported 250 licensed fish processing establishments, which was up from the 209 plants it licensed in 1986. In 2016, however, there were only 92 licensed fish-processing plants. St. Anthony Seafoods is one of the few remaining.

Reading Patey's story makes me reconsider my first inclination about the family-run entrepreneurial culture here (*Who's looking out for the underdogs?*). But I can't deny spirits were definitely high during my visit in mid-September. Hynes and the plant workers alike talked about how nice it was to return to processing cod. It brought back hope, let alone additional cash for those involved. Right now, there are two-dozen workers employed, but Hynes is hopeful they'll bring in closer to thirty workers if they can get another cod-processing line going.

"More hoppers, more machinery, more production crew," he says, "and that's a start. But nothing in the fishery comes without some degree of

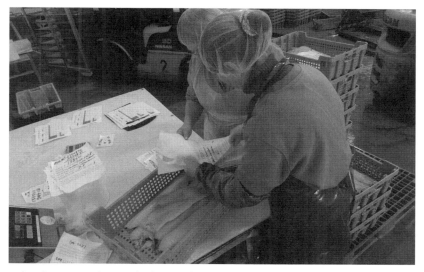

Cod grading at St. Anthony Seafoods, St. Anthony, Newfoundland, 2018.

politics," Hynes says. "I'll say the politics of the fishery in Newfoundland, for my part having come in, knowing what it was like before the mortarium, it's a completely different story. Completely, completely changed. There's more paperwork to the fishery now than fishing."

The cod-quality program that was introduced in 2000 as a joint industry–government effort to improve the quality of commercial fisheries, in this case cod, has introduced a great deal more paperwork too. "I mean, we're talking nightmare amounts of paper to make sure everything is just right," Hynes says.

The paper trail starts at the front door, when the fish is delivered to the plant. The fish is graded, the plant assigning every fisher's catch a grading sheet. The grading is based on the cod's texture, smell, weight, and overall quality. This is what determines the price paid to each fisher.

"I understand some of the rationale," Hynes says about the grading process. "I mean, [it's] getting the fishermen to be better fishers. I understand it discourages leaving fish for five or six days [e.g., in their gillnets]. But most fishermen are on board with the program, they are good with the program. [But] you don't control the wind. So, if you can't get out [to retrieve the fish from your gillnet], then you know you're going to have a lower grade. But a lot of fishermen, they do step up to the plate."

As part of the grading process, the total weight of the catch per fisher is taken; then samples are removed from the cod to be assessed and compared to the filleted portions later in the process. If the fish are dropped off early in the day, then they are processed on the day of; however, if they come in late, they are put in a chilled room for the following day.

"It comes up to the table here," Hynes says, "The girls take it out, lay it out, however many—say if it's 500 pounds, 5 fish are used for grading, if it's 1,000 pounds, then 10 fish; 1,500 pounds, then 15 fish. They grade each one, lay it out and grade it, colour, texture, everything. Then they write it up and move on to the next basket."

From there, the whole fish is run through the hoppers, where its head and fins are removed. At the filleting machine, which follows, the cod is split. Then it's onto the trim line, where the fillets are hand-trimmed to perfect the cut, removing any defects. From there, it's onto packaging—packing the fish into blue plastic inside 10-kilogram cardboard boxes. It's then placed on a shelf, where it will be moved by a forklift to the blast freezers, and kept there for twenty-four hours to bring the temperature down to below minus 18 degrees Celsius. Then it's onto the storage facility and shipped to its final destination, all over the world.

As the fillets are cut, the graders assess each box of cod—as the cod runs the line, it stays in grey plastic boxes so the fish can continue to be tracked by its origin (the individual fisher). The paperwork must follow the boxes—the plastic one that runs the processing line, as well as the cardboard box to be shipped out.

I observe the processing line, familiarizing myself with the process: hoppers, filleting machine, trimmers, packers, repeat. The whirring continues and so too does the intermittent squeaking sound. The smell in the factory surprises me—it's fishy, yes, but with a clean, sterile quality; it's like standing between a fish stand and a cleaning supply closet.

As the work slows down, I take the opportunity to chat with Juanita Elliott from Raleigh. She's finished work for the day and is busy cutting cod tongues for personal use. These are best enjoyed fried, Elliott says. Wearing two different coloured gloves—one blue, one orange—Elliott is making swift work cutting tongues with a large-bladed knife, filling her clear plastic bag. She stands at the edge of a plastic tub as tall as her waist and as big as a hot tub. It's filled with severed cod heads and slushy ice that's turned pink in places from the bloodshed.

These heads are destined for Main Brook, where Northern Lights Seafoods has a plant for processing salt cod. The cod are salted in tubs just like this one. In Main Brook, plant workers cut out the cheeks and tongues, sold mostly to the local market. Meanwhile, all of the other bits and pieces are, for now, on ice.

"We're looking for, hopefully, getting a line going on pet food or whatever with the rest of the carcass," Hynes says. "We're hoping that's going to play out. We have 50,000 pounds of it frozen just trying to hit a market."

It's the waste-not, want-not approach taken in places like Iceland, too—trying to secure high value means making use of as many parts of the fish as possible. Meanwhile, cutting cod tongues, Elliott is eager for her moment in the spotlight. She's thrilled I'm writing a book.

"I started work when I was twenty-seven and now I'll be seventy-seven in November," Elliott says, all the time smiling, looking to see if I'm writing that down. "And I do berry-picking and firewood too."

"Wow," I offer earnestly, thinking of the difficult labour. Not to mention those fields are seeing their workers age out of the work.

I met Kier Knudsen of The Dark Tickle Company in St. Lunaire-Griquet after speaking with Juanita Elliott. Knudsen is one of Elliott's berry-buyers and his family's company is considered among the first "économusée" shops in the province, promoting and selling artisanal goods alongside a museum-like exhibit showcasing some of the settler history of the surrounding area. Young people are not getting into berry-picking the way the older generation did, Knudsen tells me. In part, it's because the young people aren't here to do it, but they also don't want to be at the hard labour, he says. Berry-picking requires going deep into the bogland, repeatedly crouching to pick the berries, then carrying out your load. It also takes patience. I had hoped to go berry-picking for partridgeberries while in the area in September, but they still weren't ripe. Knudsen is a thirtysomething who left and then returned to Newfoundland take over the family business with his wife. His family was once a merchant family and, in many ways, the couple carry on that tradition, buying local goods like berries and turning them into jam, chocolate, and other confectionery items. Their café and giftshop has become a common pitstop for those en route to the Viking village.

Meanwhile, Elliott figures she'll keep on picking berries until she can't do it anymore. Her work brings her purpose and a paycheque. She's thrilled to be back at the cod. When the cod ran out twenty-five years ago, she was mostly processing shrimp and squid, she says, while supplementing her income with other manual labour like berry-picking.

"That's my daughter over there, Diane, the one with the ponytail," Elliott says, surprising me even more. Elliott's rectangular, black-rimmed glasses have slid down her nose, but she doesn't adjust them. Diane is fifty-eight and learning the grading scheme. That's how I pick her out. Without the hairnets, the ponytail would have made an especially good marker in a place where most woman have cropped their hair by the time they reach forty-something.

"In terms of grading, what are the types of things that's dependent on?" I ask Diane.

"Well, weight of the fillet compared to the full weight of the cod," Diane begins, "you have the colour. You have the smell. You have the texture. Then, the overall look and feel of the fillet is what you're going for. Then, you give it a grade."

There's more paperwork than fish at this table. Each page includes a placeholder for the commercial fishing vessel (a number, like a license plate, identifying which vessel caught the fish), date the fish are caught, the buyer, pounds and boxes in the lot, and a note: "one label per box of fish to go on top of ice in box. Traceability form 117 to be filled out with each shipment and sent with papers on truck or faxed."

This is a different world than in Pop's day, I think. But I can spot evidence along St. Anthony's harbour that, at least, some things are comparable. The fish plant is open and operable, with fishing vessels docked nearby. A flock of seagulls have congregated over a nearby wharf. The fishers are gone, but the leftovers from their labour have attracted the birds. Plenty of people are walking along the side of the road too—down around the harbour's fishing stages and wharves and across the way by the local hospital and International Grenfell Association (or what people commonly call the Grenfell Mission). I come to realize these are not locals, but visitors, having stopped off for a daytrip during their Viking Sea cruise. Still, there are people here. There's life here.

Back in Quirpon, I settle in for an early evening at Bartlett and McCarron's B&B. Sleep comes easily. I wake up to the morning sky on fire with the sun rising, but it quickly dulls white with overcast skies. The air is crisp and cool with autumn. I head upstairs for breakfast, where Bartlett and McCarron are up and at 'em. They plate me two eggs over easy, homemade bread toasted with partridgeberry jam, crispy bacon, coffee, and orange juice. I look out over Quirpon Harbour, where the sun makes

Singer-songwriter Wayne Bartlett plays a tune in his kitchen at The Big Blow B&B, Quirpon, Newfoundland, 2018.

itself known again, pouring over the bay, calm and still. I'm reminded of how quickly the weather changes here. "Come fall, the wind will blow a gale all winter long," Bartlett says. Quirpon is known for its nor'easters, winds that can blow shingles and sidings off the houses. In a grand sweep, they can transport docks and other structures from land out to shore. I glance out the window and just like that, the clouds are rolling in again.

I ask Bartlett and McCarron about their online radio program, Quirpon Radio. They've taken a hiatus but expect to bring the popular show back again, which is surely music to the ears of their more than 3,500 listeners. The local radio program, which is broadcast around the world, showcases Newfoundland and Labrador's culture and music. Through the program the couple continues a discovery legacy of sorts; though different than the explorations of the more well-known Captain Bob Bartlett, they unearth the rich scenes and sounds of undiscovered talent.

Wayne Bartlett brings a bar stool into the kitchen along with his Juniper acoustic guitar. He starts to strum that familiar 1991 tune.

The old man looked down in his dory,
As he stood on the wharf one more time;
With the wind in his hair, he stood there and stared,
"Look at her now, what a crime!"
He said, "I can recall when I built her,
When I lived in the place I called home;
'Twas a good life back then, but never again,
'Cause now, she's gone, boys, she's gone.

Life as it once was is gone, but what remains is what inspires.

CHAPTER 9:
Newfoundland *de Novo*

The January 30, 2019, headline in the St. John's *Telegram* has a touch of hope in it: Cod recovery still far off: DFO

It reminds me of the conversations I've had with leading northern cod scientist Sherrylynn Rowe from the Marine Institute in St. John's. Rowe holds out hope because she's observed the stock make a remarkable recovery from near destruction. A full recovery has not and may not happen, but it *could*.

Cod scientist George Rose offered us wisdom in his introduction to Wade Kearley's 2012 book, *Here's the Catch—The Fish We Harvest From The Northwest Atlantic*. Rose wrote: "Despite the 40 years of excess, the 450 years of sustainable production should not be forgotten." He goes on to write that the world needs the sustenance the North Atlantic provides and, as such, we need sustainable approaches—ones that show we've learned from the destructive behaviours of our past. Rose continues: "Unlike land animals, there have been almost no extinctions of marine fish. And habitat destruction is nowhere near as complete in the ocean as on land. It is far easier to envision rebuilt cod stocks than herds of bison on the North American plains."

Even if that sounds dismal, there's hope in it, too. Northern cod is, at once, one of the most devastating cases of the depletion of a marine species in our lifetime, but it's also one of the most astonishing cases of a species attempting a serious comeback. No one can say if the stocks will fully recover, but we do know cod only stands a chance of improving if, to Kearley's point, we care about the fish as much, and arguably more, than we care about the fishery. To me, that point reads like a call to action.

But as I look at the big picture, I worry we don't care as much as we should about the fish *or* the fishery, even with everything they have each afforded us. Cod fishing is, after all, the source of what defines us and our culture here in Newfoundland and Labrador. Even today, you cannot visit this province without feeling the lasting influence of the cod fishery.

"We have to be willing to harvest less than the ecosystem produces, so resources can increase in abundance over time," Bob Verge of the Canadian Centre for Fisheries Innovation writes in his column, "Making Do With Less," for *The Navigator* magazine. The statement echoes Kearley's powerful point. We must be willing to fish less, while seeking higher-quality and higher-value catch. We must take this cautious approach to fishing now—for groundfish like cod, pelagics like capelin, shellfish like shrimp and crab, and everything in between. At a time when nearly all marine stocks are not at the levels they once were, humans must reconsider the ways we fish, too. The climate crisis—also the result of human destruction—has created a warming ocean that perversely created a more hospitable environment for cod for a time. The warmer temperatures arguably gave cod an added and needed push that helped the stock flourish under otherwise dire circumstances. But without serious intervention on humanity's part, rising ocean temperatures will continue to rise. And if that's the case, then, combined with overfishing, we will most certainly lose the gains we've seen to date.

While it's clear we cannot undo the behaviours of our past, we can learn from our actions. On the one hand, we've made enormous, lunar-landing-type strides in fishing technology—bigger, faster boats with more accurate instruments, efficient gear giving us better capabilities to harvest, pack, and ship direct from ocean to customer—but with our current management model, these strides became unwieldy; we're constantly seeking more, more, more. Decades of industrialization overturned centuries of what traditional fishing methods had sustained. In the past, "[w]e were more concerned with catching more fish, than we were with increasing the value we got from each fish," Verge writes in that same column. Perhaps part of the problem is that we yield more value now from the fish we harvest than ever before.

As the 1992 moratorium intended to last two years continues, marking more than twenty-five years, DFO permits a "stewardship" cod fishery—a limited seasonal commercial fishery with gear restrictions (on the amount and type of gear). Commercially, there are fewer fishing vessels and processing plants in operation and, likewise, there are fewer fishers and processors (or plant workers) across the province. And yet, while the commercial value of cod has fallen alongside cod landings, the years that followed the moratorium led to a redefinition of the fishery—one that became more dependent on shellfish like shrimp and crab than groundfish like cod. Now, even though total landings (across all species) are down, the value of the fish we catch is the highest on record and the commercial fisheries remain a major economic driver for the provincial economy.

"The market-driven approach to the fishery has been focused on getting volumes of fish out of the water to monetize it," says Professor Dean Bavington. A focus on monetizing the catch is short-sighted, he says, and history is our greatest evidence of that fact. Without question, we are getting value from the fish we catch, but it's suboptimal, he says. "The fishery is actually extremely successful when you look at it in terms of money coming in," he adds. "There's more money coming into the thing now than there ever has been, yet the fish are gone. There's lots of millionaires that have been made off this, but they're not fishermen, they're investors."

Bavington believes the fishery's "boom or bust" mentality explains how and why people continued to fish after the moratorium. It's that same mentality that likens the fish and fishers to commodities. Instead, Bavington says, the fishery has been and remains a central way of life in this province. The move to call fishers *harvesters* furthers the concept of the ocean as a farm, but wild fisheries do not operate the way agriculture does. There will always be fluctuations in the stock levels of marine species, and fishers traditionally learned to accommodate these fluctuations by diversifying, so they could make do during the less abundant seasons. Today, we farm fish in aquaculture or aquafarming projects in an attempt to further our harvesting efforts, but not all species are conducive to such approaches, cod included.

So, as we focus on monetizing our catch, are we doing enough to preserve our wild fish for the future? And are we garnering the greatest value from our wild fisheries? After talking to Dean Bavington, Sherrylynn Rowe, and Bob Verge among others, I am convinced that sustainable fishing requires a return to more traditional methods— methods that protect the fish and their ecosystem, while also preserving a future fishery, the fishers, and rural communities who still depend on it. Garnering full value also extends beyond a focus on fillets over fish sticks; priorities should include making use of the whole fish in an effort to reduce fisheries waste as well as considerations of how the fishery can contribute to the local community—through sharing skills, creating better jobs, and focusing on food security.

First, on the fillets, there is a market for high-value cod, as the Fogo Island Fish experience shows. I have visited a half-dozen restaurants in Ottawa and Toronto for a feed of Fogo Island cod, caught by Fogo Island fishers and sold and delivered to the restaurant market by Fogo Island Fish. Yes, it requires paying a premium—one that I am willing to and have forked out—but isn't that what we want, to give value to fish and fishing in a way that privileges high-quality cod fillets over mass-produced quantities of breaded fish sticks? To Sherrylynn Rowe's point, why bother taking cod out of the water for anything less? Because when we place a higher value on cod, we can also place a higher value on the fishers, too, by paying them better wages. Better pay, in turn, has positive ramifications on communities and culture, allowing a five-centuries-old practice to continue.

Fair pay is a topic I didn't delve into in this book, but I'm aware that fishers and plant workers often struggle to make ends meet, while big companies can reap big profits. Take the case of fishers who make less now per pound of cod than they did before the moratorium; Ryan Cleary, president of FISH-NL, says that's why many fishers would "rather fucking spit on a codfish than catch it." Or take the case of plant worker Audrey Patey, who didn't clear enough earnings in the 2018 season in St. Anthony to qualify for employment insurance. The vision of Fogo Island Fish, says Tony Cobb, is to yield more profit to the fishers, while preserving the catch. "The economists like to call that *disintermediation*, [a] right fancy word for 'eliminate the middle man,' and that's what we've done," Cobb says. No doubt he's a savvy businessperson, but he cares not at all about academic business and pseudo-economics; his motivation has everything to do with building up his home, community, and people. Building things, he says, is a sign of hope. When people stop building things, they stop caring about their futures.

The statement rings true to me. This book is the thing I've built. The research and interviews were like house plans; the outline was the frame; the words were the bricks and mortar; the characters and the details were the rooms and contents. I built this book to find out where I came from and to learn what I can do to help preserve its places and people—even if, sometimes, that means preserving their memories.

The fishery in Newfoundland and Labrador has given so much to me—and yet, I left. Like so many other Newfoundlanders who continue to leave. At times, I've worried my perspective won't count, having lived in Ontario nearly as long as I've spent on the island. "Don't apologize for the fact that you're spending some part of your life in Ontario and some part of it in Newfoundland," Cobb said to me when I voiced this concern. "I think it's a great gift to yourself and to Newfoundland." Those were the words I needed to hear. Cobb is someone who shows just how great a gift it can be to leverage your perspective and pursuits to the benefit of the place you call home. It's with that distance that organizations like Shorefast and the Fogo Island Inn came to fruition. It's not that I place myself anywhere near those entities and their success, but I understand the germination of their motivations as well as the limitations of their achievements. The Cobb family's roots and accomplishments run deep, and yet neither are deep enough to keep the fishery afloat on their own.

"Fogo Island Inn was built on the idea that we have always been an active fishing community and that we will always be an active fishing community," says Tony Cobb."If we didn't believe that, we wouldn't have built [Fogo Island Inn]. The inn was not built as something that we thought was necessary because we were losing our fishery. It was built on the belief that we're not going to lose our fishery and that the inn can exist and can only be successful if it's part of a vibrant fishing community. It's part of what makes the inn work and it's a key aspect of why people are interested in it." Case in point: yielding the full potential value of cod (and all landings) will take more than the first-value focus, one that Fogo Island Fish practices, delivering high-value fillets instead of low-value fish sticks. Second, it requires making every possible use from every part of the fish. Harvesting the fillets, the tongues, the cheeks, then using the bones and head for animal food or other products. And the uses can extend beyond food to skincare, medications and supplements, and leather goods. Harvesting cod to its fullest potential is commonly practiced in Iceland—and doing so is a step toward reducing the waste from commercial fisheries. And that is, in turn, a step toward reducing our carbon footprint.

Value also comes from giving back to the community in every way the fishery can. The fishery has succeeded in this province because of its communities, particularly the outports, and now the outports need the fishery more than ever. Towns like Grand Bank will continue to try to diversify their economies, and they must, but the boats in harbour and the plants in town remain central beacons of the local economy.

For-profit business models fall short of what ouport communities need: social enterprises. Like Shorefast and Fogo Island Fish. And like Island Rooms of Petty Harbour, home of Fishing for Success, co-founded by fishing captain Kimberly Orren. Orren is yet another example of a Newfoundlander who left and returned—bringing back ideas and programs that focus on building up the fishery, the outports, the people, and the fish too.

In addition to tourism (recreational or food fishing) programs, which bring in the non-profit's revenue, Fishing for Success, the heart of this organization, offers youth and community programming. The programs include Girls Who Fish, Wild Family Nature Club, and Youth Cod Fishery, and Dory Club, the names of which hint at their underlying causes. Through these programs, one child, one woman, one family at a time— often those without the means—are learning the "traditional fishing knowledge and skill of their ancestors," reports the non-profits' website. With that vision, comes "a sense of pride, of place, and a longing to protect and conserve their natural home."

This is a vision to which I can relate. I can no longer rely on my grandfather to pass on his traditional fishing knowledge to me or to my daughter. This is what academic types call our *intangible cultural history*, or ICH, which goes beyond the tangible parts of our heritage—things like buildings, clothing, and so on that are physical remnants of the past— and highlights the customs, knowledge, and traditions that comprise our collective cultural identity. These intangibles are usually passed down by word of mouth or by one person demonstrating a practice to another. Newfoundland and Labrador has an ICH strategy to preserve its intangible culture through documentation, celebration, transmission, and cultural industry. But as far as traditional fishing skills are concerned, many of us are or will become dependent on organizations like Fishing for Success to provide these skills.

More than connecting us to our pasts, these socially minded programs are busting stereotypes, too. There remains a long-held belief that men fish, while women tend home and family, for example, and that fishing is an exclusive practice, while in fact, it's a shared human heritage. "Talk to people all over the world and they have fishing stories. Right away you can start connecting with people from anywhere," says Orren. If we grow local, we can reach global, she adds, but we should start by building the solutions here first. Part of that rebuilding process is getting children, women, and immigrants involved in fishing, too. Orren knows this: she returned to Newfoundland and Labrador after years of teaching high school science in Florida, and trained to be a fish harvester and captain. She was the only woman in her cohort at the Marine Institute in St. John's. It was an uphill battle of cost, time, and perseverance, not to mention battling the gender stereotypes.

Kimberly Orren and her partner Leo Hearn's vision for Fishing for Success goes beyond passing on fishing skills—although that's the underlying goal—to planning for a sustainable future. "Teaching kids to fish in a sustainable way is a cornerstone to teaching kids to fish," she says. Petty Harbour fishers do not use gillnets; they've preserved a tradition of handlining to protect the fish, their ecosystem, and their own livelihoods. "Handlining is not damaging the ocean floor; it's not leaving behind microplastics; it's not leading to ghost-fishing," Orren says. "When you're done, you roll up your gear and go home." Orren's work also focuses on food security and food sovereignty. Just before Christmas in 2018, winter storms hampered delivery of goods and services to the island of Newfoundland. People took to social media to showcase evidence of empty shelves at major grocery chains. The province's climate and soil conditions are unconducive to growing fresh local produce—in fact, only one-tenth of the produce consumed here originates here. As a result, Newfoundlanders and Labradorians have relied on imported foods, particularly over winter, since colonization.

That's one of the main reasons Kimberly Orren and Dean Bavington are advocates of the province's recreational fishery, which gives everyone, visitors and residents alike, the chance to fish. But Orren argues the name "recreational fishery" doesn't adequately capture the fishery or the reasons people fish. For starters, the groundfish that garners the most interest is still cod. As to why, there's the culture and heritage experience (linking us with our ICH) but there's also the primary reason people have gone fishing since the beginning of time—for food. Provided the shipments arrive, Newfoundlanders who live near a grocer or wholesaler can buy cod fillets for $9–10 per pound from Russia, Norway, and Iceland. Alternatively, they can buy cod locally, either from a local restaurant selling local cod or for about $3.50 to $4 per pound, directly from a NL commercial fish harvester. The cost of catching the fish oneself through the recreational fishery (more commonly called the food fishery) is greater than these options, especially for those without the means—the boat, the gear, and the time off on weekends—readily at their disposal. But in this water-to-table world, many want to support locally harvested foods—and they want the option of doing it themselves. Or learning from those who do it themselves.

"I think where I see the hope or the difference coming from for the future [of the fishery] is Indigenous fishers learning about the Indigenous history of the island and the idea of a food fishery," says Dean Bavington. "We have to think about food on the island because we're exporting 90 per cent of our seafood, and we're importing 90 per cent of our fruits and vegetables. We should have no exporting of fish so long as food supply is limited."

There's a pride that comes in harvesting the food for one's own table. And it's a pride that Newfoundlanders and Labradorians have known since they took up residence on these rocky shores. We may not have had wealth, but we had our pride—and that was the greatest riches of all. Fish and the fishery are about more than garnering wealth (commercially) or trophies (recreationally). If we want to recognize the full breadth of why people fish—beyond the recreation to the time-honoured tradition and putting local food on the table—and if we want to make it more affordable and accessible to everyone, then perhaps we should reconsider its name. In 2017, the Standing Committee on Fisheries and Oceans called on DFO to rename this fishery the "public groundfish food and recreational fishery." Kimberly Orren suggests the "heritage fishery." A name change may seem like window dressing, but I believe it can signal attention to the barriers and inequities that exist in this fishery. It can also redirect policy action to follow the renamed practice; for example, investing in programs that reach our communities. Orren and Bavington want to see more done to deliver the fish we harvest to the plates of Newfoundlanders and Labradorians; for example, reaching children in school meal programs or patients and families using hospital food services. As chronic disease rates sore in the province (and Atlantic Canada), Bavington adds that diseases like diabetes and obesity are often treated as individual problems. Instead, they ought to be treated, at least in part, as a broader food sovereignty problem: our population has a food supply problem, but is not making use of the nutritious and fresh fish harvested from our own waters. Why not—especially when the reasons to do so are compelling.

When it comes to community-building, Orren says she also wants to see our wharves become community hubs once again. While she lived away, the transformation of the community wharf—from a hub of the community to an industrial setting—was among the biggest reasons she wanted to return to the province. As she explains, she wanted to help restore the wharves to their previous glory:

> I would come home, and I could just see a drastic change. The community wharf wasn't a community wharf anymore. It was something that was now a workplace. You didn't see children and families come down to see what the fish catch was. And because there were forklifts, and there were things swinging overhead, and the boats were bigger, and everything's concrete now, there wasn't this central place where communities were gathering, especially the small communities. The outdoor places are important in connecting with who we are and where we are.

Again, that's a vision I can relate to as a new parent, wanting my child to have what I realize now are the luxuries I had: of getting out in nature, seeing where our food comes from, learning about the earth and our role as its caretakers. If we want to raise a generation that cares about the planet, then we must offer them the planet. Unless we want our fishery to become an intangible part of our heritage, then we must take measures to make it tangibly ours once again. "We are compelled to think about and engage with fisheries differently," sociologist Nicole Power says, "in ways that do not simply position fish as commodities (something for sale)—and we also shouldn't be lulled into some romantic nostalgia for past fisheries either. It's time for new approaches—ones that understand fishing in ways that not only do the least harm but also allow for diverse forms of marine life in our bays and ocean to flourish."

I've looked for the signals across Newfoundland and Labrador as to which entities are prioritizing the fish, the fishers, and the fisheries. And my findings are painfully obvious: they are few and far between. The Department of Fisheries, Forestry and Agrifoods in 2016 replaced the former Department of Fisheries and Aquaculture and the former Forestry and Agrifoods Agency in an effort to streamline the delivery of programs and services and consolidate the support for these agencies. In 2017 it was renamed again to the Department of Fisheries and Resources, consolidating the lands branch, wildlife division, and fish and wildlife division with the former department. The offices were then moved to

Corner Brook, where the majority of agriculture and forestry activity in Newfoundland and Labrador occurs.

Since the merger, fisheries no longer receive the government attention it once did. It's a sub-issue in a broader portfolio with an economically driven mandate focused primarily on the promise of big energy projects. Economics continues to be a primary mandate of this and all Newfoundland governments, as the province claws its way back from one economic downturn after another. The economy here showed steady growth from the early 2000s into 2013 with a Gross Domestic Product of 5.8 per cent, the highest of all provinces, mostly due to the main export of crude oil averaging US $108.15 a barrel. But those conditions started to soften in 2014, particularly as the price of oil dropped to US $63 a barrel, then $40 a barrel by year's end. In 2016 the oil royalties that accounted for 30 per cent of the government's annual revenue had dropped to 7 per cent, forcing the NL government to spend nearly $1 billion to service its debt of $14.7 billion, and growing. The government responded with tax hikes (representing an approximate $3,000-a-year year increase for a family in Newfoundland and Labrador), laid off 450 public service employees (cuts that continued in 2017–18), increased class sizes, and reduced subsidies (including a $1,000 baby bonus, an important measure in a province where the population is shrinking, while all of our neighbours' populations grow). Higher offshore oil production beginning in 2018 promises a return to front-of-the-pack economic status that Newfoundland enjoyed for a short period, but for now residents still pay a premium to live in a province that may as well be asking them to leave. And how can we measure the environmental costs of ongoing oil spills—for which we are dependent on oil companies to self-report and self-manage?

Another piece of evidence showing how far the fishery has fallen is the recent 2019 provincial election. "There's been no discourse about the fishery or fishing in the election talks so far. And I'm wondering where is it?" Kimberly Orren told CBC News in May 2019. In a campaign called "Five Fishy Questions for NL Provincial Parties & Candidates," Orren's organization, Fishing for Success, teamed up with Too Big To Ignore, a global think tank on issues affecting sustainability of small-scale fisheries, and the Ocean Frontier Institute, a research collaborative involving local universities, government, industry and international partners, to pose questions to parties during the election period. The campaign raised the profile of five fishery-related issues: employment, food security, communities (specifically, their dependency on the fishery), access, and sustainability. Without the campaign's intervention, it's possible party platforms may have ignored the fishery as an election issue entirely.

Meanwhile, Fisheries and Oceans Canada could just as well be asking the cod to go quietly. The rub is this: more than a quarter of a century after the moratorium—which, you'll remember, was expected to last two years, but continues today—there's no fisheries management plan for the recovery of northern cod.

The situation reminds me of a story my father and Uncle Reg told me about a time when Pop and one of his brothers, probably Uncle Ches, were caught in a dense fog, adrift in their dory for hours. It was the kind of fog people here often call *pea soup* fog, a term for smog, though this fog can be every bit as deadly. The same mixture of Labrador Current and Gulf Stream that creates optimal fishing conditions underwater contributes to often perilous, dense fog conditions above it. It was customary practice for a captain to ask the crew to be all ears when sight failed. Knowing this, Pop and Uncle Ches likely listened for the sound of waves breaking on the shore. After all, without visibility or navigation equipment, their paddles and sails were useless. Survival called for creativity. "They licked the gunwales stem to stern," Dad had told me, recalling Pop talking about the condensation on the rails of the dory, as his and Ches's only water source. Operating a cod fishery—if even a limited stewardship fishery—without a recovery plan is like being in survival mode, rowing blind in a dense fog.

There is talk of hope on this horizon, as proposals to revise the Fisheries Act call for a federal role in rebuilding fish stocks. For now, we must wait and see what from the proposed bill to amend the Fisheries Act is translated into legislation and how that legislation, in turn, is translated into policy and practice.

What's perhaps more surprising to me than having no cod recovery management plan after everything cod and its fishery has endured is why the public doesn't seem to care. On January 30, when I read that northern cod headline in *The Telegram*, I might have expected people to riot in the streets, but beyond a few angry calls to VOCM radio and some angry comments on social media, the day's news came and went without so much as a small outburst.

Why wouldn't the public want measures to be taken to protect this resource for its people's future? What would our ancestors make of what's happening? Why does the Government of Newfoundland

and Labrador continue to look beyond its borders for the next big megaproject, thinking we are but one successful hydroelectric or oil and gas investment away from economic prosperity—especially when that hasn't played out in the past? What will it take to put in place protective measures to grow the inshore fishery, to retrain fishers in the traditional, sustainable fishing methods, for example, moving away from gillnets toward handlines and pots; and carving out a niche, high-value market the way Iceland has shown is possible and prosperous? Do most people think all of this is an impossible task? A task not worthy of pursuit at all?

Martin Hynes, the manager of Northern Lights Seafoods, whom I met in St. Anthony, says fishers have been kicked out so many times, it's not worth the fight: "If you look through the rules that Newfoundland fishermen have to go through, as compared to any other province in Canada, we're tagged, taxed, beaten back and forth by every part of the fishing organization," Hynes says. "It's actually from even as far back as the time as merchants. If you were outspoken, then maybe you wouldn't get your share and you'd worry about how you'll make it through the winter. Maybe it was all the way back from then. I don't know."

Maybe our history is partly to blame. Our ancestors were put here to fish to benefit a kingdom far away, brokering deals that benefitted others more so than ourselves. And why would we expect DFO to operate any differently now than it always has? For starters, the science is more reliable now. We also know better what happened to northern cod—in excruciating detail, in fact. Granted, new lessons still come—like the recent Rose and Walters 2019 study that argues overfishing played a greater role in the collapse of cod and its slow rebuilding than originally assumed. So then, why aren't we compelled to do better now?

Sherrylynn Rowe says we ought to:

> One of the key things I think we need to do to really improve the situation at present is get a lot more focus on what we're optimizing for. Northern cod, it's been under moratorium since 1992 and under DFO policy, the sustainable fisheries framework with the precautionary approach, there's all kinds of stuff in there saying how management actions must promote stock growth and removals by all human sources kept at the lowest possible level and so on. But nonetheless, for northern cod right now, we still don't have a plan.

And yet, arguably, we are as unlikely to get such a plan now as the day Newfoundland and Labrador handed over its right to manage its fishery to Canada. The year 2019 marks seventy years since the province joined Confederation. It's been sixty-five years since Canada assumed responsibility for Newfoundland and Labrador's fishery. How is it that we are situated right next to the stocks that brought our ancestors here but have no greater claims to them than anyone else?

To regain control of our locational advantage would take a rewriting of the Fisheries Act as it relates to an adjacency principle, granting those in proximity to the resource a greater stake in its decision-making and use. We must also re-examine the terms of the Atlantic Accord, which is silent on this matter but should specify Newfoundland and Labrador as a primary beneficiary of its fishery. And we must re-open the Terms of Union with Canada. But before any of that can happen, we need some gumption.

Newfoundlanders and Labradorians may be more like a jigged cod than we are willing to admit. Perhaps it's our past, the fisher–merchant relationship, being put here to work for someone else's primary interests, or the years of fishers being voiceless—the guise of politics and science legitimizing the unworthiness of fishers' experience. I'm reminded of a fisher's quote from Dean Bavington's *Managed Annihilation*: "We have to wait for them [DFO scientists] to say there is or there isn't fish, our experience don't mean a thing." But that's how it is; fishers are not speaking up for themselves and whether it's learned or inherent, it's not helping their case.

Ryan Cleary is the one who drew the comparison to jigged cod for me. I met Cleary at Zachery's on Duckworth Street in St. John's on the same day as the northern cod headline. He too wasn't surprised by it, but said it showed the continued mismanagement of our fisheries as well as public apathy. Cleary lives in this neighbourhood and knows this place so well he calls it *Zac's*. In our conversation he calls his wife *da misses*, always stops the conversation for the sake of politeness with the waitress, and listens and speaks to me intensely. I share with Cleary one of my observations about the fishers I've interviewed: many are willing to share things on the wharf, things affecting their livelihood, things they wouldn't dream of saying on record, let alone to their local politicians or union representatives.

"Have you ever fished—have you ever jigged a cod?" Cleary asks.

"Yeah. I have," I reply.

"How much fight does a cod give you on the way up?"

"Not very much."

"No, it doesn't, does it? I mean, you can feel the initial weight on the hook, but then it just—" Cleary pauses, and I know where he's going with this. The fish succumbs at that point, falling, to use the familiar phrase, hook, line, and sinker, for the draw.

"I've often thought when I was jigging fish that this is pretty much how fishermen have become. There's no fight in them." I take Cleary's point. Where is the vision of the fighting Newfoundlander from the First World War? Did we leave that reputation behind on the battlefield, he asks, failing to fight our own battles at home?

Looking back through my research notes, I am reminded of Dean Bavington's point about the introduction of the cod jigger, which signalled a power shift between fishers and merchants. Merchants encouraged fishers to use the double-hooked lead weight (which would later become single-hooked) because it could attract cod without bait. Eliminating the problem of waiting for a hungry fish meant fishers could catch more cod and merchants would make more money. But the new practice also flew in the face of sustainable wild-fisheries management. Bavington relayed the story to me: "Sir John Hope Simpson, one of the commissioners of government that came to Newfoundland when we lost our nation and went back to being a British colony, he came in and explicitly said, 'We know enough about fishing. We need knowledge and arithmetic, and we need to organize the fishery according to that, not the knowledge of fisherman.'" Today's challenge, Bavington says, is to once again reorganize wild fisheries management based on the traditional knowledge of fishing.

"We're breeding spineless cowards," Martin Hynes had said to me back up in St. Anthony at the fish plant. "The fishermen will all stand up and fight when it comes to something in their own town, right? If something happened in their own town, they'd kill somebody. But when it comes to their livelihood, it seems like they just sit back [and say,] 'Well, I've got better things to do than to worry about that.'" The communities out on the Northern Peninsula near where Martin Hynes lives have been among the hardest hit by the cod fisheries collapse. Wayne Bartlett's "Resettlement Song" tells the story of a ghost in the doorway of the last standing house in the resettled Northern Peninsula community of Fortune, which was abandoned in 1974 under the Fisheries Household Resettlement Program. In the music video Bartlett produced about Fortune's resettlement, the footage travels through buttercups toward the doorway of an abandoned house, as if a ghost is walking through the field. I kayaked by Fortune this fall with outport excursion company Heave Away or Hang-a-shore Adventures NL. From the distance, I could see only a couple of structures still standing. But as I watched, my kayak bouncing on the ocean, the sound of waves crashing nearby, I saw fishers motoring to their fishing grounds directly ahead of Fortune to tend to their nets. The community was resettled, but the fishers, even today, return to the old fishing grounds where codfish remain, forty-five years later. Some things have changed irreversibly, and yet, some things never change.

For too long, the story of what happened to Newfoundlanders and Labradorians after the cod moratorium has been told by outsiders. The story may well be thought to be over—just this spring (2019), an Ottawa businessperson who bought a fishing plant with plans to turn it into a brewery and restaurant in Salvage, Newfoundland, said in a CBC NL News story, "tourists are the new cod"—but it's still unfolding, and will for generations to come. How that story plays out remains up to us. We can have our cod—fillets over fish sticks—and our tourism too. There are many out there who believe in an *alternative possible,* a different future than the one we're headed towards. Fogo Island Fish, Fishing for Success, and their partners who posted five fishy questions are among those setting a new vision.

For all that's changed, including the smaller numbers involved in an aging fisheries workforce, scarcer fish stocks, and a global fisheries market that's taken a stronghold, Newfoundland and Labrador remains a fishing nation. Tourists flock here from all over the world wanting to see a glimpse of our unique culture, how we live, our music, our food, our art, and our stories. And many want to see our rural, fishing outport lifestyle because it has influenced all of those aspects of our lives and still does today. Tourists may well be the new cod, but they come for the cod, too—so can we realistically have one without the other? Unquestionably, we have opportunities at our fingertips that we can amplify, but we still have serious questions, too. Just thinking about the people I've profiled in this book, here are some of mine:

1. Who will take over for the inshore fishers once they fold up their gear for good? And what can be done to support the Brad Watkins types, who have been arguably left as abandoned as the *Atlantic Charger* is at the bottom of Baffin Bay?

2. How can we help get Newfoundlanders and Labradorians back out in boats with people like Captain Wayne Maloney—if not to fish, to appreciate what we have on our own doorsteps?

3. How can we preserve our heritage structures, keeping the buildings April MacDonald photographs from turning to dust?

4. Who will support the upcoming musicians Wayne Bartlett profiles on Quirpon Radio? What about the other artists, documenting our culture so it can live beyond our lifetime?

5. And then, I have my own family to think about. What can I do?

It's early in the morning on February 3, 2019. I've spent the last three hours by my father's side; he sits in a lounge chair in the living room and it's where he spent the night. I'm lying on the sofa next to him. I heard him wake up, calling out my mother's name. *Pauline.* But my mother is hard of hearing and refuses to wear her hearing aids. Dad needed water and was feeling especially nauseated this morning. I convince him to take his pain medication and get him a warm facecloth to place on his forehead.

During this trip home to Corner Brook, I witness Dad's entire world slowing down. He gets up only to move from the bed to his favourite chair and to and from the washroom as absolutely necessary. His appetite is also gone, and he's mostly existing on a diet of vitamin shakes and water, accented by the odd food craving—mostly for canned peaches and pears—that vanishes long before it could ever be satisfied. What a transition from the man of last summer, scarfing down fried chicken and fish and chips.

My daughter, Navya, now fifteen months old, barrels around Mom and Dad's house, circling from the living room through the dining room, the kitchen, the main entryway, and back to the living room again, unaware of her grandfather's worsening condition. In her innocence, she plays with the remote for his favourite recliner, uses his pill bottles as maracas, and hides under his walker. Seeing this, Dad places a throw overtop the walker, creating a tent. My four-year-old niece, Lauren, and Navya play along, giggling inside the tent. They are too young now to remember this later, I think. The thought hits me in my gut. My father has reached the two-year mark of the "two to five years" the doctors predicted he had left when we first learned the prostate cancer had spread to his bones. The pain at times is so great, my father forcibly shakes his legs and moans aloud to get through it, waiting for the extra dose of pain medication to catch up.

Fast-forward a couple of weeks and Mom and Dad have travelled to Ottawa for a nuclear medicine consult. Dad will be the second Newfoundlander with stage IV cancer in the bones to receive a radioisotope treatment here at The Ottawa Hospital. "I'm not sure that's anything to brag about," Dad says to the specialist, laughing; it's difficult for me to laugh along, so I feign a smile. We learn the treatment will take six months and, on average, prolongs patients' lives by three months. Three months. It also won't help the pain and may actually worsen it, bringing on more flashes of pain. I look at Dad, his body thinning out even more and losing mobility by the day. He also complains now about his failing hearing and eyesight. "I'm getting all kinds of calls to fix accordions, but can't fix 'em," Dad says, "It's a shame, you know." I know, but I don't say anything. Every day, he has to relinquish a part of himself he's not ready to. Last week, it was driving. In reality, he couldn't have gotten behind the wheel of his truck anyway, but his doctors told him as much, so that's when it became real for him. "I'm gonna fix my own accordions and sell them," Dad says. He's not ready to accept he may not fix any at all. He's here in Ottawa and the piles of accordions are back in Corner Brook.

That night, Dad is unable to walk up or down the stairs to a bedroom, so I make a bed for him on the living room sofa. I turn on the baby monitor, pointing it at Dad (Navya is fast asleep and rarely wakes these days; if she does, she'll make sure I hear her with loud cries). I grab my copy of *The Magic Fish*, the one I took from the abandoned house, and sit next to dad, waiting until he falls asleep. On its cover is a fisher, a slight man with a beard, fisherman's cap, rubber boots, and vest over a shirt, with rolled-up sleeves and jeans. He stands before a blue fish, who has risen above the land, on a pedestal of water. The fish wears a pointy white crown and the fisher could almost be praying, his eyes fixated on the fish and his arms bent, hands pressed together toward this god. The book is marked with the name *Bryon R.* (*Thank you, Bryon*, I think.) It smells so dreadfully musty I have to keep it wrapped inside of a plastic bag, inside of another plastic bag. But still, the residual odour lingers. It even stays on my hands and fingers after flipping through its pages—which is itself a necessarily delicate job. I turned a page too quickly, reading it the first time, inflicting a small tear in one of the pages. The yellowed pages feel and look misshapen, sometimes sticking together, symptoms of neglect and dried water or moisture damage.

I haven't yet showed this copy to Navya, knowing what her toddler hands are capable of doing (she's on a strict reading diet of cardboard books for the foreseeable future). But this story is one I want her to hear, to read, to know, to understand. It's a story Pop could have easily read to me—maybe he would have replaced the word *castle* with *wheelbarrow*, but still. The illustration, beautiful in its black line-drawing simplicity with minimal blue accents, could tell the story all on its own.

The story starts off simply enough. The fisher leaves his old hut by the sea to go fishing, his wife looking on from their window. It's what they do every day. On this day, he feels something pulling his line. The fisherman reels it in: a big, crowned fish. The fish pleads to be put back in the water. He's a magic fish, he says, a real prince. The fisher obliges and heads home without fish for supper. Upon learning this news, the fisher's wife is unhappy. She wears a blue headscarf and apron over a long black skirt, patterned short-sleeved shirt, and slip-on shoes. They are accustomed to a simple life, but the wife has an idea: they should ask the fish for a new pretty house. So the fisher asks, and they receive it. Upon returning to his new house, the fisher's wife is dressed in a ballgown, waving a fan, with her hair in a bouffant, and donning dangling earrings. But it's not enough for her. The wife wants a castle. Ask, and they receive. But again, it's not enough. She wants to be queen of the land. And so, it was. The wife is adorned in gold crown and attire, surrounded by noblemen and maid servants upon the humble fisher's return. And still, it's not enough. The wife wishes to be queen of the universe. That wish proves too much. The magic fish withdraws all of the wishes granted and the fisher returns to his hut, his wife inside, and that's how they'll live forevermore.

I fold the book and, seeing Dad's eyes are closed, turn out the lamp and pull his blanket up a little higher. Dad's life running out is beyond anyone's control. There are no wishes at this stage, despite my own bedside prayers that evening and every evening. But where the fishery is concerned, we can thrive in a world of just enough, if we are willing to let go of the pursuit of excess. If we don't let go of the vision of plentiful, we will be left with nothing. And how truly pitiful is that? For Dad, I have to focus on the time remaining. Death will come, but while there's life, let's do our best to live and let live.

The day we left Uncle Clyde and Aunt Hattie's in Little Bay East, we all piled into the car. The bay was awash with fog by then and mist rose up from the pavement. I took the driver's seat, Dad in shotgun, with Mom, Raman, and Navya in the backseat. Everyone was exhausted, so the car filled with quiet even before they slept, forcing me to be alone with my thoughts and the sinking feeling rushing over me. I drove through the feeling, around and over the road repairs covering other repairs that needed more repairs still. I tried to avoid the deep grooves, potholes, and bits of pavement broken off at the road's edge and scattered onto the narrow shoulder. I was aware of waking the family and causing Dad more pain. I bit back tears passing roadside crosses, which came to have new meaning. The souls of my family members are here, too.

Mother (Pauline) Thornhill, and Father (Don) Thornhill hold their granddaughter, Navya Verma, at Pinchgut Lake, Newfoundland, 2018. (Scott Grant, RONiN photography)

This is it, I think. I was leaving behind a place that defined me with no plans to return to it; if I did, it would likely be without my father riding shotgun. The rain washed down furiously, filling the ruts in the road until they were flowing streams. I took care to avoid the water runoff, driving through blasted rocks after blasted rocks, all the while observing those professions of love and place (the *this-person-loves-that-person* and the *so-and-sos-were-here* tags). As the rain trickled off the windshield, the mustards and greens of the creeping plants and the slate greys and maroons of rocks and boulders blurred into a rolling landscape, like dark green waves of a temperamental sea.

"A life at sea keeps you honest," Pop once told me. I didn't need the explanation. I knew what he'd survived and the odds he'd fought to do it. Those hands, the ones that held mine and flipped the pages of my storybook, calling out wheelbarrows, were the source of what prosperity he had. Those same hands untangled, secured, and retrieved fishing nets. And they were the same hands to knit and weave the nets. The hand-blown glass floaters suspending the nets were also his handiwork. Mostly they were translucent greens or browns but also clear, amber, and blue, pieces of glass easily camouflaged against glassy ocean waters. Those hands, the glass, these were not at all delicate things, but precious just the same.

As a child, I remember Pop showing me those old nets, quick to scratch my amateur skin. My grandfather checked over my translucent hands for wounds, but seeing only grazes and no scrapes, reassured me by placing a glass float, as big as a cantaloupe, in my palms. It was round but bumpy all over with a knobbed spot where the blown glass was sealed, making it airtight. I keep those fish floats in my living room now and can see the signs they've been etched by sand, sun, and salt water. The glass has something of a mystical quality, like a crystal ball, only this glass holds stories of the past. The way a conch shell breathes winds of the ocean when held against the ear, these trinkets tell tales of a fisher at sea.

One day, I'll put this glass float in Navya's palms in just the same way. I'll trace her fingers over the bumps of the beautiful baubles, souvenirs of lives lived at sea. I'll tell her how the blown glass granted the fishnets buoyancy once released from her great-grandfather's hands. Hands that surely felt the sea water, as thick as blood, course through his veins; and blood that still gushes, through ours.

Endnotes

Chapter 1

p. 6 "Don't fall me down, Pop, don't fall me down": Jennifer Verma. Letters from Pop (Newfoundland and Labrador's Poor Literacy Legacy). *Maisonneuve*, March 2018.

p. 7 "1929, a wrecking ball of a tsunami rose up out of an earthquake rumbling under the ocean": Alan Ruffman; Violet Hann, January 2001. "The Newfoundland Tsunami of Nov. 18, 1929: An Examination of the 28 Deaths of the 'South Coast Disaster,'" *Newfoundland and Labrador Studies*, Volume 21, Number 1.

p. 9 "Portuguese and Basque are thought to have fished the Grand Banks before that time," Joseph Gough, August 2013. *History of Commercial Fisheries*. The Canadian Encyclopedia website.

p. 10 "By the mid-nineteenth century, there were as many as 300 settlers on Brunette Island": "Lighthouse Explorer: Brunette Island Light." *Lighthouse Digest*.

p. 10 "The bay, which appears on maps in the early sixteenth century likely received its name from the Portuguese word *fortuna*, meaning 'place of good fortune.'" D Penny, 1981. Communities: Brunette Island, Fortune Bay. *The Livyre*, Volume 1, pp. 21–24.

p. 10 "80,000 by 1840, doubling the population from 40,568 in 1815 and quadrupling from 21,975 in 1805" Census of Canada, 1851–2, Vol. 2 and Statistics Canada, November 2010. *Progress of Population, 1700 to 1825.* Government of Canada.

p. 11 "In the 1870s, it is estimated that the Newfoundland commercial fishing fleet alone had grown to eighteen thousand small boats and twelve hundred larger vessels." *History of Fishing in Canada, Early Years Fishing in Canada.* Canadian Council of Professional Fish Harvesters website.

p. 11 "the Canadian-wide commercial fishing fleet today (based on 2016 numbers) is about eighteen thousand vessels": Fisheries and Oceans Canada, March 2018. Canada's Fisheries Fast Facts 2017. Government of Canada.

p. 11 "The seal hunt continued into the mid-1900s, but has faced difficulties ever since," CW Sanger, 1998. *Seal Fishery, Background: History, Resource and Natural Environment.* Heritage Newfoundland website; Fisheries and Aquaculture, April 2019. *Sealing: History.* Government of Newfoundland and Labrador.

p. 11 "By the 1890s, there were double the number of fishers than in the 1850s": Dean Bavington. *Managed Annihilation: An Unnatural History of the Newfoundland Cod Collapse.* UBC Press, 2010.

p. 11 "With existing methods of fishing, it is inconceivable that the great sea fisheries such as those for cod, herring and mackerel, could ever be exhausted.": Thomas Henry Huxley, 1883, International Fisheries Exhibition Keynote Address, London, UK.

p. 12   "Mercer's Cove, a fishing community on Brunette Island whose residents were resettled elsewhere in the late 1950s": Robert D. Pitt, October 2014, Brunette Island, *The Canadian Encyclopedia, Historica Canada.*

p. 12   "the bison and moose introduced as part of a provincial wildlife reserve in the 1960s—have died" Robert D. Pitt, October 2014, Brunette Island, *The Canadian Encyclopedia, Historica Canada*

p. 13   "In Little Bay East and all along Newfoundland's coastlines, codfish was split, salted, and dried on flakes" Mark Ferguson. *Hard Racket for a Living–Making Light-Salted Fish on the East Coast of Newfoundland.* Material Culture Review, January 1997.

p. 13   "The word "flake" is of Nordic origin, deriving from Old Norse, a language spoken by Vikings or Norsemen": Richard Whitbourne. *Newfoundland*, p.57, 1623.

p. 13   "the [Great] Depression was largely responsible for later reductions as capital became scarce and demand dropped": Keith Collier. "20th Century Salt Fish Markets, 1914–1992." *Newfoundland and Labrador Heritage* website, 2011.

p. 13   "global market price for salt-fish dropped at the end of the century, saw a brief comeback, then tanked again": David Alexander. "Newfoundland's Traditional Economy and Development to 1934." *Acadiensis*, p. 56, April 1976.

p. 13   "By the 1930s, one-quarter of the population was dependent on government relief": C. D. Howe, 1950. *Newfoundland: An Introduction to Canada's New Province.* Department of External Affairs, Dominion Bureau of Statistics.

p. 13   "reports the non-profit Canadian Council for Professional Fish Harvesters": "History of Fishing in Canada, Early Years Fishing in Canada." *Canadian Council of Professional Fish Harvesters* website.

p. 13   "Since colonization, Newfoundlanders and Labradorians have relied on imported foods, particularly over winter.": Chad Pelley. "Everybody Eats: Taking a Bite Out of Food Security Issues in NL. *The Overcast* online, April 2018; "Grow your own: How N.L. plans to produce more of its own food," *CBC News* online, February 2017; "MUN entrepreneur looking to improve food security in Newfoundland and Labrador." *CBC News* online, May 2018.

p. 14   "conditions like beriberi (caused by vitamin B-1 deficiency, often leading to heart failure) and tuberculosis spreading rampantly": Keith Collier, 2011, "Malnutrition in Newfoundland," *Newfoundland and Labrador Heritage* online.

p. 14   "salt-codfish trade exports fell by half and fifteen thousand fishing jobs were lost in the decade following 1947": Dean Bavington. *Managed Annihilation: An Unnatural History of the Newfoundland Cod Collapse*, Nature xiii [Foreword].

p. 14   "a six-person commission (three Brits and three Newfoundlanders) along with the governor in 1934.": Melvin Baker. "The Tenth Province: Newfoundland joins Canada, 1949." *Horizon*, 10:111, 1987.

p. 14   "just over half of Newfoundlanders voted, in 1949, in favour of joining the Canadian Confederation": Melvin Baker, *Falling into the Canadian Lap: The Confederation of Newfoundland and Canada, 1945–1949.* Government of Newfoundland and Labrador, March 2003.

p. 21   "The Grand Banks and the Flemish Cap sprawl over an area of 280,000 square kilometres": Fisheries and Oceans Canada, *The Grand Banks and the Flemish Cap,* June 2012.

p. 22   "A meal of *fish and brewis* (pronounced *brews*), salt cod boiled with hard bread, and *scrunchions*, salted fried pork fat, would have been a particular favourite among crews.": Jenny Higgins, "Social History 1760–1830." *Newfoundland and Labrador Heritage* online, , 2015.

p. 23   "Deckhands would earn a small sum for the season as well as any fish they managed to catch": Allan Stoodley, "Down Memory Lane–From Catchee to Captain." *The Southern Gazette*, September 2017.

p. 25 "The *Florence* was an American-made Bank fishing schooner": Robert C. Parsons, *Lost at sea: a compilation*. Creative Book Publishing, 2001.

p. 26 "what they would have measured as 40 *quintals*.": G. M. Story, W. J. Kirwin and J. D. A. Widdowson. "Dictionary of Newfoundland English: quintal." *Newfoundland and Labrador Heritage* online.

Chapter 2

p. 38 "(Newfoundland had its own currency from 1865 to 1949; the Newfoundland dollar was on par with the Canadian dollar.) ": Joseph Roberts Smallwood and Robert D. W. Pitt, 1981, *Encyclopedia of Newfoundland and Labrador, volume 1 [Extract: letter C]*.

p. 39 "many fishers quadrupled their earnings, and between 1935 and 1945, their average annual income jumped from $135 to $641": Jenny Higgins, 2007, "Economic Impacts of WW II," *Newfoundland and Labrador Heritage* online.

p. 39 "In 1939, $28.50 CAD/week was the minimum budget for a family of five in Canada": Emil Bjarnason and Bert Marcuse, *The Case of the Dwindling Dollar*, Trade Union Research Bureau, 1948.

p. 40 "The same was true of infections like tuberculosis, which plagued Newfoundland at a rate far higher than Canada": Keith Collier, 2011, "History of Tuberculosis and Its Prevalence in Newfoundland," *Newfoundland and Labrador Heritage* online.

p. 40 "Throughout the 1940s and 1950s, any schooners that weren't wrecks had been converted to gasoline and diesel power": Jenny Higgins, "Fisheries Technology Since Confederation," *Newfoundland and Labrador Heritage* online.

p. 40 "draggers were equipped to drag nets along the ocean floor, scooping up everything in their path": *Ibid*.

p. 40 "Some continued working on the ocean in coastal freighting or the merchant navy" Jenny Higgins, "Impacts of New Harvesting Technology on NL Fishery," *Newfoundland and Labrador Heritage* online, 2007.

p. 41 "more commonly called a *make and break*, recognized for its *putt-putt* sound": Intangible Cultural Heritage. Make and Break Engines. Memorial University of Newfoundland.

p.42 "Handlining involves deploying a line with hooks, lures, or bait (squid or capelin for attracting cod)": Elizabeth Brown-Hornstein, "Fishing Gear 101: Handlines – Entice and Hook," The Safina Centre, June 2016,

p. 42 "Handlining and trapping are considered more sustainable methods": *Ibid*.

p. 48 "Longlining was a relatively new practice for the Canadian swordfish fishery" J. L. Hart, 1962–63. *Annual Report and Investigators' Summaries*. Fisheries Research Board of Canada. p. 24

p. 50 "a winter storm wreaked havoc across Canada's eastern seaboard": Allan Stoodley, September 2017. *Down Memory Lane—The Blue Wave Tragedy*. The Southern Gazette.

p. 52 "By the early 1950s, when many schooners had been forced out of the fishery by the factory freezer trawlers": Jenny Higgins, 2009. "Cod Moratorium," *Newfoundland and Labrador Heritage* online.

p. 53 "*steamers*, as they were once called, were owned and operated by the Canadian National Railway (CNR)": Robert Cuff, "Steamers," *Newfoundland and Labrador Heritage* online, 2001.

p. 54 "There was a Congregational Church erected in Little Bay East in 1909": Pamela Bruce, "The Congregational Church in Newfoundland," *Newfoundland and Labrador Heritage* online, 2000.

p. 58 "Perhaps most scathing are the estimates by fisheries biologists Jeffrey Hutchings and Ransom Myers": J. A. Hutchings and R. A. Myers, 1995. The biological collapse of Atlantic cod off Newfoundland and Labrador: an exploration of historical changes in exploitation, harvesting technology and management, *The North Atlantic fisheries: Successes, failures and challenges*, vol. 3, pp. 37-93, 1995.

p. 58 "By 1995, all major cod and flounder fisheries on the Grand Banks were closed": Fisheries and Oceans Canada, *The Grand Banks and the Flemish Cap*, June 2012.

Chapter 3

p. 63 "Unemployment rates reached a high in Newfoundland and Labrador that year" :Statistics Canada, Labour Force Survey, January 2018. *Annual Average Unemployment Rate Canada and Provinces 1976-2017.*

p. 63 "The thirty to forty thousand Newfoundlanders and Labradorians who were put out of work": Jenny Higgins, "Economic Impacts of the Cod Moratorium," *Newfoundland and Labrador Heritage* online, 2008.

p. 64 "Two of the core programs were the Northern Cod Adjustment and Rehabilitation Program (NCARP) and The Atlantic Groundfish Strategy (TAGS).": *Ibid.*

p. 65 "When it came to TAGS, more than half of those eligible participated in one or more of the programs offered." Government of Newfoundland and Labrador. *The Atlantic Groundfish Strategy: An Analysis of the Program on a Regional Basis.* Department of Finance, May 1997.

p. 65 "Both NCARP and TAGS met with limited success" Jenny Higgins, "Economic Impacts of the Cod Moratorium," *Newfoundland and Labrador Heritage* online, 2008.

p. 65 "it received $750 million (announced in July 1998 from then Human Resources Development Canada)": Beaton Tulk and Laurie Blackwood Pike, May 2018. *A Man of My Word.* Flanker Press, 2018.

p. 67 "Newfoundland and Labrador's population dropped by a record 10 per cent.": Statistics Canada, Demography Division, September 2018, *Annual Estimate of Population for Canada, Provinces and Territories 1971–2018.*

p. 67 "But by 2014, it had started to slow once again; and by 2017, the population was shrinking again." Newfoundland Statistics Agency. *Population and Demographics 1971–2019.* Government of Newfoundland.

p. 68 "The first recorded public use of the term was on the radio program, *The Barrelman,* in 1938" Ruth King and Sandra Clarke, December 2002, *Contesting meaning: Newfie and the Politics of Ethnic Labelling,* Journal of Sociolinguistics

p. 69 "numbskulls too dumb to realize their own "ineptitude and alien status." P. Byrne, 1997. *Booze, ritual and the invention of tradition: The phenomenon of the screech-in.* p. 232-248. Utah State University Press

p. 69 "Like the colloquial renaming of the Canadian National Railway passenger train from the Caribou to The Newfie Bullet.": Canadian Railroad Historical Association, July–August 1967. *Canadian Rail,* No. 190, p. 156

p. 70 "the number of licensed tourist establishments increased by over 100 per cent": Newfoundland Statistics Agency, November 1994, *Number of Licensed Tourist Establishments and Number of Accommodation Units in Newfoundland and Labrador,* Historical Statistics of Newfoundland and Labrador, p. 220.

p. 72 "The minimum wage in this province is also among the lowest in the country at $11.40/hour": *CBC News Newfoundland and Labrador*, February, 2019; "Minimum wage going up in Newfoundland and Labrador on April 1." *CBC News* online.

p. 72 "nearly two-thirds of the population (twelve years and older) report having at least one chronic disease": "Health Status Report: Chronic Disease," *Eastern Health,* August 2016, p. 1.

p. 73 "Until 1983, secondary education in the province ended at Grade 11": Kerri Neil, The Economic History of Women in Newfoundland and Labrador. Memorial University of Newfoundland, 2011.

p. 76 "Newfoundland became the unexpected host of thirty-eight planes and their seven thousand displaced passengers.": CBC News: World, September 2011. Gander honoured by U.S. for 9/11 help.

p. 80 "Oil prices would tank the following year, resulting in an unprecedented provincial deficit": Government of Newfoundland and Labrador, December 2014, *The Economic Review* 2014, pp. 12–13

p. 80 "Fogo Island Inn is a social business, funnelling wealth back into the local community in the form of employment": *Fogo Island Inn* website.

p. 81 "Shorefast, a registered Canadian charity with the mandate to promote cultural and economic resiliency": *Shorefast* website, 2018

Chapter 4

p. 87 "the province's real estate market levelled out in 2018 after dropping for the past several years": Government of Newfoundland and Labrador, December 2018, *The Economic Review 2018*, pp. 41–43.

p. 87 "J.B. Foote & Sons Ltd. storefront, built in 1908 by fish merchant and captain John Benjamin Foote.": Registered Heritage Structures Bibliography. "J. B. Foote House (Grand Bank)." *Newfoundland and Labrador Heritage* online, June 2005.

p. 88 "Over the last year, Clearwater (including its Grand Bank processing plant) has been the subject of local and national and local news media attention": Quentin Casey, "How Ottawa bungled Indigenous reconciliation in the Arctic surf clam fishery." *Natural Resources Magazine* web site, January 2019.

p. 89 "The official word on that decision from the federal government, under newly appointed federal fisheries minister Jonathan Wilkinson": "Decision to cancel lucrative surf clam contract remains shrouded in mystery." *CBC News*, August 2018.

p. 89 "A columnist for the *Halifax Examiner*, Stephen Kimber, summarized the debacle": Stephen Kimber, "Clearwater wins. Again. Still. Always. And forever." *Halifax Examiner*, March 2019.

p. 90 "The situation raises a fundamental point about fisheries management in not only the province but the country": Ryan Cleary, "Ottawa's failure to include adjacency principle in Fisheries Act amendments 'grave injustice': FISH-NL." *The Federation of Independent Sea Harvesters of Newfoundland and Labrador* website, February 2018.

p. 90 "The economy of a fishing industry with no adjacency [is] no economy, at all.": *Fish, Food and Allied Workers* website.

p. 90 "I don't believe that Newfoundland and Labrador will have a real future as a fishing province until we control the quotas of fish off our shores": "FISH-NL wants better management of the industry in this province." *The Telegram*, October 2017.

p. 90 "He raises the adjacency principle, the idea that those who live alongside resources should benefit most from the resource's development": *Fish, Food and Allied Workers* website.

p. 90 "When the French sailed more than 4,300 kilometres across the sea to get here": Joseph Roberts Smallwood and Robert D. W. Pitt, 1981, *Encyclopedia of Newfoundland and Labrador*, volume 2 [Extract: letter G], p. 677.

p. 91 "The introduction of the cod jigger—likely in the 1850s—signalled a particular shift in power between fishers and merchants, says Bavington": Sean Cadigan, "The Moral Economy of the Commons: Ecology and Equity in Newfoundland Cod Fishery, 1815–1855," *Labour/Le Travail* 43 (Spring 1999), 9–42.

p. 91 "When Captain James Cook surveyed the south coast of Newfoundland in 1765, he visited Grand Bank and reported it having the largest fishery in Fortune Bay.": V. R. Taylor, 1985. "The Early Atlantic Salmon Fishery in Newfoundland and Labrador." Department of Fisheries and Oceans, Newfoundland.

p. 91 "The price of a quintal (100 kg) of fish on the merchant's book was tied to the cost of a barrel of flour": Rosemary Ommer, "Fishing Places, Fishing People: Traditions and Issues in Canadian Small-scale Fisheries," p. 27, University of Toronto Press, 1999.

p. 92 "Domestic and foreign fleets sailed to the Grand Banks, with schooners replacing shallops, and trawling replacing the handlining": W. H. Lear, 1998. "Histories of Fisheries in the Northwest Atlantic: The 500-Year Perspective." *Journal of Northwestern Atlantic Fishery Science*, vol. 23, p. 59.

p. 94 "In its heyday, Captain John Thornhill's home, the Thorndyke, was an architectural beauty" Registered Heritage Structures Bibliography, "The Thorndyke (Grand Bank)." *Newfoundland and Labrador Heritage* online, August 2016.

p. 98 "ineffective in curbing the overexploitation, mainly because enforcement was ineffective, and catches exceeded them in many cases.": W. H. Lear, *Underwater World: Atlantic Cod.* Communications Directorate, Fisheries and Oceans Canada, 1993.

p. 105 "the Canadian Centre for Fisheries Innovation (CCFI), a non-profit organization owned by Memorial University and predominantly funded by the Marine Institute in St. John's": "Cod: Building the Fishery of the Future." *Canadian Centre for Fisheries Innovation* website.

p. 103 "Fisheries and Oceans uses what it calls a "precautionary approach framework"": Fisheries and Oceans Canada, "A fishery decision-making framework incorporating the precautionary approach." Government of Canada, March 2009.

p. 104 "DFO had already allowed the northern cod quota to more than double—from 4,000 t in 2015 to 10,000 t in 2016 and 13,000 t in 2017.": Janelle Kelly, Northern Cod Stock Down by 30%, Still in 'Critical Zone'. *CBC News*, March 2018.

p. 104 "A 2019 paper in the journal *Fisheries Research* by George Rose and Carl Walters argues": George A. Rose and Carl J. Walters, November 2019 (future). "The state of Canada's Iconic Northern cod: A second opinion." *Fisheries Research*, Volume 219.

p. 105 "Lobster was the only shellfish species to actually increase over that period,": *Canadian Fisheries Statistics 2004.* Fisheries and Oceans Canada. Government of Canada.

p. 106 "The Committee on the Status of Endangered Wildlife in Canada (COSEWIC), in its 2010 assessment of the northern cod stock": *Press Release: Risk of Extinction Increases for Atlantic Cod.* Committee on the Status of Endangered Wildlife in Canada, Government of Canada, May 2010.

p. 107 "There is evidence to suggest grey seals in the Gulf of St. Lawrence are impeding recovery of the cod stock there": M. Kurtis Trzcinski et al. "Continued Decline of an Atlantic Cod Population: How Important is Gray Seal Predation?" *Ecological Applications*, vol. 16, no. 6, December 2006.

p. 107 "In 1992 fishing accounted for 20 per cent of all employment in Newfoundland and Labrador.": Jenny Higgins, "Economic Impacts of the Cod Moratorium," *Newfoundland and Labrador Heritage* online, 2008.

p. 108 "In 1989 the fishery employed about 37,665 seasonal workers and the pre-moratorium cod market brought in approximately $500-million annually": Government of Newfoundland and Labrador, December 2018, *The Economic Review 2018*, pp. 41–43.

p.108 "In Canada, in 2018, the average age is forty to forty-one, while in Atlantic Canada it's forty-five and in Newfoundland and Labrador it's forty-six to forty-seven years old.": Statistics Canada, *Annual Demographic Estimates: Canada, Provinces and Territories*. Government of Canada, November 2015.

p. 108 "new fishery opportunities, like fish farming salmon and *smolt*": Government of Newfoundland and Labrador, December 2018, *The Economic Review 2018*, p. 31.

p. 108 "In 1999 approximately 20 per cent of registered fish harvesters were under the age of thirty compared with 9 per cent in 2009": M. MacDonald, 2013. Report of the Community-University Research for Recovery Alliance Globalization Group. *Globalization, fisheries and recovery.*

p. 108 "A more recent figure suggests in 2019 almost one-third (32 per cent) of fish harvesters in the province will reach age fifty-four or older.": "Media Release: Five Fishy Questions for NL Provincial Parties," *Too Big to Ignore* online, Global Partnership for Small-scale Fisheries Research.

p. 108 "Newfoundland and Labrador's population, as with the rest of Atlantic Canada, is aging faster than the rest of the country" Minister of Industry, January 2019. *Annual Demographic Estimates: Canada, Provinces and Territories 2018*. Statistics Canada; Statistics Canada, July 2019. *Population estimates on July 1ˢᵗ, by age and sex.* Government of Canada.

p. 110 "A 2019 statistic suggests women comprise about one-fifth (23 per cent) of professional fish harvesters in the province.": "Media Release: Five Fishy Questions for NL Provincial Parties." *Too Big to Ignore*, Global Partnership for Small-scale Fisheries Research, May 2019.

p. 111 "A 2015 report in the *Globe and Mail* claimed crewmembers often earn day rates of $200–250": Scott Munn. "I want to be a commercial fisherman. What will my salary be?" the *Globe and Mail*, Salaries Series, April 2015.

Chapter 5

p. 117 "Newfoundland and Labrador Tourism is reporting a strong outlook for the industry, showing no signs of letting up.": Jenny Higgins, "Tourism After Confederation," *Newfoundland and Labrador Heritage* online, 2012.

p. 117 "Gros Morne alone welcomed 240,000 visitors in 2017.": *Newfoundland and Labrador Provincial Tourism Performance 2017. Gros Morne National Park Visitation (Table 13).* Department of Tourism, Culture, Industry and Innovation.

p. 119 "Cod is Iceland's biggest fish export, supplying much of the British demand for fresh and frozen fresh cod" Alexander Simoes. "Iceland, Exports," *The Observatory of Economic Complexity* website.

p. 119 "As a result, Iceland has one of the most profitable fishing industries in the world, hauling in more than $1-billion (converted to CAD) annually.": "Catch by region of landings and region of buyers," Statistics Iceland.

p. 119 "Between the 1950s and '80s, Iceland's annual cod catch varied between approximately 200,000 to 300,000 tonnes (t)," Statistics Iceland.

p. 120 "cod landings in Newfoundland and Labrador dropped from approximately 250,000 t annually up to the 1970s": "Seafisheries Landings," Fisheries and Oceans Canada, Government of Canada, January 2019.

p. 120 "Of Newfoundland and Labrador's $777 million fishery earnings in 2017, cod contributed about $28 million.": *Newfoundland and Labrador Fishing Industry Highlights 2016 (Revised) and 2017 (Preliminary).* Government of Newfoundland and Labrador, January 2018.

p. 120 "Most of that cod is exported to the United States (about 44 per cent), followed by the United Kingdom (30 per cent).": *Seafood Industry Year in Review 2018*, p. 36, Government of Newfoundland, 2018.

p. 120 "using whatever it can for food (including pet food) and the rest for various skincare, pharmaceutical, and other goods.": Sarah Smellie, July 2008. "Waste not, want not: Would you wear shoes made of fish?" *CBC News* Newfoundland and Labrador.

p. 120 "while Newfoundland and Labrador's numbers are decreasing (8,712 vessels total).": Fisheries and Land Resources. 2016 List of Licensed Processors in Newfoundland and Labrador. Government of Newfoundland and Labrador.

p. 120 "In 2014 Iceland had about 2,000 small-size (less than 15-metre) vessels, and 52 larger vessels." Gunnar Þórðarson and Jónas R. Viðarsson. 2014. *Coastal Fisheries in Iceland*. Matis website.

p. 120 "while Newfoundland and Labrador had more than three times as many, at about 6,614 (the majority which were of the smaller variety.": *Vessel Information*, Fisheries and Oceans Canada, Government of Canada, 2014.

p. 121 "from over 24,500 people in the fishing industry overall to 5,400 from 1987 to 2017": Noel Roy, *The Newfoundland Fishery: A Descriptive Analysis. Department of Economics*, Memorial University of Newfoundland; Statistics Canada, *Labour Force Survey*, September 1997; *Annual Average Unemployment Rate Canada and Provinces 1976-2017*, January 2018.

p. 121 "The Atlantic Fisheries Fund, a Canadian federal and provincial financial contribution program": Fisheries and Oceans Canada, Atlantic Fisheries Fund. Government of Canada, December 2018.

p. 124 "fishing as the third leading cause of employment-related death in the country (between 1996 and 2005)": Andrew Jackson, 2009. *Work and Labour in Canada: Critical Issues*. Second ed., p. 77.

p. 126 "frozen cod fillets from Russia ($8.48 a pound) and Norway ($10.02 a pound) or fresh cod fillets from Iceland ($10.43 a pound)": Jennifer Thornhill Verma. *Letter: The reasons we fish: calling it 'recreational' misses the mark. The Telegram* website, October 2018.

p. 127 "The Total Allowable Catch, or TAC, remains low, having built up to about 20,000 tonnes for cod annually." Government of Newfoundland. *Seafood Industry Year in Review 2017*, p. 45.

p. 127 "The commercial and recreational fisheries were subsequently closed in April 2003, in response to what was called a "mortality event" for the cod stock in Smith Sound": "Stock Assessment of Northern Cod," *Canadian Science Advisory Secretariat Science Advisory Report 2016*. Fisheries and Oceans Canada.

p. 127 "2,000 pounds from August 15 to September 4, then 3,000 pounds from September 4 to December 16": Fisheries and Oceans Canada. *Science Response 2017/034 – Northern Cod Stock Update*. Government of Canada.

p. 128 "The majority comes from the stewardship/recreational fishery and other causes contributing minority shares" Jennifer Thornhill Verma, October 2018. *Letter: The reasons we fish: calling it 'recreational' misses the mark. The Telegram* website.

p. 128 "as low as $0.20 a pound (Grade C) to $0.38-0.40 a pound (Grade B) to as high as $0.70–0.83 a pound (Grade A)" "Cod Prices 2018." *Fish, Food and Allied Workers* website.

p. 128 "Of the harvest levels at the time, which totalled 13,500 tonnes, the commercial fishery took home 10,525 tonnes": Scott Simms, "Newfoundland and Labrador's Northern Cod Fishery: Charting a New Sustainable Future." *Report of the Standing Committee on Fisheries and Oceans*, p. 7. House of Commons, Canada, March 2017.

p. 128 "as per legislation under the 2006 Fishing Industry Collective Bargaining Act." "Standing Fish Price Setting Panel," Government of Newfoundland and Labrador website, June 2019.

p. 128 "The grading scheme is based on what's colloquially called the *cod quality program*": *News Releases: New cod grading program another step forward in quality efforts.* Fisheries and Aquaculture, Government of Newfoundland and Labrador, July 2000.

p. 129 "In what's become known locally as the "Fogo Process,"island residents let a National Film Board (NFB) documentary crew follow them in 1967": Welcome to Fogo Island Co-Operative Society LTD." *Fogo Island Co-op* website, 2019.

p. 131 "DFO had recently cut the overall catch quota for the upcoming season by 22 per cent.": Terry Roberts, "DFO Slashes Crab Quota in Latest Blow to N.L. Fishing Industry." *CBC News*, Newfoundland and Labrador, April 2017.

p. 132 "Harvesting and processing have experienced reductions of 35.2 and 50.8 per cent, respectively, between 1989 and 2010": Nicole G. Power et al., 2014. "The Fishery Went Away." *Ecology and Society*. Memorial University of Newfoundland.

p. 133 "from an average price of $2.98 per pound in 2016 to $4.39 per pound in 2017.": Government of Newfoundland and Labrador. *Seafood Industry Year in Review 2017.* p. 10.

p. 133 "Now, twenty-five years on, total landings for shellfish—including until recently lobster—are declining.": T. H. Spanos and E. O. Hreinsson, April 2016. *Canada Seafood Market Report.* Islandsbanki Research.

p. 136 "A 2003 Royal Commission on the management of Newfoundland and Labrador's fishery reported" David Vardy and Eric Dunne, March 2003. *New Arrangements for Fisheries Management in Newfoundland and Labrador.* Royal Commission on Renewing and Strengthening Our Place in Canada.

p. 139 "Back in Corner Brook, Dad is making swift work on an accordion repair. It's his *newish* hobby, but one he picked up out of necessity.": Jennifer Thornhill Verma, "Accordion to Don: How a Squeezebox Became a Barometer for My Father's Health." *Newfoundland Quarterly*, Summer 2019.

Chapter 6

p. 141 "Anyone who go to sea for fun would go to hell for pastime.": Jennifer Thornhill Verma. "Half a Century a fisherman—'til they closed it," *Saltscapes*, First Person Feature, Winter 2018.

p. 147 "the latest unemployment rate in Canada was 5.4 per cent, while Newfoundland and Labrador's rate was more than double that at 12.4": Statistics Canada: The Daily, May 2019. *Labour Force Survey, April 2019.* Government of Canada.

p. 148 "new developments built for this purpose has become a "bedroom community": for those working in St. John's" "Our sense of St, John's is going to change dramatically." *CBC News* Newfoundland and Labrador, June 2012.

p. 149 "With higher offshore oil production in 2018, Newfoundland and Labrador expects to once again regain its short-lived title of one of the front-of-the-pack economies across Canada": Equinor Canada LTD, *Bay du Nord Development Project.* Project Description Summary, June 2018.

p. 149 "The company is responsible for implementing its own internal and environmental safety plans, approved by the Canada-NL Offshore Petroleum Board": *Canada-Newfoundland and Labrador Offshore Petroleum Board* website.

p. 149 "off of the coast of British Columbia, the federal government put a moratorium on oil and gas exploration.": "Will Trudeau Government action on tanker ban re-open painful wound," *Resource Works website*, June 2016.

p. 149 "in late 2018, spilling 250,000 litres of oil into the Atlantic Ocean.": David Maher, "'We followed our procedures,' Husky says of oil spill in Newfoundland offshore." *The Telegram*, November 2018.

p. 150 "the Witless Bay Ecological Reserve, a collection of four islands": Parks and Natural Areas Division, Department of Environment and Conservation, *Witless Bay Ecological Reserve*. Government of Newfoundland and Labrador, 1994.

p. 150 "2017, the Government of Canada introduced Bill C-48, the proposed Oil Tanker Moratorium Act, in Parliament.": Jed Chong and Nicole Sweeney, *Bill C-48*. Library of Parliament, May 2017.

p. 161 "spans pirates, shipwrecks, secret midnight meetings and even a supposed visit from the *Mayflower* en route to Plymouth Rock": "Renews-Cappahayden." *Irish Loop* website. "The *Florizel* was among the first steel ships in the world designed to navigate through ice" Admiralty House, Communications Museum est. 1915. *The Florizel* exhibit.

Chapter 7

p.167 "April MacDonald was a teenager the first time she photographed an abandoned house." Jennifer Thornhill Verma, December 2017. *Abandoned Architecture as Art: Newfoundland Resettlement in Photographs.* Downhome magazine web site.

p. 167 "It is estimated the provincial government encouraged some thirty thousand residents spread over 250 communities to resettle into "designated growth centres.": Caroline Hillier, December 2017. *How do you deal with dwindling tiny towns? Newfoundland and Labrador will pay you to leave.* CBC Radio Special.

p. 170 "The subject of garter snakes comes up: about a decade ago, news reports indicated they had been introduced to western Newfoundland" CBC News, Newfoundland and Labrador, September 2010. Snakes Found Breeding in Western Newfoundland.

p. 176 "The same oil that inspired the Conference Board of Canada to dub the province": "Newfoundland and Labrador Likely to Lead Provincial Economic Growth in 2013," Conference Board of Canada, June 2013.

p. 177 "The largest island in the Bay of Islands, Woods Island sits due north of the Lewis Hills with views to the Long Range Mountains.": Richard Park, March 1968. *A History of Bay of Islands With Special Reference to Gillams, One of Its First Settlements.*

p. 230 "Predating the 1965 fisheries resettlement program was the 1954 provincially led Centralization Programme." Government of Newfoundland, Education and Early Childhood Development. *Smallwood's Social Policies*, Topic 6.3, p. 534.

p. 188 "The Maritime History Archive at Memorial University in Newfoundland and Labrador" Maritime History Archive, 2004. *"No Great Future"*. Memorial University of Newfoundland.

p. 189–190 "Media reports indicate eligible homeowners in both communities received or will be eligible for up to $270,000 per household to move." *CBC News Newfoundland and Labrador*, February, 2019. Lindsay Jones, "The day the lights went out in William's Harbour." *Macleans Magazine* website, November 2017.

p. 190 "A CBC News story about the planned Little Bay Islands resettlement indicates the department quoted a projected $20 million savings over twenty years": CBC News Newfoundland and Labrador, "Little Bay Islands votes unanimously to resettle." *CBC News* online, February, 2019.

Chapter 8

p. 192 "Tablelands mark an ancient collision of North America and Africa.": Newfoundland and Labrador Tourism. "Tableland Trail—Parks Canada Gros Morne National Park." *Newfoundland and Labrador* website.

p. 192 "500-million-year-old fossil of a trilobite, an extinct marine arthropod vaguely resembling a horseshoe crab": "500 Million Year Old Fossils Lead to Economic Development Opportunities Today." Innovation, Trade and Rural Development, Government of Newfoundland and Labrador, June 2011.

p. 193 "Last year, the Viking settlement nearby, L'Anse Aux Meadows, had more than 37,000 new visitors.": "Newfoundland and Labrador Provincial Tourism Performance 2017." Government of Newfoundland and Labrador, Department of Tourism, Culture, Industry and Innovation, 2017.

p. 198 "*As fishing was a way of life in that area, a few of us naturally had to try it.*": Jack J. Ronald, *Canadian Military Biography*, vol. 1, no. 2, November 1989.

p. 193–94 "the Norse referred to the Indigenous people as *skrælingjar*, meaning barbarians. ": Mike Cohen, "The Vikings and the Barbarians." *Schuylkill Valley Journal Online*.

p. 195 "In 1508 Quirpon Island first appears on the map as the *Isle of Demons.*": Joel A Sutherland, 2015. *Haunted Canada 5: Terrifying True Stories*, p. 9

p. 195–96 "Marguerite de La Rocque, who was marooned here in the mid-sixteenth century": R. La Roque de Roquebrune, "Marguerite de La Rocque," *Dictionary of Canadian Biography*. Vol. 2., 2003.

p. 196 "Migratory fishers frequented Quirpon harbour in the early to mid-1500s.": Intangible Cultural Heritage. "Quirpon." *Memorial University* website.

p. 196 "Built in 1892 by William Henry Pynn and Henry Bartlett": Registered Heritage Structures Bibliography, 2005. "J. B. William Henry Pynn House (Quirpon)." *Newfoundland and Labrador Heritage* online.

p. 197 "During the Second World War, the US military had an overseas Radar Unit (No. 30 RU) on Cape Bauld " L. W. (Bill) Lloyd, "Cape Bauld—Wartime Isolation—RCAF," *Canadian Military Biography*, November 1989.

p. 197 "Which Newfoundland and Labrador Tourism cites as both the one-time salt fish capital of the world and as unofficial capital of Labrador.": "Welcome to Battle Harbour," Newfoundland and Labrador Tourism. *Newfoundland and Labrador* website.

p. 197 "Located on a small island in the Labrador Sea, this historic fishing village has been preserved by the non-profit organization, the Battle Harbour Historic Trust": "History," *Battle Harbour* website.

p. 198 "The annual *capelin roll*, as it's called": "Capelin Roll—a glittery, spectacular pop-up festival," *Government of Newfoundland and Labrador* website, 2019.

p. 199 "in 2018, harvesters were collectively allowed to harvest up to 9,500 tonnes (t), which is a 25 percent reduction over last year's total allowable catch (TAC) limits.": Stantec, "Newfoundland Orphan Basin Exploration Drilling Program," *Existing Socio-Economic Environment*, sec. 7, p. 42, September 2018.

p. 200 "One can trace the region's rich culture based on cod": "Society and Culture." *Newfoundland and Labrador Heritage* online, 1997.

p. 200 "Over the last ten years, the song has garnered nearly 330,000 YouTube views.": Quirpon123, "She's Gone, Boys, She's Gone." *YouTube*, September 2008.

p. 212 "In 1992, the then provincial department of fisheries reported 250 licensed fish processing establishments": "Tripartite Committee Implications of Resource Crisis for Newfoundland's Fish Processing Sector." Department of Fisheries and Oceans, December 1992.

Chapter 9

p. 219 "The climate crisis—also the result of human destruction—has created a warming ocean that perversely created a more hospitable environment for cod for a time.": Robert McSweeney, "The contrasting fortunes of Atlantic cod in warming oceans," *Carbon Brief* website, October 2015.

p. 222 "Fogo Island Inn was built on the idea that we have always been an active fishing community.": "Enterprise," *Fogo Island Inn* website.

p. 223 "And like Island Rooms of Petty Harbour, home of Fishing for Success, co-founded by fishing captain Kimberly Orren" *Island Rooms* website.

p. 222 "the uses can extend beyond food to skincare, medications and supplements and leather goods." Sarah Smellie, "Waste not, want not: Would you wear shoes made of fish?" *CBC News Newfoundland and Labrador*, July 2008.

p. 223 "*intangible cultural history*" Intangible Cultural Heritage. *Memorial University of Newfoundland and Labrador* website.

p. 224 "Newfoundlanders and Labradorians have relied on imported foods, particularly over winter" Chad Pelley, April 2018. "Everybody Eats: Taking a Bite Out of Food Security Issues in NL." *The Overcast*, Newfoundland's Alternative Newspaper web site; CBC News Newfoundland and Labrador, February 2017. "Grow your own: How N.L. plans to produce more of its own food," *CBC News* website; CBC News Newfoundland and Labrador, May 14. "MUN entrepreneur looking to improve food security in Newfoundland and Labrador." *CBC News* website.

p. 224 "But Orren argues the name "recreational fishery" doesn't adequately capture the fishery or the reasons people fish.": Jennifer Thornhill Verma, "Letter: The reasons we fish: calling it 'recreational' misses the mark." *The Telegram* website, October 2018.

p. 226 "The Department of Fisheries, Forestry and Agrifoods in 2016 replaced the former Department of Fisheries and Aquaculture": Executive Council, News Release, *Premier Ball Announces Changes to Structure of Government*. Government of Newfoundland and Labrador, August 2016.

p. 227 "The economy here showed steady growth from the early 2000s into 2013 with a Gross Domestic Product of 5.8 per cent, the highest of all provinces": Minister of Finance and President of Treasury Board. *Fall Update 2013–14*. Government of Newfoundland and Labrador.

p. 227 "The government responded with tax hikes (representing an approximate $3,000 a year increase for a family in Newfoundland and Labrador": Terry Roberts, April 2016. "N.L. Budget: $1.83B deficit, across-the-board tax hikes and layoffs," *CBC News Newfoundland and Labrador*.

p. 227 "There's been no discourse about the fishery or fishing in the election talks so far. And I'm wondering where is it": CBC News Newfoundland and Labrador, "Politicians mum on fisheries during election campaign, says advocate," *CBC News* website, May 2019.

p. 227 "In a campaign called 'Five Fishy Questions for NL Provincial Parties & Candidates' Orren's organization, Fishing for Success, teamed up with Too Big To Ignore": CBC News Newfoundland and Labrador, "Politicians mum on fisheries during election campaign," says advocate. *CBC News* website, May 2019.

p. 231 "Fortune, which was abandoned in 1974 under the Fisheries Household Resettlement Program." Melanie Martin, "The Second Resettlement Programme." *Heritage Newfoundland and Labrador* online, 2006.

Acknowledgements

Visiting lots of *places*, talking to many *people*, and scouring plenty of *paper*—that's how this book came to fruition. With my daughter on my hip and my family by my side, we traversed one end of Newfoundland to the other, visiting *places* along the Avalon, Burin, and Northern Peninsulas and the west and south-central coasts. Among the *people* to whom I am most grateful are those who opened up their homes and histories to me along the way: Brad Watkins, Wayne Maloney (and his father, Eugene "Gene" Maloney), April MacDonald, and Wayne Bartlett. The cod moratorium connects all of us in how it shaped our lives— becoming a fisher with his father just as most were exiting the fishery (Watkins), setting out by boat as his father did, but to view sealife rather than harvest it (Maloney), taking photos of communities like her own resettled by fisheries closures (MacDonald), and writing music to tell the stories behind the cod fishery collapse that shuttered communities in his region (Bartlett).

The moratorium has been captured in precise detail on *paper* by authors, historians, and researchers from every angle (whether it be what happened to the fish, the people, or the communities). I benefitted from books like Dean Bavington's *Managed Annihilation*, Michael Harris's *Lament for an Ocean*, Mark Kurlansky's *Cod,* Wade Kearley's *Here's the Catch*, Jean Pierre Andrieux's *The Grand Banks*, and Jeff A. Webb's *Observing the Outports*; research by cod fisheries scientists Sherrylynn Rowe and George A. Rose, as well as those at Fisheries and Oceans Canada; studies and data examining sociodemographics factors and the evolution (and devolution) of outport Newfoundland and Labrador by George Withers, Nicole Power, Rosemary E. Ommer, Statistics Canada and the Newfoundland

and Labrador Statistics Agency; library and archives materials at Memorial University of Newfoundland (including Marine Institute) and Heritage Newfoundland and Labrador; and exhibits at The Rooms (St. John's), Provincial Seamen's Museum (Grand Bank), and Admiralty House Communications Museum (Mount Pearl). Similarly, when it came to understanding the circumstances and consequences of various disasters at sea, Jim Wellman's *Challenges of the Sea*, Raoul Andersen's *Voyage to the Grand Banks*, and Robert C. Parsons's *Lost at Sea* filled in the gaps about the sinking of the *Atlantic Charger* (Wellman), and the *Florence* (Andersen and Parsons), while Sebastien Junger's *The Perfect Storm* provided an invaluable reference for reporting a disaster at sea no one survived to tell.

Researching this book has felt like an emotional roller coaster. When I spoke to inshore fishers (like Alec Roberts in Quirpon and Rachel Durnford in Grand Bank, and those who are not quoted in this book but were references just the same, like Lee Tremblett in Bonavista), I often felt I was talking to a dying breed. I was angered to learn that twenty-five years after the cod moratorium, there remains no recovery management plan for northern cod, the mighty fish that brought settler families to this place. But I found hope in talking to a number of sources, most notably: Kimberly Orren of Fishing for Success, Anthony "Tony" Cobb of Fogo Island Fish, Robert "Bob" Verge of the Canadian Centre for Fisheries Innovation, and Ryan Cleary of the Federation of Independent Sea Harvesters of Newfoundland and Labrador (FISH-NL). While I didn't interview anyone at the Fish, Food and Allied Workers Union (FFAW-Unifor), I must note that their resources were invaluable to my learning—and I want to thank Dwan Street who pointed me to resources she's written about women and youth in the fishery.

I also found plenty of fishery solutions in news media reports, especially that of CBC (news and programs like *The Broadcast*; *Land and Sea*); *Navigator Magazine*; local newspapers and national ones. These and other news media helped make what is important both interesting and a pleasure to read, upholding the role of responsible journalism.

Planning and developing this book were only possible through the mentorship I received from the University of King's College Master of Fine Arts program. I am especially thankful to my mentors, Ken McGoogan and David Hayes. I am also grateful to the research assistance of graduate student Hannah Gillis (University of Ottawa). And to my publisher (Nimbus) and editors, Simon Thibault and Whitney Moran: thank you for believing in me and this book as well as helping to make the words on each page sing.